IRISH WRITERS
on Writing

What does it mean to be a writer in the context of Ireland's centuries of uncertainty and upheaval? How does an Irish writer define Irish writing? The writers here, who range from early legends to modern masters, address these questions through their sources: the land, the Church, the past, changing politics, and literary styles. Irish Writers on Writing raises a toast to one of the world's most vital literary traditions.

CONTRIBUTORS

John Banville
Sebastian Barry
Samuel Beckett
Brendan Behan
Dermot Bolger
Elizabeth Bowen
Marina Carr
Ciaran Carson
Austin Clarke
Padraic Colum
Daniel Corkery
Anthony Cronin
Gerald Dawe
Seamus Deane
Greg Delanty
Emma Donoghue
Theo Dorgan
Roddy Doyle
Paul Durcan
Anne Enright
Padraic Fallon
Brian Friel
Lady Augusta Gregory
Michael Hartnett
Seamus Heaney
John Hewitt

Rita Ann Higgins
Jennifer Johnston
James Joyce
Patrick Kavanagh
John B. Keane
Molly Keane
Brendan Kennelly
Benedict Kiely
Thomas Kilroy
Thomas Kinsella
Mary Lavin
Francis Ledwidge
Hugh Leonard
Michael Longley
Louis MacNeice
Derek Mahon
Colum McCann
Thomas McCarthy
John McGahern
Medbh McGuckian
Frank McGuinness
Conor McPherson
Paula Meehan
Máire Mhac an tSaoi
John Montague
George Moore

Paul Muldoon
Richard Murphy
Tom Murphy
Myles na Gopaleen
Eiléan Ní Chuilleanáin
Nuala Ni Dhomhnaill
Conor Cruise O'Brien
Edna O'Brien
Kate O'Brien
Sean O'Casey
Frank O'Connor
Joseph O'Connor
Sean O'Faolain
Liam O'Flaherty
Mary O'Malley
Micheal O'Siadhail
Tom Paulin
A. E. Russell
George Bernard Shaw
Francis Stuart
John Millington Synge
Colm Tóibín
William Trevor
William Yeats

THE WRITER'S WORLD
Edward Hirsch, SERIES EDITOR

The Writer's World features writers from around the globe discussing what it means to write, and to be a writer, in many different parts of the world. The series collects a broad range of material and provides access for the first time to a body of work never before gathered in English. Edward Hirsch, the series editor, is internationally acclaimed as a poet and critic. He is the president of the John Simon Guggenheim Foundation.

Irish Writers on Writing
EDITED BY Eavan Boland

Mexican Writers on Writing
EDITED BY Margaret Sayers Peden

Polish Writers on Writing
EDITED BY Adam Zagajewski

Trinity University Press gratefully acknowledges the generous support of the following Patrons of The Writer's World:

Sarah Harte and John Gutzler
Mach Family Fund, Joella and Steve Mach

IRISH WRITERS

on Writing

EDITED BY

Eavan Boland

TRINITY UNIVERSITY PRESS

San Antonio, Texas

Published by Trinity University Press
San Antonio, Texas 78212

Cover design by Karen Schober
Book design by BookMatters, Berkeley

♾ The paper used in this publication meets the minimum requirements of the American
National Standard for Information Sciences—Permanence of Paper for Printed Library
Materials, ANSI Z39.48-1992.

Printed on 100% post-consumer waste recycled text stock.

Library of Congress Cataloging-in-Publication Data
   Irish Writers on writing / edited by Eavan Boland.
      p. cm. — (Writer's world)
   Includes index.
      SUMMARY: "Drawing on sources such as the land, the Church, the past, changing politics,
      and literary styles, Irish writers ranging from W. B. Yeats, James Joyce, and Augusta
      Gregory to Roddy Doyle, Kate O'Brien, Colm Toibin, John Banville, and Seamus Heaney
      explore what it means to be a writer in Ireland."—PROVIDED BY PUBLISHER.
   Includes bibliographical references.
      ISBN-13: 978-1-59534-029-0 (alk. paper)
      ISBN-10: 1-59534-029-7 (alk. paper)
      ISBN-13: 978-1-59534-032-0 (pbk. : alk. paper)
      ISBN-10: 1-59534-032-7 (pbk. : alk. paper)
   1. English literature—Irish authors—History and criticism.   2. Authors, Irish—
Political and social views.   3. Literature and history—Ireland—History.   4. Politics
and literature—Ireland—History.   5. Civilization, Modern, in literature.   6. Ireland—
Intellectual life.   7. Ireland in literature.   I. Boland, Eavan.
PR8718.175   2007
820.9'9417—dc22   2006037075

11   10   09   08   07   —   5   4   3   2   1

Contents

Preface

In one of the darkest moments of Irish history, Thomas Davis, a young patriot, wrote an essay. The year was 1846. Ireland was on the brink of another failed revolution. Within months famine would engulf the island. Within two years Davis himself would be dead. In his essay, he warned and promised, "This country of ours," he wrote, "is no sandbank thrown up by some recent caprice of earth. It is an ancient land, honored in the archives of civilization, traceable into antiquity by its piety, its valor, and its sufferings. Every great European race has sent its stream to the rivers of the Irish mind."

It is hard to resist Davis's eloquence. Yet this book shows how complicated that apparently simple concept became. It took another half century for the Irish nation to emerge. With that emergence came stresses, resistances, and counterclaims. In the process the Irish mind was shown to be anything but the paradigm of tranquil reception that Davis suggested. The Writer's World series is about writers and writing. But what exactly does that mean in the Irish context? How does an Irish writer define Irish writing? To start with, not with theory or abstraction. That is not the Irish way. In the nineteenth century, in a preface to a book of short stories, Yeats wrote, "The old men tried to make one see life plainly, but all written down in a kind of fiery shorthand."

This is a book of fire and shorthand. The pieces are often brief. The writers here address Irish writing through its sources: the land, the Church, the past; a dream of eighteenth-century writers, a reproach to twentieth-

century ones; a celebration of a provincial town and a satire on urban manners — this is the way it is done. If this sounds like a wide net, it is. But
though the references are multiple, the source is single. That source is the
Irish imagination. If most Irish writers are reluctant to define it, nearly all of
them included in this anthology address it here in some way.

For that reason I have wanted these pages to be a rich, various, unlikely
account of a small island and its writers — not a textbook but a theater. The
best way of framing that heraldry of argument and meditation is to show
Irish writers not in reflection, which is not an Irish mode, but in conversation, which is. It is not an ideal conversation; nor should it be. To be ideal it
would have to be idealized. No editor of a book of Irish writing, given its
richness and dissonance, would wish that. I certainly don't.

I began to write and publish poetry in the Ireland of the early sixties. One
evening, when I was in my late teens, I talked with Padraic Colum, a sweet-
natured and approachable poet. He was then in his late seventies. He had
been on the margins of the Irish Revival. Now he lived in the United States.
I asked him about those days; if, for instance, he remembered Yeats. He
paused for a moment. His voice had a distinctive, treble resonance. When
he answered, it was high and emphatic. "Yeats hurt me," he said, "he
expected too much of me."

His answer stayed with me. From then on, adding other conversations to
his, I began to see Irish writing differently. It ceased to be the triumphant
emergence that announced itself when I was a schoolgirl, which kept its
radiance when I was a beginning poet. Gradually it took on edges, angles, a
new aspect. I began to understand Irish literature as a living web of influences and inheritances, of injuries done, of continuous, fierce disagree-
ments. The more I came to this view, the less it seemed a diminishment. In
fact, the opposite. There was something thrilling and hopeful in thinking
about what was being written on a small island as a continuing process.
There was something sustaining in knowing that Irish literature was not a
closed canon but an open tradition.

This anthology opens with works by William Yeats and Lady Augusta
Gregory. Their meditations on the founding of the National Theatre are

nothing less than an attempt to define a new Irish imagination. To illustrate this, I chose Yeats's essay "The Galway Plains." It is a beautiful and compact manifesto on the subject. Lady Gregory supplies chapter and verse.

But this is only a beginning. I have also wanted this book to be a sound chamber rather than a single voice. And so almost a century after these essays were written, Colm Tóibín's witty and thoughtful retrospect on Lady Gregory adds acoustical depth to her earlier entry. Twenty years before, Kate O'Brien's reflections on Lady Gregory add a meaning that is reinforced decades later by the way the fine Irish novelist Anne Enright speculates about Kate O'Brien.

If this sounds like a series of circles, it is. But the circles have a purpose. If the Irish literary tradition is a living web, it is also a nonstop conversation between the present and the past. This is the way writers reflect on writing: through ghosts of style, memory, cadence, and change. The old Ireland anticipates the new one on almost every page in this book. In the same way the new Ireland can't resist returning to that earlier country — and to those writers who lived there — to challenge, accuse, subtract, and alter.

I have given great space in this anthology to the way these voices consider and reconsider each other. Daniel Corkery on the Gaelic poets; Frank O'Connor on Corkery. Sean O'Casey on Yeats; Roddy Doyle and Mary O'Malley on John Millington Synge; Conor McPherson on Samuel Beckett. The list goes on: Derek Mahon's powerful poem on Louis MacNeice and Seamus Heaney's on Francis Ledwidge; Edna O'Brien's wonderful, mercurial side-glance at James Joyce; Hugh Leonard's discovery of O'Casey; and Thomas Kilroy's memories of Mary Lavin — these writings all continue this pattern.

I have used this sound effect in preference to any theory or aesthetic, because it stands in for both. Ireland is an intimate, powerful place. I have not wanted to include lengthy analysis or abstract argument. I doubt if I could have found them — and the truth is, I didn't look. No abstraction can adequately explain how a small island could break free of a larger one and fashion a great literature. I wanted the participants, the makers of the fiery shorthand to do that — to provide those snapshots of inner dialogue that are the real truth of a tradition in its time. These passionate, abrading conversations happening on and off the page — all the time, with all our hearts — go a long way toward explaining what happened. Wherever they happened, I have tried to include them. As I did, I kept remembering Brian Friel's phrase, quoted in the chapter on Friel, about the dialogue between Turgenev and Chekhov: "So they gave life to each other."

Irish literature came to greatness in the twentieth century. When I was young, I believed I knew why. If that seems presumptuous, there were reasons. Lightning had struck a small island. And struck again. There were plays, novels, short stories to prove it. Not to mention poetry. "The standing army of Irish poets," said Patrick Kavanagh, "never falls below 20,000."

At a more analytical level what happened seemed obvious. Ireland — in the dark and darker nineteenth and eighteenth centuries — had lost one language and received another. Through this new language — English — came all the humiliations history can offer a defeated people: The orders of the garrison. Injustice in the courts. The landlord's rent rules. The bailiff's shouted instructions to the battering-ram party.

But history relented. A battle was joined; a new state emerged. Given another chance, Irish writers took the language of their country's abasement and forced it — poem by poem, novel by novel — to retell the story. The sight of a language that had formerly been an instrument of power and colony, now being made to voice the imaginative redress of a whole people, was and is a spectacle to behold.

There is truth in that approach. I believed it entirely once. I believe some of it still. But this book also shows its flaws. Within the new situation were profound stresses; rich and fertile angers. One writer's politics became another's exclusion. While Yeats and Synge crafted a new theater, Daniel Corkery, an important and disaffected contemporary, railed against their one-sidedness. Looking at the Irish Revival, he wrote: "Though we may think of this literature as a homogenous thing we cannot think of it as an indigenous one." Corkery's fear that the Irish were losing their nationhood and their identity a second time — once at the hands of the British, but now in the toils of a new inauthentic literature — is a real one.

When the reaction is not fear or anger, it can be skepticism and satire. Even then, it is a conversation — and well worth eavesdropping on — between Irish writers. The acidic excerpt reprinted in this book from

George Moore's *Hail and Farewell* about Yeats's demeanor and Lady Gregory's reverence is a case in point. Then again, it was Moore who said: "A literary movement consists of five or six people who live in the same town and hate each other cordially."

The tense conversations continued. A hundred years after Synge, Mary O'Malley wrote of how it felt to have a writer idealizing her own people before they were even real to her. "When I read *The Playboy* sometime in my teens," she says, "I thought it was ridiculous. I was mildly offended, not at anything in the play, but that educated people thought it had something to say about the kind of life lived by my ancestors and their like." Her vivid, brave critique raises a crucial issue. Irish poems, plays, and novels have often shadowed the lives of future writers by simplifying them in advance. Patrick Kavanagh had reason to feel he could have been trapped in the background of a Yeats poem. Emma Donoghue, in her eloquent interview on being a lesbian Irish writer, suggests the exclusions that force consciousness. John Banville writes a lively siduswiping article on Bloomsday and notes the "exasperation many of us feel at the pervasiveness and bathos of the Joyce myth."

Perhaps most important, the lost language was mourned and the new one not quite accepted. Nuala Ni Dhomhnaill's superb essay on the Irish language is excerpted in this book, registering decline and expressing outrage. Sean O'Faolain takes an opposite view, castigating the new state for hypocrisy. The debates on the Irish language are central to this volume. They are the unfinished business of Irish writing. Máire Mhac an tSaoi has a wonderful tribute to the past, and Conor Cruise O'Brien an exasperated statement of the present. Theo Dorgan provides a wide-angled and welcome reassessment of poetry in Irish. John Montague has a heartbreaking poem about it. All of these contributions are revealing. The issue weaves in and out of these pages — a music of pain, accusation, and recovery.

There is the opposite theme also. In certain places here past and present rejoice in each other. Seamus Heaney's tenderhearted, lyric re-creation of Francis Ledwidge is a subtle calibration of different identities. Roddy Doyle's wonderful piece on teaching Synge is, in merry disguise, an arranged marriage between traditions and eras. Edna O'Brien celebrates Joyce and Derek Mahon commemorates MacNeice. Thomas Kinsella deflates the

Irish poetic persona. Anthony Cronin's splendid and comic account of Brendan Behan and Kavanagh's unhappy Christmas does not conceal its dark and beautiful subject: the oldest duty one generation of writers owes another — to bury the dead and compose their elegy.

On winter evenings, when I was a student in Trinity, I sometimes went with friends the short distance from College Green to Duke Street. There, in the Bailey or in some other pub, I would look around me with wonder. At every table, in every corner, voluble, noisy arguments began and ended. Ashtrays filled. Blue smoke curled to the ceiling. Fog crept in and out, as the door opened and shut. The handles at the bar were pulled back and forth all night. Names pierced the air. Reminiscences began and ended. The ghost of the young Joyce, nearsighted and waspish, could have entered and been at ease. The figure of Yeats could have come and gone and known exactly where he had been. That visceral, quarrelsome aura of a Dublin evening, I was sure, could have held its own against any city and any situation in the world.

I know now that at least some of it was an illusion. The conversation was incomplete on several grounds. Certainly, as I found later, there were too few women. They wrote less in the first decade of the twentieth century, and in the twenties, thirties, and forties than I might wish. By the time of the seventies and eighties, they are powerful and often commanding voices. Nevertheless, all through, they are strong and wonderful: Elizabeth Bowen, Eiléan Ní Chuilleanáin, Emma Donoghue, Anne Enright, Lady Augusta Gregory, Rita Ann Higgins, Jennifer Johnston, Medbh McGuckian, Paula Meehan, Máire Mhac an tSaoi, Edna O'Brien, Kate O'Brien, Mary O'Malley — they provide an array of voices and essential insights.

In tribute to those evenings, and the memory of that cornucopia of talk and opinion, I have made certain choices throughout this book. I have, for instance, chosen a cut-off birth date of 1971. Younger writers, born after that, have not been included. This is a matter of space, and not talent. The more obvious one has to do with the number of writers and the length of entries. The increase of the first has meant the decrease of the second. The balance, I feel, is right. Irish writing is not a canon; it is a tradition. Despite my affection for those long-ago occasions, time has left them far behind. There are new conversations; different arguments. If I cannot hear them all, I can at least try to represent some of them — and their relationship to earlier versions of themselves — however briefly. The brevity, of course, is a source of frustration. Often I could not include a lengthy, eloquent argument, or even reprint the whole of an essay. So I have given a flavor or a sampler where I would have liked to have had an expansive, open-ended evening of text. Often the pieces are off the beaten track of a writer's work — quirky, revealing, in deep conversation with other writers of the Irish past. In most cases the entries, however short, are dense with argument and rich in meaning. They stand on their own.

I have included as many Irish writers as possible. I have chosen the comments on Irish writing that I think are most germane — even when most oblique. When John McGahern is writing, in his plangent, powerful piece on the Catholic Church, I consider — indeed I know — that he is writing about the Irish imagination. The same is true of Francis Stuart on meeting Yeats. When Elizabeth Bowen writes on Anglo-Irish history and Molly Keane on Elizabeth Bowen, when Louis MacNeice considers Dublin and John Montague the lost language, when William Trevor dwells on and in his Munster Arcadia and Paula Meehan writes her dark and beautiful account of the statues of the Virgin Mary at Granard, the same is true. This is the way I remember it. This is how I found my way to seeing Irish literature as festive and self-renewing — and do still.

I have noted the work of these Irish writers and excerpted some of it. In the head notes that accompany each writer's selection in this anthology, I have listed the books they have written. Readers can follow them off these pages, as I have done time out of mind, and back to the poems, the novels, the stories, the plays that come from the sources they describe. Which is as it should be.

Eavan Boland, Dublin 2006

Thanks to Barbara Ras, Sarah Nawrocki, and Amy Smith Bell for their help and care with this book. To Edward Hirsch who invited me to be part of this series. And to Kevin Casey for his support throughout.

William Butler Yeats

(1865–1939)

"The Galway Plains"

William Yeats was born in 1865. Although a portion of his life was lived in the nineteenth century, he is remembered as a defining twentieth-century figure: modernist, activist, and a great Irish poet. Yeats's childhood was marked by a wounding contradiction. His father, the painter John Butler Yeats, was agnostic, yet all around him, in the lore of Sligo and the west of Ireland, the child gathered in and was nourished by a sense of an invisible world. Yeats's hunger for the unseen—for a community of purpose that could encompass it—marks all of his work. This propensity is evident in the idealization of the Irish literary imagination, formulated in his essay "The Galway Plains," which is reprinted below.

Yeats was educated in Dublin and London. In 1884 he attended the Metropolitan School of Art in Dublin. In London he drew inspiration from such poets as Lionel Johnson and Ernest Dowson, with whom he met regularly in the Cheshire Cheese pub on the Strand. Yeats's first book, *The Wanderings of Oisin and Other Poems*, published in 1889, showed an early turn toward Irish themes. He was prolific in poetry, drama, and criticism. His later poetry— especially his 1928 volume *The Tower*—redefined the relation between the lyric self and the outward world.

A modernist who said of himself and his friends "We were the last Romantics," Yeats could be both bleak and clear about the limitations of the imagination, as he was in one of his last poems, "The Circus Animals' Desertion." But in 1899, when he founded the Irish National Theatre with Lady Augusta Gregory and Edward Martyn, he was intent on defining the Irish imagination in a fresh, radical way. His definitions would become, in time, founding tenets of the Irish Literary Revival.

Yeats's seminal essay "The Galway Plains," written in 1903, is a central text. It may also be the single most beautiful critique he made of the possibilities for a new Irish literature. It is idealistic and may today seem unrealistic. But at the time, struggling against the odds, it was a bold attempt to found a national art in a visible location. It was also Yeats's attempt to find, in Galway and the history of its people, those invisible strengths that had been shunned by Yeats's father and therefore made elusive in his childhood. "There is still in truth upon these great level plains," he wrote, "a people, a community bound together by imaginative possessions." Those words have formed a part of the hopes and the heritage of all Irish writers who followed Yeats. They echo still.

Lady Gregory has just given me her beautiful *Poets and Dreamers*, and it has brought to mind a day two or three years ago when I stood on the side of Slieve Echtge, looking out over Galway. The Burren Hills were to my left, and though I forget whether I could see the cairn over Bald Conan of the Fianna, I could certainly see many places there that are in poems and stories. In front of me, over many miles of level Galway plains, I saw a low blue hill flooded with evening light. I asked a countryman who was with me what hill that was, and he told me it was Cruachmaa of the Sidhe. I had often heard of Cruachmaa of the Sidhe even as far north as Sligo, for the countrypeople have told me a great many stories of the great host of the Sidhe who live there, still fighting and holding festivals.

I asked the old countryman about it, and he told me of strange women who had come from it, and who would come into a house having the appearance of countrywomen, but would know all that happened in that house; and how they would always pay back with increase, though not by their own hands, whatever was given to them. And he had heard, too, of people who had been carried away into the hill, and how one man went to look for his wife there, and dug into the hill and all but got his wife again, but at the very moment she was coming out to him, the pick he was digging with struck her upon the head and killed her. I asked him if he had himself seen any of its enchantments, and he said, "Sometimes when I look over to the hill, I see a mist lying on the top of it, that goes away after a while."

A great part of the poems and stories in Lady Gregory's book were made or gathered between Burren and Cruachmaa. It was here that Raftery, the wandering country poet of ninety years ago, praised and blamed, chanting fine verses, and playing badly on his fiddle. It is here the ballads of meeting and parting have been sung, and some whose lamentations for defeat are still remembered may have passed through this plain flying from the battle of Aughrim.

"I will go up on the mountain alone; and I will come hither from it again. It is there I saw the camp of the Gael, the poor troop thinned, not keeping with one another; Och Ochone!" And here, if one can believe many devout people whose stories are in the book, Christ has walked upon the roads, bringing the needy to some warm fireside, and sending one of His saints to anoint the dying.

I do not think these country imaginations have changed much for centuries, for they are still busy with those two themes of the ancient Irish poets, the sternness of battle and the sadness of parting and death. The emotion that in other countries has made many love-songs has here been given, in a long wooing, to danger, that ghostly bride. It is not a difference in the substance of things that the lamentations that were sung after battles are now sung for men who have died upon the gallows.

The emotion has become not less, but more noble, by the change, for the man who goes to death with the thought —

It is with the people I was,
    It is not with the law I was,

has behind him generations of poetry and poetical life.

The poets of today speak with the voice of the unknown priest who wrote, some two hundred years ago, that *Sorrowful Lament for Ireland* Lady Gregory has put into passionate and rhythmical prose:

I do not know of anything under the sky
That is friendly or favourable to the Gael,
But only the sea that our need brings us to,
Or the wind that blows to the harbour
The ship that is bearing us away from Ireland;
And there is reason that these are reconciled with us,
For we increase the sea with our tears,
And the wandering wind with our sighs.

There is still in truth upon these great level plains a people, a community bound together by imaginative possessions, by stories and poems which have grown out of its own life, and by a past of great passions which can still waken the heart to imaginative action. One could still, if one had the genius, and had been born to Irish, write for these people plays and poems like those of Greece. Does not the greatest poetry always require a people to listen to it? England or any other country which takes its tunes from the great cities and gets its taste from schools and not from old custom may have a mob, but it cannot have a people. In England there are a few groups of men and women who have good taste, whether in cookery or in books; and the great multitudes but copy them or their copiers. The poet must always prefer the community where the perfected minds express the people, to a community that is vainly seeking to copy the perfected minds. To have even perfectly the thoughts that can be weighed, the knowledge that can be got from books, the precision that can be learned at school, to belong to any aristocracy, is to be a little pool that will soon dry up. A people alone are a great river; and that is why I am persuaded that where a people has died, a nation is about to die.

Lady Augusta Gregory
(1852–1932)

[EXCERPT FROM]

Our Irish Theatre:
A Chapter of Autobiography

Augusta Gregory was born Isabella Augusta Persse in 1852, one of sixteen children, in Roxborough in Galway. Her family were Anglo-Irish landlords. The west of Ireland remained central to her imagination until her death in 1932. She liked to quote the words of Ireland's legendary hero Fionn mac Cumhaill: "We would not give up our own country—Ireland—if we were to get the whole world as an estate." But behind those words of general attachment, there was a more local passion for the sawmill, the gooseberry bushes, the hills and distances of her own Galway birthplace.

In photographs and paintings Lady Gregory is a small, downright woman, very much the person George Moore describes on his first meeting (excerpted later in this book)—"broad, handsome, intellectual brow en-framed in iron-grey hair." The qualities writers like Yeats and Sean O'Casey recall of hers, however, are her warmth and inspiring friendship. As Yeats put it in a later tribute: "She has been to me mother, friend, sister and brother. I cannot realise this world without her."

In 1880, at the age of twenty-eight, she married Sir William Gregory, then sixty-three, a former governor of Ceylon. Their only child, Robert Gregory—the subject of a celebrated elegy by William Yeats—was born in 1881. The Gregorys traveled widely. When Sir William died in 1892, Lady Gregory retired to the Coole Park estate in Galway that he had owned. There the preliminary discussions occurred that led to the founding of the Irish Literary Theatre in 1899. This was replaced by the Irish National Theatre in 1904. She herself had many plays performed there, the best known of which were *Hyacinth Halvey* (1906) and *The Rising of the Moon* (1907).

Lady Gregory's literary achievement has been viewed differently at different times. At one stage she was seen merely as a facilitator and catalyst of the Irish Literary Revival. Later, her contribution would move and illuminate other Irish writers. In this book alone Colm Tóibín, Austin Clarke, and Kate O'Brien at different moments and in different ways reassess her influence.

The selection below is from *Our Irish Theatre: A Chapter of Autobiography*, published in 1913. The writing is plainspoken and modest, but the existence of this text, in an age when far too few Irish writers kept an account of literary happenings, is little short of a miracle. It provides a rare, day-to-day glimpse of one of the defining moments of Irish writing: the foundation of a national theater. Here Lady Gregory describes the first months of setting it up—an account full of irony, understatement, and charm.

On one of those days at Duras in 1898, Mr. Edward Martyn, my neighbour, came to see the Count, bringing with him Mr. Yeats, whom I did not then know very well, though I cared for his work very much and had already, through his directions, been gathering folk-lore. They had lunch with us, but it was a wet day, and we could not go out. After a while I thought the Count wanted to talk to Mr. Martyn alone; so I took Mr. Yeats to the office where the steward used to come to talk, — less about business I think than of the Land War or the state of the country, or the last year's deaths and marriages from Kinvara to the headland of Aughanish. We sat there through that wet afternoon, and though I had never been at all interested in theatres, our talk turned on plays. Mr. Martyn had written two, *The Heather Field* and *Maeve*. They had been offered to London managers, and now he thought of trying to have them produced in Germany where there seemed to be more room for new drama than in England. I said it was a pity we had no Irish theatre where such plays could be given. Mr. Yeats said that had always been a dream of his, but he had of late thought it an impossible one, for it could not at first pay its way, and there was no money to be found for such a thing in Ireland.

We went on talking about it, and things seemed to grow possible as we talked, and before the end of the afternoon we had made our plan. We said we would collect money, or rather ask to have a certain sum of money guaranteed. We would then take a Dublin theatre and give a performance of Mr. Martyn's *Heather Field* and one of Mr. Yeats's own plays, *The Countess Cathleen*. I offered the first guarantee of £25.

A few days after that I was back at Coole, and Mr. Yeats came over from Mr. Martyn's home, Tillyra, and we wrote a formal letter to send out. We neither of us write a very clear hand, but a friend had just given me a Remington typewriter and I was learning to use it, and I wrote out the letter with its help. That typewriter has done a great deal of work since that day, making it easy for the printers to read my plays and translations, and Mr. Yeats's plays and essays, and sometimes his poems. I have used it also for the many, many hundreds of letters that have had to be written about theatre business in each of these last fifteen years. It has gone with me very often up and down to Dublin and back again, and it went with me even to America last year that I might write my letters home. And while I am writing the leaves are falling, and since I have written those last words on its keys, she who had given it to me has gone. She gave me also the great gift of her friendship through more than half my lifetime, Enid, Lady Layard, Ambassadress at Constantinople and Madrid, helper of the miserable and the wounded in the Turkish-Russian war; helper of the sick in the hospital she founded at Venice, friend and hostess and guest of queens in England and Germany and Rome. She was her husband's good helpmate while he lived — is not the Cyprus treaty set down in that clear handwriting I shall never see coming here again? And widowed, she kept his name in honour, living after him for fifteen years, and herself leaving a noble memory in all places where she had stayed, and in Venice where her home was and where she died.

Our statement — it seems now a little pompous — began:

"We propose to have performed in Dublin, in the spring of every year certain Celtic and Irish plays, which whatever be their degree of excellence will be written with a high ambition, and so to build up a Celtic and Irish school of dramatic literature. We hope to find in Ireland an uncorrupted and imaginative audience trained to listen by its passion for oratory, and believe that our desire to bring upon the stage the deeper thoughts and emotions of Ireland will ensure for us a tolerant welcome, and that freedom to experiment which is not found in theatres of England, and without which no new movement in art or literature can succeed. We will show that Ireland is not the home of buffoonery and of easy sentiment, as it has been represented, but the home of an ancient idealism. We are confident of the support of all Irish people, who are weary of misrepresentation, in carrying out a work that is outside all the political questions that divide us."

I think the word "Celtic" was put in for the sake of Fiona Macleod whose plays however we never acted, though we used to amuse ourselves by thinking of the call for "author" that might follow one, and the possible appearance of William Sharp in place of the beautiful woman he had given her out to be, for even then we had little doubt they were one and the same person. I myself never quite understood the meaning of the "Celtic Movement," which we were said to belong to. When I was asked about it, I used to say it was a movement meant to persuade the Scotch to begin buying our books, while we continued not to buy theirs.

We asked for a guarantee fund of £300 to make the experiment, which we hoped to carry on during three years. The first person I wrote to was the old poet, Aubrey de Vere. He answered very kindly, saying, "Whatever develops the genius of Ireland, must in the most effectual way benefit her; and in Ireland's genius I have long been a strong believer. Circumstances of very various sorts have hitherto tended much to retard the development of that genius; but it cannot fail to make itself recognised before very long, and Ireland will have cause for gratitude to all those who have hastened the coming of that day."

I am glad we had this letter, carrying as it were the blessing of the generation passing away to that which was taking its place. He was the first poet I had ever met and spoken with; he had come in my girlhood to a neighbour's house. He was so gentle, so fragile, he seemed to have been wafted in by that "wind from the plains of Athenry" of which he wrote in one of his most charming little poems. He was of the Lake School, and talked of Wordsworth, and I think it was as a sort of courtesy or deference to him that

I determined to finish reading *The Excursion*, which though a reader of poetry it had failed me, as we say, to get through. At last one morning I climbed up to a wide wood, Grobawn, on one of the hillsides of Slieve Echtge, determined not to come down again until I had honestly read every line. I think I saw the sun set behind the far-off Connemara hills before I came home, exhausted but triumphant! I have a charming picture of Aubrey de Vere in my mind as I last saw him, at a garden party in London. He was walking about, having on his arm, in the old-world style, the beautiful Lady Somers, lovely to the last as in Thackeray's day, and as I had heard of her from many of that time, and as she had been painted by Watts.

Some gave us their promise with enthusiasm but some from good will only, without much faith that an Irish Theatre would ever come to success. One friend, a writer of historical romance, wrote: "October 15th. I enclose a cheque for £1, but confess it is more as a proof of regard for *you* than of belief in the drama, for I cannot with the best wish in the world to do so, feel hopeful on that subject. My experience has been that any attempt at treating Irish history is a fatal handicap, not to say absolute *bar*, to anything in the shape of popularity, and I cannot see how any drama can flourish which is not to some degree supported by the public, as it is even more dependent on it than literature is. There *are* popular Irish dramatists, of course, and very popular ones, but then unhappily they did not treat of Irish subjects, and *The School for Scandal* and *She Stoops to Conquer* would hardly come under your category. You will think me very discouraging, but I cannot help it, and I am also afraid that putting plays experimentally on the boards is a very costly entertainment. Where will they be acted in the first instance? And has any stage manager undertaken to produce them? Forgive my tiresomeness; it does not come from want of sympathy, only from a little want of hope, the result of experience."

George Bernard Shaw

(1856–1950)

[EXCERPT FROM]

John Bull's Other Island

George Bernard Shaw was born in Dublin in 1856, to poor Church of Ireland parents. In later life he referred with pain and resentment to the economic harshness of his youth. He left for London in the 1870s and never returned to Ireland.

His first play was *Widowers' Houses* in 1892. After that, even the most incomplete list of his plays is an inventory of the distinction of British drama at the end of the nineteenth century and the beginning of the twentieth: *Mrs. Warren's Profession* (1893), *Arms and the Man* (1894), *Caesar and Cleopatra* (1898), *Major Barbara* (1905), *The Doctor's Dilemma* (1906), *Pygmalion* (1912–13), and *Saint Joan* (1923).

Shaw is a blunt critic and had a name for being oppressively didactic. G. K. Chesterton, the British writer, called him "a very prefatory sort of person." Shaw's advocacy of pure reason did not always sit well with fellow Irish writers either. Yeats called him "a notorious hater of romance." Shaw was also impatient with what he saw as shibboleths and superstitions of nationalism. "I am a typical Irishman," he once said curtly. "My family came from Yorkshire." Nor did he confine his idiosyncratic views to Ireland: he opposed World War I, and his work became deeply unpopular in Britain as a result.

Shaw's caustic, forthright view of the Irish made it impossible for him to show much empathy for the Irish Revival. And yet the combination of intellectual lucidity with a sweet-natured, obstinate flair for theatrical effect made his a commanding presence in British theater. Shaw's wit and insistent reasoning have continued to enchant audiences.

Shaw's play *John Bull's Other Island* is an ambitious attempt to deal with a difficult topic: the imagination as a force that sapped the Irish of purpose and progress. He offered it to the Abbey Theatre in 1904, but it was—not surprisingly—rejected. In the play Lawrence Doyle, a melancholy Irishman, angrily attacks the escapism and dreaming that, in his view, characterize the Irish imagination. Meanwhile, Thomas Broadbent, a bumbling Englishman with far more colonial instincts than he could ever admit, praises and condescends to the Irish. The dialogue is a cautious *ars poetica* by Shaw—a manifesto salted with the regret, love, and anger of the perpetual exile.

The conversation between Broadbent and Doyle offers a bleak, sharp view of Ireland. "An Irishman's imagination," Shaw has Doyle say, "never lets him alone, never convinces him, never satisfies him; but it makes him that he can't face reality nor deal with it nor handle it nor conquer it."

BROADBENT: What! Here you are, belonging to a nation with the strongest patriotism! the most inveterate homing instinct in the world! and you pretend you'd rather go anywhere than back to Ireland. You don't suppose I believe you, do you? In your heart —

DOYLE: Never mind my heart: an Irishman's heart is nothing but his imagination. How many of all those millions that have left Ireland have ever come back or wanted to come back? But what's the use of talking to you? Three verses of twaddle about the Irish emigrant "sitting on the stile, Mary," or three hours of Irish patriotism in Bermondsey or the Scotland Division of Liverpool, go further with you than all the facts that stare you in the face. Why, man alive, look at me! You know the way I nag, and worry, and carp, and cavil, and disparage, and am never satisfied and never quiet, and try the patience of my best friends.

BROADBENT: Oh, come, Larry! do yourself justice. You're very amusing and agreeable to strangers.

DOYLE: Yes, to strangers. Perhaps if I was a bit stiffer to strangers, and a bit easier at home, like an Englishman, I'd be better company for you.

BROADBENT: We get on well enough. Of course you have the melancholy of the Celtic race —

DOYLE (bounding out of his chair): Good God!!!

BROADBENT (slyly): — and also its habit of using strong language when there's nothing the matter.

DOYLE: Nothing the matter! When people talk about the Celtic race, I feel as if I could burn down London. That sort of rot does more harm than ten Coercion Acts. Do you suppose a man need be a Celt to feel melancholy in Rosscullen? Why, man, Ireland was peopled just as England was; and its breed was crossed by just the same invaders.

BROADBENT: True. All the capable people in Ireland are of English extraction. It has often struck me as a most remarkable circumstance that the only party in parliament which shows the genuine old English character and spirit is the Irish party. Look at its independence, its determination, its defiance of bad Governments, its sympathy with oppressed nationalities all the world over! How English!

DOYLE: Not to mention the solemnity with which it talks old-fashioned nonsense which it knows perfectly well to be a century behind the times. That's English, if you like.

BROADBENT: No, Larry, no. You are thinking of the modern hybrids that now monopolize England. Hypocrites, humbugs, Germans, Jews, Yankees, foreigners, Park Laners, cosmopolitan riffraff. Don't call them English. They don't belong to the dear old island, but to their confounded new empire; and by George! they're worthy of it; and I wish them joy of it.

DOYLE (unmoved by this outburst): There! You feel better now, don't you?

BROADBENT (defiantly): I do. Much better.

DOYLE: My dear Tom, you only need a touch of the Irish climate to be as big a fool as I am myself. If all my Irish blood were poured into your veins, you wouldn't turn a hair of your constitution and character. Go and marry the most English Englishwoman you can find, and then bring up your son in Rosscullen; and that son's character will be so like mine and so unlike yours that everybody will accuse me of being his father. (*With sudden anguish.*) Rosscullen! oh, good Lord, Rosscullen! The dullness! the hopelessness! the ignorance! the bigotry!

BROADBENT (*matter-of-factly*): The usual thing in the country, Larry. Just the same here.

DOYLE (*hastily*): No, no: the climate is different. Here, if the life is dull, you can be dull too, and no great harm done. (*Going off into a passionate dream.*) But your wits can't thicken in that soft moist air, on those white springy roads, in those misty rushes and brown bogs, on those hillsides of granite rocks and magenta heather. You've no such colors in the sky, no such lure in the distances, no such sadness in the evenings. Oh, the dreaming! the dreaming! the torturing, heartscalding, never satisfying dreaming, dreaming, dreaming, dreaming! (*Savagely.*) No debauchery that ever coarsened and brutalized an Englishman can take the worth and usefulness out of him like that dreaming. An Irishman's imagination never lets him alone, never convinces him, never satisfies him; but it makes him that he can't face reality nor deal with it nor handle it nor conquer it: he can only sneer at them that do, and (*bitterly, at* BROADBENT) be "agreeable to strangers," like a good-for-nothing woman on the streets. (*Gabbling at* BROADBENT *across the table.*) It's all dreaming, all imagination. He can't be religious. The inspired Churchman that teaches him the sanctity of life and the importance of conduct is sent away empty; while the poor village priest that gives him a miracle or a sentimental story of a saint, has cathedrals built for him out of the pennies of the poor. He can't be intelligently political, he dreams of what the Shan Van Vocht said in ninety-eight. If you want to interest him in Ireland you've got to call the unfortunate island Kathleen ni Hoolihan and pretend she's a little old woman. It saves thinking. It saves working. It saves everything except imagination, imagination, imagination; and imagination's such a torture that you can't bear it without whisky. (*With fierce shivering self-contempt.*) At last you get that you can bear nothing real at all: you'd rather starve than cook a meal; you'd rather go shabby and dirty than set your mind to take care of your clothes and wash yourself; you nag and squabble at home because your wife isn't an angel, and she despises you because you're not a hero; and you hate the whole lot round you because they're only poor slovenly useless devils like yourself. (*Dropping his voice like a man making some shameful confi-*

dence.) And all the while there goes on a horrible, senseless, mischievous laughter. When you're young, you exchange drinks with other young men; and you exchange vile stories with them; and as you're too futile to be able to help or cheer them, you chaff and sneer and taunt them for not doing the things you daren't do yourself. And all the time you laugh, laugh, laugh! eternal derision, eternal envy, eternal folly, eternal fouling and staining and degrading, until, when you come at last to a country where men take a question seriously and give a serious answer to it, you deride them for having no sense of humor, and plume yourself on your own worthlessness as if it made you better than them.

George Moore
(1852–1933)

Hail and Farewell

George Augustus Moore was born in 1852, in Lough Carra, County Mayo. A writer of immense charm, skill, and interest, he is also the Lord of Misrule of the Irish Revival. His book *Hail and Farewell*, from which a brief excerpt is included below, punctured the earnest intentions of Lady Gregory and Yeats. In merciless prose he lampooned them for their faith in a native dialect and national theater, and for their solemn, reverent interactions. He particularly turned his satiric efforts on the high estimate Lady Gregory had of Yeats's talents, and the sanctuary she provided for him at Coole.

Moore came late to the revival. He returned to Dublin from Europe— where he had been involved with the new art movements—in 1901. By then Yeats, Lady Gregory, and Moore's cousin, Edward Martyn, had already set up the Irish Literary Theatre, which would ultimately become the Irish National Theatre. It is Moore's strength and weakness—as well as his gift to generations of readers—that he found it hard to take the revival seriously. Mercurial, rivalrous, deeply skeptical of Yeats, his prose reflects his disbelief that a large-scale literary endeavor could come from a small country he had intellectually abandoned years earlier.

Moore's powerful realist novels include *A Modern Lover* (1883), *A Mummer's Wife* (1885), *A Drama in Muslin* (1887), *A Mere Accident* (1887), *Confessions of a Young Man* (1888), *Spring Days* (1888), *Mike Fletcher* (1889),

Vain Fortune (1891), and *Esther Waters* (1894). Their delicate, serious tone—as well as their obvious affinity with such French writers as Emile Zola—do little to prepare the reader for the acid-etched wit of *Hail and Farewell*.

In the excerpt below Moore describes an early visit to Coole Park at the start of the century. He gives a straight-faced, barbed account of the enclosed environment he found there; of Lady Gregory's concern for Yeats's poems and Yeats's solemnity. Moore is an unreliable witness. As far as the history of Irish writing goes, however, it is not at all necessary to believe him to find him both essential and entertaining.

After long ringing the maidservant opened the door and told me that Lady Gregory had gone to church with her niece; Mr. Yeats was composing. Would I take a seat in the drawing-room and wait till he was finished? He must have heard the wheels of the car coming round the gravel sweep, for he was in the room before the servant left it — enthusiastic, though a little weary. He had written five lines and a half, and a pause between one's rhymes is an excellent thing, he said. One could not but admire him, for even in early morning he was convinced of the importance of literature in our national life. He is nearly as tall as a Dublin policeman, and preaching literature he stood on the hearth-rug, his feet set close together. Lifting his arms above his head (the very movement that Raphael gives to Paul when preaching at Athens), he said what he wanted to do was to gather up a great mass of speech. It did not seem to me clear why he should be at pains to gather up a great mass of speech to write so exiguous a thing as *The Shadowy Waters*; but we live in our desires rather than in our achievements, and Yeats talked on, telling me that he was experimenting, and did not know whether his play would come out in rhyme or in blank verse; he was experimenting. He could write blank verse almost as easily as prose, and therefore feared it; some obstacle, some dam was necessary. It seemed a pity to interrupt him, but I was interested to hear if he were going to accept my end, and allow the lady to drift southward, drinking ale with the sailors, while the hero sought salvation alone in the North. He flowed out into a torrent of argument and explanation, very ingenious, but impossible to follow. Phrase after phrase rose and turned and went out like a wreath of smoke, and when the last was spoken and the idea it had borne had vanished, I asked him if he knew the legend of Diarmuid and Grania. He began to tell it to me in its many variants, surprising me with unexpected dramatic situations, at first sight contradictory and incoherent, but on closer scrutiny revealing a psychology in germ which it would interest me to unfold. A wonderful hour of literature that was, flowering into a resolution to write an heroic play together. As we sat looking at each other in silence, Lady Gregory returned from church.

She came into the room quickly, with a welcoming smile on her face, and I set her down here as I see her: a middle-aged woman, agreeable to look upon, perhaps for her broad, handsome, intellectual brow en-framed in iron-grey hair. The brown wide-open eyes are often lifted in looks of appeal and inquiry, and a natural sympathy softens her voice till it whines. It modulated very pleasantly, however, as she yielded her attention to Yeats [. . .] Lady Gregory chattered on, telling stories faintly farcical, amusing to those who knew the neighbourhood, rather wearisome for one who didn't, and I was waiting for an opportunity to tell her that an heroic drama was going to be written on the subject of Diarmuid and Grania.

When my lips broke the news, a cloud gathered in her eyes, and she admitted that she thought it would be hardly wise for Yeats to undertake any further work at present; and later in the afternoon she took me into her confidence, telling me that Yeats came to Coole every summer because it was necessary to get him away from the distractions of London, not so much from social as from the intellectual distractions that Arthur Symons had inaugurated. The Savoy rose up in my mind with its translations from Villiers le l'Isle Adam, Verlaine and Maeterlinck; and I agreed with her that alien influences were a great danger to the artist. All Yeats's early poems, she broke in, were written in Sligo, and among them were twenty beautiful lyrics and Ireland's one great poem, *The Wanderings of Usheen* — all these had come out of the landscape and the people he had known from boyhood.

For seven years we have been waiting for a new book from him; ever since *The Countess Cathleen* we have been reading the publisher's autumn announcement of *The Wind among the Reeds*. The volume was finished here last year; it would never have been finished if I had not asked him to Coole; and though we live in an ungrateful world somebody will throw a kind word after me some day, if for nothing else, for *The Wind among the Reeds.*

I looked round, thinking that perhaps life at Coole was primarily to give him an opportunity of writing poems. As if she had read my thoughts, Lady Gregory led me into the back drawing-room and showed me the table at which he wrote, and I admired the clean pens, the fresh ink, and the spotless blotter; these were her special care every morning; I foresaw the strait sofa lying across the window, valued in some future time because the poet had reclined upon it between his rhymes. Ah me! the creeper that rustles an accompaniment to his melodies in the pane will awaken again, year after year, but one year it will awaken in vain, . . . My eyes thanked Lady Gregory for her devotion to literature. . . .

A. E. Russell

(1867–1935)

"On Behalf of Some Irishmen Not Followers of Tradition"

George William Russell was born in Lurgan, in Northern Ireland, in 1867. He moved to Dublin as a boy. From his youth on he was a friend of the Irish cause. Throughout his life he became a progressive activist and journalist, an accomplished poet, and a generous mentor to emerging Irish writers. In all these pursuits, he was better known by his pen name, A. E. Legend had it that he had initially chosen a different pen name—AEon—but when the typesetter could only decipher the first two letters, and printed those, Russell was pleased with the change and adopted it.

In 1894, he was appointed organizer of the Irish Agricultural Organisation Society (IAOS) by Horace Plunkett. Thereafter Russell became a spokesman for the cooperative movement in Ireland, which promoted the benefits of agricultural and commercial self-reliance for the Irish people. From 1905 until 1923 he served as editor of the IAOS journal *Irish Homestead*. As the national and language movements strengthened, Russell was at the center of Dublin's literary circles. Less doctrinaire than other writer-politicians, more flexible in his sense of the requirements of a national literature, he was sought out and admired by several different constituencies.

Russell was a close friend of William Yeats. He cultivated friendships among young writers, meeting James Joyce in 1902 and introducing him to others. But Russell's literary judgment faltered at times. In an article written

in the *New York Times* in 1922, Padraic Colum recalled the relationship
between Joyce and A. E.: "A. E. said to him when Joyce showed him his first
poem: 'I don't know whether you are a fountain or a cistern.' And again he
said to him: 'I'm afraid you have not enough chaos in you to make a world.' "

Russell's books include *Homeward Songs by the Way* (1894), *The Earth
Breath and Other Poems* (1896), *The Nuts of Knowledge* (1903), *The Divine
Vision and Other Poems* (1904), *By Still Waters* (1906), *Deirdre* (1907),
Collected Poems (1913), *Gods of War, with Other Poems* (1915), *Imaginations
and Reveries* (1915), *The Candle of Vision* (1918), *Midsummer Eve* (1928),
Enchantment and Other Poems (1930), *Vale and Other Poems* (1931), *Songs
and Its Fountains* (1932), *The House of Titans and Other Poems* (1934), and
Selected Poems (1935).

Russell's diction was ornate, and some of it appears dated today.
Nevertheless, the force of his argument in the poem reprinted here is fresh
and exact and even applicable to this moment. Addressing the Irish
nationalists, at the moment of their gathering strength, Russell warns that not
all Irishmen and -women will think their way.

They call us aliens, we are told,
Because our wayward visions stray
From that dim banner they unfold,
The dreams of worn-out yesterday.
The sum of all the past is theirs,
The creeds, the deeds, the fame, the name,
Whose death-created glory flares
And dims the spark of living flame.
They weave the necromancer's spell,
And burst the graves where martyrs slept,
Their ancient story to retell,
Renewing tears the dead have wept.
And they would have us join their dirge,

This worship of an extinct fire
In which they drift beyond the verge
Where races all outworn expire.
The worship of the dead is not
A worship that our hearts allow,
Though every famous shade were wrought
With woven thorns above the brow.
We fling our answer back in scorn:
"We are less children of this clime
Than of some nation yet unborn
Or empire in the womb of time.
We hold the Ireland in the heart
More than the land our eyes have seen,
And love the goal for which we start
More than the tale of what has been."
The generations as they rise
May live the life men lived before,
Still hold the thought once held as wise,
Go in and out by the same door.
We leave the easy peace it brings:
The few we are shall still unite
In fealty to unseen kings
Or unimaginable light.
We would no Irish sign efface,
But yet our lips would gladlier hail
The firstborn of the Coming Race
No blazoned banner we unfold —
One charge alone we give to youth,
Against the sceptred myth to hold
The golden heresy of truth.

John Millington Synge

(1871–1909)

[EXCERPT FROM]

The Aran Islands

John Millington Synge was born in Rathfarnham, County Dublin, in 1871. He came from an Anglo-Irish background. He attended the Royal Academy of Music and was an accomplished musician, playing both piano and violin. In 1888 Synge entered Trinity College Dublin. He met William Yeats in Paris in 1894. "I did not see what was to come," said Yeats in his Nobel address of 1923, "when I advised John Synge to go to a wild island off the Galway coast and study its life because that life had never been expressed in literature."

Synge first visited the Aran Islands in 1898. He was already in frail health by then, despite his relative youth. He had been treated for Hodgkin's disease earlier in the year. He spent the next five summers on Aran, listening to the language, talking to the islanders, and beginning to craft his dramatic contribution to the Irish Revival. In 1902 Synge finished two plays—*Riders to the Sea* and *Shadow of the Glen*. They were accepted by Lady Gregory and performed the following year. He became an adviser to the Abbey Theatre—the theater was then situated on Abbey Street—and his play *The Well of the Saints* was performed in 1905. But it was *The Playboy of the Western World* in 1907 that provided the Irish Theatre with its defining play and the Irish Revival with a controversy that would continue long after. Nationalists attacked the play as "a vile and inhuman story told in the foulest language." Within two years Synge was dead.

Synge's artistic quest was to discover an Irish way of life where language was stripped bare of custom and intellectual ornament; in which gesture, style, purity, and instinct were uppermost. He found it in the Aran Islands. He articulated this in the exuberant poetry of *The Playboy*. Synge's dream and the high language in which he executed it have been a profound influence on Irish writing ever since.

In this poignant extract from *The Aran Islands*, published in 1907, Synge gives an account of his first visit there. He also celebrates the power of a life he both idealized and simplified. This encounter between a hard-pressed island culture and a reticent, inward Irishman, from a completely different history, is one of the enigmas and marvels of the Irish Revival. This, as near as Synge could come to it, was his truth of the meaning of the Irish imagination.

I am settled at last on Inishmaan in a small cottage with a continual drone of Gaelic coming from the kitchen that opens into my room.

Early this morning the man of the house came over for me with a four-oared curagh — that is, a curagh with four rowers and four oars on either side, as each man uses two — and we set off a little before noon.

It gave me a moment of exquisite satisfaction to find myself moving away from civilisation in this rude canvas canoe of a model that has served primitive races since men first went to sea.

We had to stop for a moment at a hulk that is anchored in the bay, to make some arrangement for the fish-curing of the middle island, and my crew called out as soon as we were within earshot that they had a man with them who had been in France a month from this day.

When we started again, a small sail was run up in the bow, and we set off across the sound with a leaping oscillation that had no resemblance to the heavy movement of a boat.

The sail is only used as an aid, so the men continued to row after it had gone up, and as they occupied the four cross-seats I lay on the canvas at the stern and the frame of slender laths, which bent and quivered as the waves passed under them.

When we set off it was a brilliant morning of April, and the green, glittering waves seemed to toss the canoe among themselves, yet as we drew nearer this island a sudden thunderstorm broke out behind the rocks we were approaching, and lent a momentary tumult to this still vein of the Atlantic.

We landed at a small pier, from which a rude track leads up to the village between small fields and bare sheets of rock like those in Aranmor. The youngest son of my boatman, a boy of about seventeen, who is to be my teacher and guide, was waiting for me at the pier and guided me to his house, while the men settled the curagh and followed slowly with my baggage.

My room is at one end of the cottage, with a boarded floor and ceiling, and two windows opposite each other. Then there is the kitchen with earth floor and open rafters, and two doors opposite each other opening into the open air, but no windows. Beyond it there are two small rooms of half the width of the kitchen with one window apiece.

The kitchen itself, where I will spend most of my time, is full of beauty and distinction. The red dresses of the women who cluster round the fire on their stools give a glow of almost Eastern richness, and the walls have been toned by the turf-smoke to a soft brown that blends with the grey earth-colour of the floor. Many sorts of fishing-tackle, and the nets and oil-skins of the men, are hung upon the walls or among the open rafters; and right overhead, under the thatch, there is a whole cowskin from which they make pampooties.

Every article on these islands has an almost personal character, which gives this simple life, where all art is unknown, something of the artistic beauty of medieval life. The curaghs and spinning-wheels, the tiny wooden barrels that are still much used in the place of earthenware, the homemade cradles, churns, and baskets, are all full of individuality, and being made from materials that are common here, yet to some extent peculiar to the island, they seem to exist as a natural link between the people and the world that is about them.

The simplicity and unity of the dress increases in another way the local air of beauty. The women wear red petticoats and jackets of the island wool stained with madder, to which they usually add a plaid shawl twisted round their chests and tied at their back. When it rains they throw another petticoat over their heads with the waistband round their faces, or, if they are young, they use a heavy shawl like those worn in Galway. Occasionally other wraps are worn, and during the thunderstorm I arrived in I saw several girls with men's waistcoats buttoned round their bodies. Their skirts do not come much below the knee, and show their powerful legs in the heavy indigo stockings with which they are all provided.

The men wear three colours: the natural wool, indigo, and a grey flannel that is woven of alternate threads of indigo and the natural wool. In Aranmor many of the younger men have adopted the usual fisherman's jersey, but I have only seen one on this island.

As flannel is cheap — the women spin the yarn from the wool of their own sheep, and it is then woven by a weaver in Kilronan for fourpence a yard — the men seem to wear an indefinite number of waistcoats and woollen drawers one over the other. They are usually surprised at the lightness of my own dress, and one old man I spoke to for a minute on the pier, when I came ashore, asked me if I was not cold with "my little clothes."

As I sat in the kitchen to dry the spray from my coat, several men who had seen me walking up came in to me to talk to me, usually murmuring on the threshold, "The blessing of God on this place," or some similar words.

The courtesy of the old woman of the house is singularly attractive, and though I could not understand much of what she said — she has no English — I could see with how much grace she motioned each visitor to a chair, or stool, according to his age, and said a few words to him till he drifted into our English conversation.

For the moment my own arrival is the chief subject of interest, and the men who come in are eager to talk to me. Some of them express themselves more correctly than the ordinary peasant, others use the Gaelic idioms continually and substitute "he" or "she" for "it," as the neuter pronoun is not found in modern Irish.

A few of the men have a curiously full vocabulary, others know only the commonest words in English, and are driven to ingenious devices to express their meaning. Of all the subjects we can talk of war seems their favourite, and the conflict between America and Spain is causing a great deal of excitement. Nearly all the families have relations who have had to cross the Atlantic, and all eat of the flour and bacon that is brought from the United

States, so they have a vague fear that "if anything happened to America," their own island would cease to be habitable.

Foreign languages are another favourite topic, and as these men are bilingual they have a fair notion of what it means to speak and think in many different idioms. Most of the strangers they see on the islands are philological students, and the people have been led to conclude that linguistic studies, particularly Gaelic studies, are the chief occupation of the outside world.

"I have seen Frenchmen, and Danes, and Germans," said one man, "and there does be a power a Irish books along with them, and they reading them better than ourselves. Believe me there are few rich men now in the world who are not studying the Gaelic." They sometimes ask me the French for simple phrases, and when they have listened to the intonation for a moment, most of them are able to reproduce it with admirable precision.

When I was going out this morning to walk round the island with Michael, the boy who is teaching me Irish, I met an old man making his way down to the cottage. He was dressed in miserable black clothes which seemed to have come from the mainland, and was so bent with rheumatism that, at a little distance, he looked more like a spider than a human being.

Michael told me it was Pat Dirane, the story-teller old Mourteen had spoken of on the other island. I wished to turn back, as he appeared to be on his way to visit me, but Michael would not hear of it.

"He will be sitting by the fire when we come in," he said; "let you not be afraid, there will be time enough to be talking to him by and by."

Francis Ledwidge

(1887–1917)

"Thomas McDonagh"

Francis Ledwidge was born in 1887 in Slane, County Meath, the eighth of nine children. His family was poor, and his father died when Francis was five. Ledwidge began writing poems early, and he published them in local newspapers. Eventually he attracted the attention and support of a local landowner, Lord Dunsany.

It is one of the ironies and puzzles of Ledwidge's career—given his death from a stray shell at the front in Pilkem, near Ieper (in western Belgium), in 1917—that he was a staunch Irish nationalist. He had joined the Gaelic League years earlier, and he was a member of the Irish volunteers. Yet within months of the conflict starting in 1914, Ledwidge joined the Royal Inniskillen Fusiliers at Richmond Barracks in Dublin. His poem reprinted below laments one of the patriots of 1916, Thomas McDonagh, who was executed for his part in the Easter Rising. The poem suggests an early and powerful thread running through Irish writing in that it took its heritage of lament and dissent from the nineteenth-century nationalist Irish poem.

And yet Ledwidge's poem for McDonagh is also a poignant restatement of the broken identities and cross-purposes that both enriched and tormented Irish writing. In Seamus Heaney's poem "In Memoriam Francis Ledwidge," included later in this book, Heaney calls him "our dead enigma."

In these lines below Ledwidge closes a circle. A young Irishman, who would soon die in a British war of attrition and empire, here celebrates and mourns the life of another young Irishman who opposed those very causes. The poem is, in its way, an elegant paradigm of the contradictions of Irish writing.

He shall not hear the bittern cry
In the wild sky, where he is lain,
Nor voices of the sweeter birds
Above the wailing of the rain.

Nor shall he know when loud March blows
Thro' slanting snows her fanfare shrill,
Blowing to flame the golden cup
Of many an upset daffodil.

But when the dark cow leaves the moor,
And pastures poor with greedy weeds,
Perhaps he'll hear her low at morn
Lifting her horn in pleasant meads.

Sean O'Casey

(1880–1964)

[EXCERPT FROM]

Autobiographies

Sean O'Casey was born John Cassidy in Upper Dorset Street, Dublin, in 1880. He was baptized into the Church of Ireland. His father died when he was young, after which his mother struggled to care for him and his older brother, Archie. Weak eyesight hindered his learning at school. At fourteen, he left school and held a succession of jobs. Finally he became a railwayman and stayed in that line of work for nine years before starting to write.

From his early twenties he adhered to the Irish cause. He joined the Gaelic League in 1906, changed his name to its Irish form, and became secretary of the Citizen Army in 1914. By the end of that decade he was writing plays. O'Casey's plays are attentive to the struggles, hardships, and verbal resistance of Dublin's working poor. This was his world; the one he had grown up in. Some of the affirmation of his work is lodged in his ability to stylize the North Dublin dialect into a superb music of love and invective. The Abbey Theatre produced three of O'Casey's earliest and most celebrated plays—*The Shadow of a Gunman* (1923), *Juno and the Paycock* (1924), and *The Plough and the Stars* (1926). This last play caused riots in the Abbey Theatre. An exasperated William Yeats defended the play on its first night, saying to the audience, "You have disgraced yourselves again."

In later years O'Casey moved away from dramatic realism, guided by new trends of expressionism in theater. *The Silver Tassie*, his experimental play on

World War I, was rejected by the Abbey. Furious and wounded, O'Casey moved to England, where *The Silver Tassie* was produced in 1929. He never returned to Ireland. His later plays include *Red Roses for Me* (1946); he also published a six-volume autobiography, from 1939 to 1956.

The following extract is taken from these *Autobiographies*. His account of the rejection of *The Silver Tassie* is both wrenching and revealing. In its way it is a watershed moment in Irish writing. It shows Yeats still determined to control the template of realism for the Irish theater. It also proves that the monolithic views of the Irish Renaissance, even then, were no longer sufficient to guide younger, more experimental Irish writers. The wounds went deep and the era of absolute authority came to an abrupt halt. O'Casey takes up the story at the point of receiving Yeats's letter of rejection.

He read the letters again: the one from Yeats was the one to be answered. Sean could not but believe that the play's rejection had been decided upon before the play had been sent. To answer Yeats would be a dangerous thing to do. Yeats in his greatness had influence everywhere, and the world of literature bowed before him. But answered he must be, and answered he would be, even though the strife meant the end of Sean. His mind tore through the letter again.

> The most considerate thing for us to do is to suggest that he withdraw the play. My letter gives an opinion, doesn't absolutely reject. He could withdraw the play "for revision" and let that be known to the Press. He should say that he himself had become dissatisfied and had written to ask it back. If he disagrees with our opinions as to its merits, he can wait a little, and offer it to some London Manager. If the London Manager accepts, then our opinion of the play won't matter to him at all. Or, on the other hand, if no Manager accepts, or if he doesn't offer it there, he can keep it by him, revising, or not revising, as he pleases. I want to get out of the difficulty of the paragraphs in the Press saying that the play has been offered to us (*and hard both you and Mr. Lennox Robinson asked that it should be offered to you. S. O'C.*). I have not told anyone what I think of the play, and I will get Lennox not to give his opinion. You have, perhaps, already written to Casey [*sic*], but even if you have, I should like you to write making this suggestion.

This to Lady Gregory and then to Sean. Obviously, Yeats was sure Sean would shake at the knees when he got this opinion; would hasten to sit down and write for the play back; would light a fire with it the first thing the following morning. Would he? He thought and thought it out: He was fenced in with money anxieties; he had now a wife and a child to guard and keep, and a rented house which needed many things more before it could become a home. Indeed, but for what his wife had brought into it from her own flat, there would have been barely enough in it to suit himself. Before they were married, she had sublet her flat; had got no rent from the tenants; and only by last-minute efforts did she manage to get her belongings back again. When he and she had come to the house they were in now, the sitting-room had had but a carpet on the centre of the floor, with a broad border around it varnished by Eileen herself; one chair, John's pictures, one of a Gitana, the other of Sean himself; a coal-scuttle and fire-irons; so that, while he sat on the floor before the fire, she sat on the chair, and wept. But not for long: they soon saw the grim humour of it, and laughed merrily over the barren way the room looked. The little they had was oozing away; now, since the child had come, what was left would depart in a steady stream; and, if *The Silver Tassie* didn't bring in enough for a further year's life, then the nights would be full of anxiety's light and the days would be gloomy and glum. Still, he had been in worse circumstances before, and had come out of them. But then he had been alone — his mother didn't count, for she had the faculty of being able to live on air, and laugh. Yeats's rejection of the play was a blow on the heart.

Casey could write for the play, and say he wanted it for revision — that was the meanest moment in the letter of Yeats. It was a bitter suggestion, and made him live with anger for a long time to come. A fight was the one honest way out of it. Almost all the literary grandees would, naturally, be on the side of Yeats, and most of the Press that mattered would, directly or indirectly, make a bow to his decision. This was inevitable because of Yeats's reputation as a literary genius; and what made it harder for Sean was that the reputation was a suitable crown for the man's achievement. But fight he should; and fight he would.

Well, here he was surrounded by Yeats's opinions. *You are not interested in the Great War; you never stood on its battlefields, never walked its hospitals, and so write out of your opinions. You illustrate those opinions by a series of almost unrelated scenes, as you might in a leading article.* Oh, God, here was a man who had never spoken to a Tommy in his life — bar Major Gregory; and to him only because he was an artist as well as a soldier — chattering about soldiers to one who had talked to them all; infantry, cavalry, and artillery; who knew most of the regimental marches; who, when a kid, had listened to them telling, in their halting way, stories about Canada, Hong Kong, India, Gibraltar, Malta, and the wilds of Shorncliffe Camp and Salisbury Plain. One who had known soldiers since he was a kid of six; whose uncle had been wounded on the field of Balaclava; whose brother had gone through the Boer War in the Dublin Fusiliers; whose elder brother had worn the khaki in the first World War; who had walked with the Tommies, and chatted with them, had sung songs with them in the hospitals of St. Vincent and of Richmond; who had followed the Great War from its first declaration, through the Russian Revolution to its final end by the surrender of Germany. And now he was being told by one who wouldn't know a Life Guard red from a Horse Guard blue, that he wasn't interested, directly or indirectly, in the Great War! Not interested to one who had talked and walked and smoked and sung with the blue-suited, wounded men fresh from the front; to one who had been among the armless, the legless, the blind, the gassed, and the shell-shocked!

Among the things that dramatic action must burn up are the author's opinions. Do you suppose for one moment that Shakespeare educated Hamlet and Lear by telling them what he thought and believed? As I see it, Hamlet and Lear educated Shakespeare, and I have no doubt that in the process of that education he found out that he was altogether a different man to what he thought himself, and had altogether different beliefs. D'ye tell me that, now, Mr. Yeats? Well, I don't know; but one thing's certain, and that is if Shakespeare became a more educated man while writing Hamlet, then it wasn't Hamlet who educated him, but Shakespeare who educated himself. But what proof — beyond an opinion — has Yeats that what he says was so? As he sees it — of course; but it doesn't necessarily follow that everyone, or anyone, will see it the same way. A man altogether different, with altogether different beliefs when he'd finished the play from what he had been before he started! Here, the poet is suggesting, or trumpeting, the opinion that he was as intimate with Shakespeare as he was with the number of his own hall-door. There are as many opinions about the character of Hamlet as there are lines in the play. Even Shakespeare wasn't sure himself, for we are told: "The variations of an early copy from the play of Hamlet in its improved state, are too numerous and striking to admit a doubt of the play having been subsequently revised, amplified, and altered by the poet." Of one thing we can be certain, namely that what Shakespeare makes Hamlet say was not what the living Prince would, or could, have said, but what Shakespeare wanted him to say; that the play is largely a biography of Shakespeare's thoughts.

Sean carried the letters of Yeats to Macmillan's. He presented them to Mr. Daniel Macmillan, remarking that if the Firm wished, after reading them, he would allow the contract to be withdrawn. Mr. Daniel read the correspondence through. He handed it back to Sean, saying, This is, of course, a matter between Mr. Yeats and you. It does not concern us. We do not agree with the criticism. We think the play worth publication, and we will publish it. We make our own decisions, and this controversy cannot alter our intentions.

Very kind, very manly, and very encouraging to Sean, for he had had a half fear that the criticism from Yeats might check, might even prevent, the play's publication. This was his first victory over the potent, almost impregnable, influence of Yeats. So he hied himself off to C. B. Cochran, and put the correspondence before him. Beyond saying to Sean that he should never have given another party the option of a production while the play was under consideration by a London Manager, Cochran was undisturbed. Sean was taken aback by Cochran's indifference to the denunciation of the play by Yeats; for denunciation it was rather than a criticism.

Padraic Colum

(1881–1972)

"Poor Scholar"

Padraic Colum was born Padraic Columb in a County Longford workhouse, where his father worked. He was the eldest of eight children. At seventeen he began work in the Irish Railway Clearing House. At the start of the twentieth century he joined the Gaelic League and eventually became a member of the first board of the Abbey Theatre, after forming friendships with William Yeats, Lady Augusta Gregory, and A. E. Russell. The publication of his first book of poems, *Wild Earth*, occurred in 1907. His plays *Broken Sail* (1903) and *Land* (1905) were successes for the National Theatre.

The founders of the Irish Revival regarded Colum as a writer of the greatest promise. "A man of genius in the first dark gropings of his thought," said Yeats. Russell remarked: "Colum will be our principal literary figure in ten years." The reason for this praise was undoubtedly the impression made by his first book, *Wild Earth*. But in a subtle, more coercive way, Colum's work and witness also suited the agenda of the revival, with its romantic version of the strength and imagination of the Irish rural poor. His lyrics convinced Lady Gregory and Yeats that his was an authentic rural voice. In fact, Colum's poems, while eloquent, now seem in retrospect both slight and uncertain, taking more from the rhetoric of Georgian England and its pastoral diction than from any Irish idiom.

In 1914 Colum emigrated with his new wife, Mary, to the United States,

where he wrote successful children's literature as well as novels, including
Castle Conquer (1923) and *The Flying Swans* (1937). In later years Colum
divided his time between Ireland and the United States and continued his
work as a folklorist, children's writer, and poet. The poem reprinted below is
from *Wild Earth*. Called "Poor Scholar," it was at first titled "A Poor Scholar of
the Forties." It is easy to see why this poem brought him to the attention of
Yeats: it is written in the voice of a hedge schoolmaster in the eighteenth
century recounting the struggle to teach Greek to the disenfranchised Irish
Catholics who came to study there.

My eyelids red and heavy are
With bending o'er the smold'ring peat.
I know the Aeneid now by heart,
My Virgil read in cold and heat,
In loneliness and hunger smart.
And I know Homer, too, I ween,
As Munster poets know Ossian.

And I must walk this road that winds
'Twixt bog and bog, while east there lies
A city with its men and books;
With treasures open to the wise,
Heart-words from equals, comrade-looks;
Down here they have but tale and song,
They talk Repeal the whole night long.

"You teach Greek verbs and Latin nouns,"
The dreamer of Young Ireland said,
"You do not hear the muffled call,
The sword being forged, the far-off tread
Of hosts to meet as Gael and Gall —
What good to us your wisdom-store,
Your Latin verse, your Grecian lore?"

And what to me is Gael or Gall?
Less than the Latin or the Greek —
I teach these by the dim rush-light
In smoky cabins night and week.
But what avail my teaching slight?
Years hence, in rustic speech, a phrase,
As in wild earth a Grecian vase!

James Joyce
(1882–1941)

[EXCERPT FROM]

A Portrait of the Artist as a Young Man

James Joyce was born in Dublin in 1882, the eldest of ten surviving children. He was educated by the Jesuits at Clongowes and Belvedere. In 1898 he enrolled at University College Dublin, where he studied English, French, and Italian. After graduation he went to Paris, returning to Dublin upon the illness of his mother. Following her death, he met his future wife, Nora Barnacle. Their first outing took place on June 16, 1904, which later became the fulcrum date of his novel *Ulysses*. Shortly afterward he eloped with her, leaving Ireland forever. Despite his exile, he became a defining Irish writer and one of the eminent modernists of the twentieth century.

Joyce may well have assembled all the constituents of a life's work in his first years in Europe. He finished *Dubliners*, his seminal book of short stories, in 1906. Before that, he made notes for a final story about a Jewish Dubliner called Leopold Bloom. Although he decided not to write the story, he would return to the character of Bloom in 1914, making him one of the central figures in *Ulysses*.

A Portrait of the Artist as a Young Man was written in Trieste, Rome, and Paris. It was serialized in *The Egoist* in 1914 and 1915, and it largely rewrites an earlier version called *Stephen Hero*. *Portrait of the Artist* was published in 1916. The book was rejected for publication by the distinguished British publisher Edward Garnett, who wrote in his reader's report: "The author shows us he has art, strength and originality, but this MS wants time and trouble spent on it, to make it a more finished piece of work." In fact, the novel represents the most conventional and cautious moment of Joyce's work: a romantic narration of the growth of a young man's commitment to art, together with his abandonment of religious faith.

Ulysses, a stylistic adventure founded on myth and intensely experimental, was serialized in the *Little Review* from 1918 to 1920 and published by Sylvia Beach in Paris in 1922. Though different from his earlier work, it maintains the great themes that made their first appearance in *Dubliners* and *Portrait of the Artist*. The meeting of Bloom and Stephen Dedalus, like the encounter between Gabriel and Greta Conroy, constitutes Joyce's deep and loving tribute to the life of instinct as well as his acute awareness of how barren the world of intellect is without it. His final book, *Finnegans Wake*, was published in 1939, two years before his death.

The excerpt below is from the end of *Portrait of the Artist*. It registers the journal entries and interior conversations of Stephen Dedalus as he prepares to leave Ireland. Joyce's characterization of Dedalus as seeking to "forge in the smithy of my soul the uncreated conscience of my race" is a celebrated and central manifesto of Irish writing.

March 20. Long talk with Cranly on the subject of my revolt.

He had his grand manner on. I supple and suave. Attacked me on the score of love for one's mother. Tried to imagine his mother: cannot. Told me once, in a moment of thoughtlessness, his father was sixty-one when he was born. Can see him. Strong farmer type. Pepper and salt suit. Square feet. Unkempt, grizzled beard. Probably attends coursing matches. Pays his dues regularly but not plentifully to Father Dwyer of Larras. Sometimes talks to girls after nightfall. But his mother? Very young or very old? Hardly the first.

If so, Cranly would not have spoken as he did. Old then. Probably, and ne-glected. Hence Cranly's despair of soul: the child of exhausted loins.

March 21, morning. Thought this in bed last night but was too lazy and free to add to it. Free, yes. The exhausted loins are those of Elizabeth and Zacchary. Then he is the precursor. Item: he eats chiefly belly bacon and dried figs. Read locusts and wild honey. Also, when thinking of him, saw always a stern severed head or death mask as if outlined on a grey curtain or veronica. Decollation they call it in the gold. Puzzled for the moment by saint John at the Latin gate. What do I see? A decollated precursor trying to pick the lock.

March 21, night. Free. Soul free and fancy free. Let the dead bury the dead. Ay. And let the dead marry the dead.

March 22. In company with Lynch followed a sizeable hospital nurse. Lynch's idea. Dislike it. Two lean hungry greyhounds walking after a heifer.

March 23. Have not seen her since that night. Unwell? Sits at the fire per-haps with mamma's shawl on her shoulders. But not peevish. A nice bowl of gruel? Won't you now?

March 24. Began with a discussion with my mother. Subject: B.V.M. Handicapped by my sex and youth. To escape held up relations between Jesus and Papa against those between Mary and her son. Said religion was not a lying-in hospital. Mother indulgent. Said I have a queer mind and have read too much. Not true. Have read little and understood less. Then she said I would come back to faith because I had a restless mind. This means to leave church by back door of sin and re-enter through the skylight of repentance. Cannot repent. Told her so and asked for sixpence. Got threepence.

Then went to college. Other wrangle with little round head rogue's eye Ghezzi. This time about Bruno the Nolan. Began in Italian and ended in pid-gin English. He said Bruno was a terrible heretic. I said he was terribly burned. He agreed to this with some sorrow. Then gave me recipe for what he calls RISOTTO ALLA BERGAMASCA. When he pronounces a soft O he protrudes his full carnal lips as if he kissed the vowel. Has he? And could he repent? Yes, he could: and cry two round rogue's tears, one from each eye.

Crossing Stephen's, that is, my green, remembered that his countrymen and not mine had invented what Cranly the other night called our religion. A quartet of them, soldiers of the ninety-seventh infantry regiment, sat at the foot of the cross and tossed up dice for the overcoat of the crucified.

Went to library. Tried to read three reviews. Useless. She is not out yet. Am I alarmed? About what? That she will never be out again.

Blake wrote:

> I wonder if William Bond will die
> For assuredly he is very ill.

Alas, poor William!

I was once at a diorama in Rotunda. At the end were pictures of big nobs. Among them William Ewart Gladstone, just then dead. Orchestra played o WILLIE, WE HAVE MISSED YOU.

A race of clodhoppers!

March 25, morning. A troubled night of dreams. Want to get them off my chest.

A long curving gallery. From the floor ascend pillars of dark vapours. It is peopled by the images of fabulous kings, set in stone. Their hands are folded upon their knees in token of weariness and their eyes are darkened for the errors of men go up before them for ever as dark vapours.

Strange figures advance as from a cave. They are not as tall as men. One does not seem to stand quite apart from another. Their faces are phosphorescent, with darker streaks. They peer at me and their eyes seem to ask me something. They do not speak.

March 30. This evening Cranly was in the porch of the library, proposing a problem to Dixon and her brother. A mother let her child fall into the Nile. Still harping on the mother. A crocodile seized the child. Mother asked it back. Crocodile said all right if she told him what he was going to do with the child, eat it or not eat it.

This mentality, Lepidus would say, is indeed bred out of your mud by the operation of your sun.

And mine? Is it not too? Then into Nile mud with it!

April 1. Disapprove of this last phrase.

April 2. Saw her drinking tea and eating cakes in Johnston's, Mooney and O'Brien's. Rather, lynx-eyed Lynch saw her as we passed. He tells me Cranly was invited there by brother. Did he bring his crocodile? Is he the shining light now? Well, I discovered him. I protest I did. Shining quietly behind a bushel of Wicklow bran.

April 3. Met Davin at the cigar shop opposite Findlater's church. He was in a black sweater and had a hurley stick. Asked me was it true I was going away and why. Told him the shortest way to Tara was VIA Holyhead. Just then my father came up. Introduction. Father polite and observant. Asked Davin if he might offer him some refreshment. Davin could not, was going to a meeting. When we came away father told me he had a good honest eye. Asked me why I did not join a rowing club. I pretended to think it over. Told me then how he broke Pennyfeather's heart. Wants me to read law. Says I was cut out for that. More mud, more crocodiles.

April 5. Wild spring. Scudding clouds. O life! Dark stream of swirling bog-water on which appletrees have cast down their delicate flowers. Eyes of girls among the leaves. Girls demure and romping. All fair or auburn: no dark ones. They blush better. Houpla!

April 6. Certainly she remembers the past. Lynch says all women do. Then she remembers the time of her childhood — and mine, if I was ever a child. The past is consumed in the present and the present is living only because it brings forth the future. Statues of women, if Lynch be right, should always be fully draped, one hand of the woman feeling regretfully her own hinder parts.

April 6, later. Michael Robartes remembers forgotten beauty and, when his arms wrap her round, he presses in his arms the loveliness which has long faded from the world. Not this. Not at all. I desire to press in my arms the loveliness which has not yet come into the world.

April 10. Faintly, under the heavy night, through the silence of the city which has turned from dreams to dreamless sleep as a weary lover whom no caresses move, the sound of hoofs upon the road. Not so faintly now as they come near the bridge; and in a moment, as they pass the darkened windows, the silence is cloven by alarm as by an arrow. They are heard now far away, hoofs that shine amid the heavy night as gems, hurrying beyond the sleeping fields to what journey's end — what heart? — bearing what tidings?

April 11. Read what I wrote last night. Vague words for a vague emotion. Would she like it? I think so. Then I should have to like it also.

April 13. That tundish has been on my mind for a long time. I looked it up and find it English and good old blunt English too. Damn the dean of studies and his funnel! What did he come here for to teach us his own language or to learn it from us. Damn him one way or the other!

April 14. John Alphonsus Mulrennan has just returned from the west of Ireland. European and Asiatic papers please copy. He told us he met an old man there in a mountain cabin. Old man had red eyes and short pipe. Old man spoke Irish. Mulrennan spoke Irish. Then old man and Mulrennan spoke English. Mulrennan spoke to him about universe and stars. Old man sat, listened, smoked, spat. Then said: —Ah, there must be terrible queer creatures at the latter end of the world.

I fear him. I fear his red-rimmed horny eyes. It is with him I must struggle all through this night till day come, till he or I lie dead, gripping him by the sinewy throat till. . . Till what? Till he yield to me? No. I mean no harm.

April 15. Met her today point blank in Grafton Street. The crowd brought us together. We both stopped. She asked me why I never came, said she had heard all sorts of stories about me. This was only to gain time. Asked me was I writing poems? About whom? I asked her. This confused her more and I felt sorry and mean. Turned off that valve at once and opened the spiritual-heroic refrigerating apparatus, invented and patented in all countries by Dante Alighieri. Talked rapidly of myself and my plans. In the midst of it unluckily I made a sudden gesture of a revolutionary nature. I must have looked like a fellow throwing a handful of peas into the air. People began to look at us. She shook hands a moment after and, in going away, said she hoped I would do what I said.

Now I call that friendly, don't you?

Yes, I liked her today. A little or much? Don't know. I liked her and it seems a new feeling to me. Then, in that case, all the rest, all that I thought I thought and all that I felt I felt, all the rest before now, in fact. O, give it up, old chap! Sleep it off!

April 16. Away! Away!

The spell of arms and voices: the white arms of roads, their promise of close embraces and the black arms of tall ships that stand against the moon, their tale of distant nations. They are held out to say: We are alone — come. And the voices say with them: We are your kinsmen. And the air is thick with their company as they call to me, their kinsman, making ready to go, shaking the wings of their exultant and terrible youth.

April 26. Mother is putting my new secondhand clothes in order. She prays now, she says, that I may learn in my own life and away from home and friends what the heart is and what it feels. Amen. So be it. Welcome, O life, I go to encounter for the millionth time the reality of experience and to forge in the smithy of my soul the uncreated conscience of my race.

April 27. Old father, old artificer, stand me now and ever in good stead.

Daniel Corkery

(1878–1964)

[EXCERPT FROM]

The Hidden Ireland

Daniel Corkery was born in Cork city in 1878, where he remained all his life. In 1917 in his prologue to his novel *The Threshold of Quiet*, he wrote of Cork as "a many-bridged river valley, jostled and jostling." He studied at University College Cork. He taught at the Christian Brothers' school, and in 1908 with Terence McSwiney and T. C. Murray he founded the Cork Dramatic Society.

Corkery wrote both novels and short stories. In a 1923 issue of *The Nation*, Padraic Colum said of him: "He has written the novel of Irish Catholic mysticism in *The Threshold of Quiet*." But it is for his critical and polemical books—*The Hidden Ireland* (1924) and *Synge and Anglo-Irish Literature* (1931)—that Corkery is most remembered. He was an entrenched opponent of the Irish Literary Revival. He deplored the ideas of William Yeats, J. M. Synge, and Lady Gregory, believing they were merely offering foreign models to native writers. "Though we may think of this literature as a homogeneous thing," he wrote, "we cannot think of it as an indigenous thing."

Corkery's passionate advocacy of an Irish Ireland, his argument with the idea of a canonical Irish Revival, offers a fascinating glimpse into the struggle for the soul of the Irish literary imagination at the start of the twentieth century—a struggle largely forgotten today. That argument, by and large, was won by adherents of the revival. Yeats and his associates triumphed. But Corkery's dream has never really died. It is present wherever cultural nationalism is argued; whenever there are fears for the survival of the Irish language; wherever there is vigilance for a national identity.

His ardent belief—that under all the damage, all the oppression, there survived almost intact the imagination of a people—is present in this glowing piece of writing from *The Hidden Ireland*, with its thrilling conclusion. In this excerpt Corkery explores and commends the greatness of the Gaelic poets of the eighteenth century.

II

Wherever they lived, in County Armagh, Mayo or Cork, the Gaelic poets of the time were peasants. They dressed like peasants, spoke like them, lived among the other peasants (yet not "unguessed at"); they shared their people's life and, indeed, their thoughts. The subject-matter of their verse — the loss of a sheep or old horse, the need of a new handle in a spade — will often surprise us if we do not remember this. Equally so will their lack of sophistication. Their wit, too, and oftentimes their coarseness, are of the fields, not of the town, while their standing by tradition speaks most clearly of all, perhaps, of life among the hills and rivers, the hills that do not renew their forms, the rivers that do not change their course.

But, and this is what we must remember, they never thought of themselves as peasants. They thought of themselves as poets, as literary men. They were sons of learning. Everywhere in their lines we come on words like clown, churl, boar, clod, boor, bear — but the word is always used of their Cromwellian overlord or his bailiff. The Cromwellian (and Cromwellianism lingered on in Ireland long after it had disappeared from English life) was no poet; poetry he could not understand, nor even the need for it. He had no learning, and, however rich he may have become, was still but an upstart. He lacked breeding. He was not fit to be named in the one breath with the Gaels, on whom he trampled. The Gaels were "children of kings, sons of Milesius," and they knew it. We have been told of an incident that happened in our own days. At a sports meeting in County Cork a rough-looking, poorly-clad onlooker had so annoyed those about him by his loudness and

want of consideration, that at last someone cried at him: "Shut up, you fool!"
The epithet stung. He flashed up, and, to the amazement of all, answered
back: "I am no fool; I know my genealogy!" Not many of the people in the
eighteenth century were without knowing their genealogy, and the poets,
most of all, were adepts in such lore; moreover, people as well as poets, they
all were aware that the Cromwellians did not know their genealogy, were,
therefore only mere upstarts.

Those poets' claim to be, first of all, literary men could not be gainsaid.
Their art was the immediate jewel of their souls; and the craft of verse the
one subject where they showed no lack of sophistication. Moreover, were
they not, at least in Munster, gathered into schools, each with its own traditions and its recognised head? And did not the names of the gods and demigods of Greece and Rome chime as sweetly to them as to any other literary
circle in Europe? By plough or spade they lived; but it was for their art they
lived. By whatever name they went in the catalogue, schoolmasters or
ploughmen, to their own people they were poets.

If they were peasants with a difference, so, too, were they literary men
with a difference. For instance, not one of them ever saw his own poems in
print; neither was there any system of copyright established among them.
Their lack of printing-press and book-making does not seem to have vexed
them; we do not find them complaining of it: the Gael had been so long at
war with the outlander that he had never been quite able to make his own of
the printing-press. The literature those poets read in Greek and Latin
existed in book-form, but the literature they read in Irish, and to which they
daily added, existed only in manuscripts. Of these manuscripts they made
new copies, occasionally adding a poem made yesterday to a collection
begun by some hand that long since had become a mere pinch of dust. And
yet, though they laboured thus to keep good songs from perishing from
men's thoughts, and laboured, too, to perfect the form of their own, aware
that only the well-wrought song endured, it does not seem to have worried
them that their fame should have only so poor a chance of spreading beyond
their own parish boundaries. They made their poem, and seem to have left
it to chance whether it should ever cross the neighbouring hills or the sundering river estuary: when it did so, they were probably glad, and still hap-
pier, it is likely, when some passing shanachy told them how, in a far-off place,

he had seen certain verses of theirs written out in good script on enduring parchment. But primarily it was for their own countryside they wrote and, the once proud literary language having split up into many dialects, the common speech of the people became more and more their medium of song. Remembering, too, their vigour and their integrity as artists, that gift that is shield and spear against the dragons of the earth, it is hard not to think of them as among those immortal ones who, in the words of John Keats,

> " . . . died content on pleasant sward,
> Leaving great verse unto a little clan."

No copyright, no printing-press, no publisher, they must, then, have been just simple wayside singers of local events: but this, again, would not be an apt description. They were literary men, very conscious of the proud part the gods had assigned them, jealous of the traditions of their craft, knowledgeable of its history: in Munster, at least, they still employed a great many words, purely literary words, intelligible to, but not used by, the common people. They aimed at literature, and often achieved it. It is, therefore, impossible to think of them as just the local singers of hidden countrysides; the clearest proof, however, that this phrase does not apply is the fact that at the same time, actually living side by side with them, were other poets, poets who produced a very different species of verse, to whom it does apply. Those anonymous poets wrote folk with, it is true, the influence of the schools showing clearly through it; but the poets of whom we shall presently be speaking did not write folk-poetry. The metres of the folk-songs, though fundamentally the same, are simpler and rougher; the message more frank and passionate; and the themes are those instituted by the beatings of the heart of all mankind. The tale of Troy was nothing to those singers — nor that of Deirdre, nothing beyond hearsay.

If we take the poems of Burns, we can easily divide them into two classes: those the Lowland ploughman wrote for the easing of his own wild head, and those the would-be literary man wrote in emulation of the *literati* of Edinburgh. His dialect poems, his most precious work, would correspond with the lyrics that certain other ploughmen were making in Ireland, also for the easing of wild hearts. His literary poems would, on the other hand, correspond to the work of the recognised poets, some of whose names we have mentioned as need served. The correspondence would be, however, not quite exact. Is there even one of Burns's literary poems, in this so unlike his songs in dialect, quite successful? Is there perfect artistic integrity in them? Is there no unwarmed material? No hesitancy in the gesture? In a word, is there not always some slight lack of mastery? If this be so, those literary poems cannot be exactly equated with the poems of men like Aodhagán Ó Rathaille or Eoghan Ruadh Ó Suilleabháin, finished craftsmen, perfect masters of language. With these it is always the mastery that one wonders at — the ease, the spontaneity, the undaunted impulse. One never wishes the poems bettered.

Such men, therefore, cannot be thought of as wayside singers who rhymed the local event. They were what they claimed to be, the *literati* of a people. Indeed, one would think that they, perhaps unfortunately, took only too much pains to earn this description. They never did what Burns did — write in two genres. *All* their work is literary, is of the schools. A French critic has written of Poussin "La force du Poussin est un composé parfait du meilleur de l'art. Elle n'est donc pas individualiste. Elle ne dit pas: Moi, mais: la Tradition." These words describe not only the work of any one of our poets, but all the work of all of them. The word in its mouth is always Tradition; and it betrays individuality only to those who have learned to perceive the subtler values.

Nowadays, to know that a piece of art-work is academic is to know that it remains unvisited, unloved of the people. The work of the Irish poets was academic, yet — strange fact! — much of it, almost two hundred years after its creation, has been found alive on the lips of fishermen and ditchers! . . .

[. . .]

V

In reading those poets, then, we are to keep in mind, first, that the nature of the poetry depends on the district in which it was written — if in Munster, it is literary in its nature; if in Ulster or Connacht, it has the simple directness of folk-song. Then we must also remember that the poets were simple men, living as peasants in rural surroundings; some of them, probably, never saw a city; not only this, but they were all poor men, very often sore-troubled where and how to find shelter, clothing, food, at the end of a day's tramping. Their native culture is ancient, harking back to pre-Renaissance standards; but there is no inflow of books from outside to impregnate it with new thoughts. Their language is dying: around them is the drip, drip of callous decay: famine overtakes famine, or the people are cleared from the land to make room for bullocks. The rocks in hidden mountain clefts are the only altars left to them; and teaching is a felony.

Not to excuse, but to explain them, are these facts mentioned; for their poetry, though doubtless the poorest chapter in the book of Irish literature, is in itself no poor thing that needs excuse: it is, contrariwise, a rich thing, a marvelous inheritance, bright with music, flushed with colour, deep with human feeling. To see it against the dark world that threw it up, is to be astonished, if not dazzled.

Austin Clarke
(1896–1974)

[EXCERPT FROM]

A Penny in the Clouds

Austin Clarke was born in Dublin in 1896. He was educated at University College Dublin, where he was taught by Thomas McDonagh, the 1916 poet-patriot who is the subject of Francis Ledwidge's poem reprinted earlier in this book. A considerable lyric poet, with a caustic critical bent, Clarke's early career showed a tendency to question and resist the myths of the Irish Revival, even though his poetry was plainly influenced by William Yeats.

His later prose—the excerpt below is an example—could turn a sharp although at times not unaffectionate satire on the earnest wishes of the revival writers to evoke a native Ireland. His early poems were mythological and erotic, with occasionally a delicate, regretful pastoral. Later he became a powerful critic of a Catholic and repressive Ireland. In his final years his poems made a rare critique of censorship and hypocrisy. Throughout his life Clarke's work could be seen as a site of dissidence, continuously anti-authoritarian.

His poetry came out during the twenties, thirties, and the following decades. His books include *Collected Poems* (1936), *Later Poems* (1961), *Flight to Africa and Other Poems* (1963), *Mnemosyne Lay in Dust* (1966), *Old Fashioned Pilgrimage and Other Poems* (1967), *The Echo at Coole & Other Poems* (1968), *Collected Poems* (1974), and posthumously *Selected Poems* (1991).

In the extract below Clarke describes a first meeting with Lady Gregory. For all its burlesque overtones, there is something substantive here: an acrid collision between styles and expectations of Irish writing. Yeats's and Lady Gregory's patrician Ireland—with their consequent idealization of rural simplicity—sat uneasily with a new generation. Accounts of that collision, however, are hard to come by. Brief as it is, this is an invaluable account of a first meeting, not just between writers, generations, and styles, but also between two different Irelands.

IV

"It's like going up to see God," exclaimed Walter de La Mare as he climbed the six or seven flights of stairs in Plunkett House to the office where A.E. edited *The Irish Statesman*. The first time that I had gone up them was during the years of *The Irish Homestead*, an agricultural periodical in which an occasional poem appeared. When I entered the room, A.E. motioned me to a chair. A small countrywoman dressed in tweed, a large basket beside her, was talking to him. I could hear her rustic accent as she went on—"dis," "dat," and "dose." I assumed that she was a farmer's wife come up to town to seek advice about butter and eggs or some local problem of the Co-operative Movement. So, as I waited, I glanced at the desk, piled high with papers and reference books, the cabinet files behind which I could see parts of the murals of gods and astral figures painted by A.E., their rich hues dimmed by time. As soon as the farmer's wife stopped for a moment, A.E. introduced me to her: "This is Lady Gregory."

I was astonished, for I had not recognized her, though I had often seen her head in the front stalls at the Abbey Theatre against the stage-light. Lady Gregory gave a stiff little bow and said shortly: "We've met before." No doubt, she had mistaken me for someone else, because she turned away and once more went on with her interminable "dis," "dat," and "dose." I sat there trying to make out the figures of celestial beings half hidden by the cabinet files. At last, Lady Gregory picked up her basket, said goodbye to A.E. and, without taking any further notice of me, walked out almost before he had time to open the door for her.

As a young writer, I resented such provinciality. Only later did I realize the remarkable achievement of Lady Gregory. She started her literary career at the age of fifty and published about thirty books — plays, collections of folklores, adaptations of Gaelic epic and legend, essay, reminiscences and diaries.

Francis Stuart

(1902–2000)

[EXCERPT FROM]

Black List, Section H

Francis Stuart was born in Australia in 1902. Both his parents were Ulster
Protestants. He returned to Ireland as a young child with his mother, following
the suicide of his father. In 1920 he changed his religion from Protestant to
Catholic. He married Maud Gonne's daughter, Iseult, and started on a lengthy
writing career that included poems, novels, and memoir-writing.

Stuart spent the thirties living in both Ireland and Europe. He was in
Germany during World War II. Among the novels that deal with his wartime
experience are *The Pillar of Cloud* (1948), *Redemption* (1949), *The Flowering
Cross* (1950), *Victors and Vanquished* (1958), and the defining masterpiece
Black List, Section H (1971). Although several of these novels were well
received at various times, his career and reputation have been shadowed
by his time in Nazi Germany. Stuart worked from 1942 to 1944 for *Redaktion-
Irland*, an initiative that involved broadcasting wartime propaganda aimed
at Ireland.

His views—and charges of alleged anti-Semitism—have offended his
writing colleagues in Ireland and were the subject of a law case involving the
Irish Times. Although some of his self-justifications are clearly reprehensible,
Stuart remains an essential, challenging Irish writer.

Black List, Section H confirms him as a masterly and disturbing chronicler
of disaffection. In the words of Colm Tóibín, who noted that Stuart's "legacy is

likely to remain difficult": "His novel *Black List, Section H* . . . had nothing to do with politics, with anti-semitism [*sic*] or fascism, or Nazism, but arose from something darkly and deeply rooted in his psyche—the need to betray and be seen to betray. It arose from something else too—a passionate belief that every organised structure, and that includes liberal democracy, is rotten."

The excerpt below from *Black List* concerns an earlier time. It locates Stuart in the earliest stages of his estrangement from conventional literary life—meeting William Yeats at the corner of St. Stephen's Green.

Aware that something, though not in his calculation, was lacking, an indication of another sort, he all the same felt too involved in time and nervous energy spent to draw back. Taking a check for ten pounds with him to cash at his bank, as he was still awaiting the dollars from his American publishers, he went to Dublin the day of the race.

After stopping to buy the morning papers and the mid-day racing edition of an evening one, H parked the car in St. Stephen's Green, onto whose greenery the window of the room in which he'd spent the first magic afternoons with Iseult in her blue, tasseled dress, over tea with hunks of Josephine's crusty bread and pear jam, had looked. Walking toward the tea shop in Grafton Street where he meant to read what the racing journalists had to say about the race — he'd yet to realize that this was pointless — he saw an imposing figure in a fawn spring suit; spring was in the air, in the park, on the distant English racecourse; coming toward him, head bowed, hands clasped behind curiously straight back.

It was too late for H to avoid Yeats, the last person he wanted to have to talk to at that moment, whose glance, in spite of its seeming blindness to what was near at hand, fastened on him with an upward jerk of the head at the last moment.

The poet, without preliminary greeting, announced, "George Shaw and I want you to become a founder member of the Irish Academy of Letters, an association we are establishing to oppose the censorship introduced by these non-entities of ours in their effort to establish a safe parochialism here."

Freddie Fox he knew, Brownie Carslake, Joe Childs, but who for God's sake was George Shaw? Then he recalled that this was how Yeats always referred to Bernard Shaw.

"We are inviting Liam O'Flaherty to join us," Yeats was saying; "I believe he's a friend of yours."

O'Flaherty was the only writer with whom H had had any contact, having been introduced to him in a Dublin pub shortly after his return from Paris, where he had been drinking, though more circumspectly than during the long nights at the Dome. He'd been struck by his handsome brown face and keen gull's eye.

H's instinct was to keep clear of literary circles. When he thought about the literary situation it seemed to him that with Joyce they'd reached a parting of the ways. *Ulysses*, far from being a novel to end the novel, as some claimed, was a revelation of the form's possibilities. Post-Joycean fiction had had two paths to choose between and it seemed to be taking the old, well-tried one, with its practitioners producing novels and stories easily recognizable as realistic portrayals of local character and situation. No great risks were being taken, the pitfalls were being safely avoided, no imagination had been set alight by Joyce's smoky torch. A few tricks had been learned from him, but his obsessive kind of writing was not inspiring any of H's contemporaries to delve deeper into themselves. And so there was little to haunt, disturb, offend, or affect in any significant way.

H thanked Yeats, ashamed at not declining there and then, but unable to partly because his resolution was weakened by the wavering of his attention between what he'd just been told and the race, and partly because of a reluctance to appear disrespectful.

Ready to discover oracles everywhere, H, on leaving the poet, took the meeting as a bad omen.

Patrick Kavanagh

(1904–1967)

[EXCERPT FROM]

Collected Pruse

Patrick Kavanagh was born in the border county of Monaghan, in the town of Inniskeen, in 1904. The farm was less than forty acres. He described his father as "a shoemaker, small farmer, hob doctor, and ditto lawyer." Despite the hard-pressed times, and the claustrophobia, Kavanagh kept a passionate attachment to his birthplace and a fondness for the vision of life his childhood brought him. "There are several fields I long to see again," he wrote later. Throughout his life the best of his poetry and prose would evoke the ditches, crossroads, frosty vistas and remembered visions of his birthplace.

Kavanagh was an unswerving critic of the Irish Revival. "It is usually taken for granted," he wrote in an article, "that there was a great literary renaissance in Ireland within the last fifty years. How little of all that writing was of the slightest merit!"

He moved to Dublin in 1939, where he lived for the rest of his life. He was a reluctant city-dweller. He wrote and published poetry as well as essays and journalism, much of it an implicit critique of the nationalism and idealism of the revival. One of Kavanagh's most ambitious poems, "The Great Hunger," was published in the British magazine *Horizon* in 1942 and brought out as a Cuala Press pamphlet by Frank O'Connor the same year. It was a scalding anti-pastoral, a testament of confined sexuality and pain. It remains his best-known poem. *A Soul for Sale*, published in 1947, was a landmark book of Irish poetry.

"A man (I am thinking of myself)," wrote Kavanagh in the preface to *The Collected Poems*, "innocently dabbles in words and rhymes and finds that it is his life." Throughout the forties and fifties his poems grew shorter, more visionary, more dissident. The early social comment was burned away by poems of private displacement. "Had I stuck to the tragic thing in *The Great Hunger* I would have found many powerful friends," he once wrote. *Come Dance with Kitty Stobling*, published in 1960, contains many of his best poems.

Kavanagh was a profoundly influential Irish writer. His dissent, anger, and lyric courage have shaped Irish poetry as much as any other force. He is fondly remembered in Anthony Cronin's *Dead as Doornails* and by Benedict Kiely elsewhere in this book. Excerpted below is a concise section of autobiography from Kavanagh's *Collected Pruse*. It registers his beginnings as a writer and his impatience with the models he found. He himself became, in the end, a powerful and enduring model for Irish writing.

My childhood experience was the usual barbaric life of the Irish country poor. I have never seen poverty properly analysed. Poverty is a mental condition. You hear of men and women who have chosen poverty, but you cannot choose poverty. Poverty has nothing to do with eating your fill today; it is anxiety about what's going to happen next week. The cliche poverty that you get in the working-class novel or play is a formula.

My father, being a shoemaker, was probably less poor than the small farmer classes. What was called the "dropping shilling" kept coming in. But as for the *scraidins* of farmers with their watery little hills that would physic a snipe, I don't know where they got any money. But the real poverty was the lack of enlightenment to get out and get under the moon.

I am afraid this fog of unknowing affected me dreadfully. But, as I have suggested earlier, all this is of little importance.

Round about the late nineteen-thirties, a certain prosperity came through and foolishly enough that was the time I chose to leave my native fields. I had no messianic impulse to leave. I was happy. I went against my will. A lot of our actions are like that. We miss the big emotional gesture and drift away. Is it possible to achieve our potential grand passion? I believe so. Perhaps that has been my weakness.

I came to Dublin in nineteen-thirty-nine. It was the worst mistake of my life. The Hitler war had started. I had my comfortable little holding of watery hills beside the Border. What was to bate it for a life? And yet I wasted what could have been my four glorious years, begging and scrambling around the streets of malignant Dublin. I could have done my smuggling stint. I could never see my own interest. I could never see love on bended knees begging me to come. I was always in the fog.

When I came to Dublin the Irish Literary affair was still booming. It was the notion that Dublin was a literary metropolis and Ireland, as invented and patented by Yeats, Lady Gregory and Synge, a spiritual entity. It was full of writers and poets and I am afraid I thought their work had the Irish quality.

The conversation in Poets' Pub had the richness and copiosity that H. W. Nevinson said all Dublin conversation had. To me, even then, it was tiresome drivel between journalists and civil servants. No humour at all. And, of course, they thought so much of poetry they didn't believe in the poet ating. I am not, I assure you, complaining, merely stating a few ridiculous facts. It was all my fault. What was I doing there? Wasn't I old enough to know the differ? Shouldn't I have cottoned on? Ah well, we live and we sometimes learn.

Now, part of my poverty-stricken upbringing was my belief in respectability — a steady job, decency. The bohemian rascals living it up in basements and in mountain hideouts horrified me. If I had joined them and endured them they'd have taken me to their bosoms. But I couldn't do it. Instinctively I realized that they were embittered people worshipping the poor man's poet. Their left-wingery was defeat. But the key to prosperity was with that sort of enemy and still is.

When I think of the indignities I endured in the cause of respectability I can kick myself. And me with health and strength to dig ditches, or to leap them anyway with a sack of white flour on me back. The Monaghan-Armagh-Louth border was not a severe test for a true stayer carrying top weight. I can kick myself for all the people I didn't kick then. Sometimes, when walking along a Dublin street, I might well be noticed making wild, vicious kicks at emptiness and scringing my teeth at the same time. Thinking over the matter in the light of hindsight, I realize it would not have been easy for a man of sensibility to survive in the society of my birth, but it could have been done had I been trained in the technique of reserve and restraint.

A poet is never one of the people. He is detached, remote, and the life of small-time dances and talk about football would not be for him. He might take part but could not belong.

A poet has to have an audience — half a dozen or so. Landor, who said he esteemed ten a sufficient audience, was very optimistic. I know about half a dozen and these are mainly London-based. It may be possible to live in total isolation but I don't understand how. The audience is as important as the poet. There is no audience in Ireland, though I have managed to build up out of my need a little audience for myself.

The real problem is the scarcity of a right audience which draws out of a poet what is best in him. The Irish audience that I came into contact with tried to draw out of me everything that was loud, journalistic and untrue. Such as:

> My soul was an old horse
> Offered for sale in twenty fairs.

Anthologists everywhere keep asking for this. Also asked for is another dreadful job about Mother Ireland:

> It would never be summer
>   always autumn.
> After a harvest always lost.

Thank God, I control the copyrights in these poems and nobody can use them. What the alleged poetry-lover loved was the Irishness of a thing. Irishness is a form of anti-art. A way of posing as a poet without actually being one. The New Lines poets of today have invented a similar system. They are also sympathetic to the Irish thing.

No young person today would think of coming to live in Dublin as a metropolis. A new awareness is in the air. A couple of years ago I remember a young chap accosting me in a Dublin street. He was from the southern part of Ireland and he was on his way to Rome — to take up the poetry trade. He was right too. At least something might happen to him there, a rich woman might take a fancy to his poetry and keep him in the decency and comfort which are a necessity of the poet.

I pause here to emphasize that I have no belief in the virtue of a place. Many misguided persons imagine that living in France or Italy is the equivalent of a liberal education. French in particular is the language of art. Still, Dublin hasn't the possibilities for getting hitched up to a rich woman, and this is about the only way a true poet can remain true and keep up an adequate supply of good whiskey.

I am wandering around Dublin when I run into a poetry lover.

"How are you getting on at all?" says he with much pity.

The instinct to do a day's good deed has always been a weakness with me, so I reply:

"Terrible."

"Poor fella."

"Sure what can I do?"

"And you're not writing any poetry those times. I never see anything by you in the *Irish Times*. The flash is gone. I say, the flash is gone."

"I suppose so."

"A terrible scandal that the Government doesn't do something for our Irish poets. There's forty or fifty major poets in this country today and if I had me way they'd all have a civil list pension. Is the health all right again?"

I cough hard and send him away happy. I won't be long in it and that City Hall booking for my lying-in-state can be taken up. And that was interesting too. When I was above in the Rialto Hospital, and the report of my impending demise spread, two well-wishers decided to do me proud in death: they would have me waked in the City Hall. A journalist friend of mine brought me the news as I lay in hospital at the end of a real tether, which was attached to the bottom of the bed and to rise sitting you pulled on the rope. It must have been disappointing that I didn't oblige.

I fear that the mood I have been evoking may give the impression that what happened to me is important and that I am important. Nobody is important. Nobody is major. We get to our destiny in the end. I am not in the least bitter over all this. In fact I am always in danger of bursting out laughing.

Padraic Fallon

(1905–1974)

"A Hedge Schoolmaster"

Padraic Fallon was born in Athenry in the west of Ireland in 1905. All around
him, as a young poet coming of age in that location, were the echoes and
whispers of a lost language and a broken past. The blind Gaelic poet, Raftery,
haunts his poems, as do the blighted fields and banished vowels of Irish
history. In historical terms this was "eighteenth-century" terrain. But as far
as poetry went—and this was crucial—it was also post-revival Ireland.

Fallon is a wayward and original poet. His work is lyric, argumentative,
and individual. His poems are often in the service of one of the most
distinctive aspects of his achievement, which is that he brokered a peace for
himself between William Yeats's high lyric project and a lost Gaelic order. He
is one of the only poets of his generation to manage this. It eluded Austin
Clarke; Patrick Kavanagh did not seek it. Fallon's work published after his
death includes *Poems* (1974), *Poems and Versions* (1983), *A Hymn of the Dawn*
(1991), *Look in the Mirror* (2003), and *Vision of MacConglinne* (2005). This last
volume collects his radio plays in one place—a form of audio-verse narrative
that he pioneered on Irish radio in the fifties.

Coming so soon after Yeats, Fallon was the inheritor of a difficult poetic
moment and—in terms of his own identity—a flawed poetic bequest. As he
struggled with his inheritance, national and poetic, he remade the Irish poem

he wanted to write. Indeed, the frame he created for Irish poetry—lyric, unprovincial, and often unabashedly heroic—is among the most interesting contexts made by any Irish poet of his or her time.

The empathetic and dark lyric reprinted here outlines the eighteenth-century hedge schoolmaster's life—whose task, the poem says, is "to create / Fine manners on salt and potatoes." It is interesting to measure it beside Padraic Colum's poem on the same subject earlier in this book. The difference is clear. Although Colum devised powerful themes, he was still hostage to a Georgian rhetoric. Fallon's language, in contrast, is fresh and truculent. This is a post-Yeatsian treatment of historic loss—antiromantic and persuasive.

Any niche is my college.
In wayside ditch roofed by a bramble
I light the small rush candle
Of knowledge in numbskulls.

No mouth-open fledglings sit
Around this Socrates on the turf
But Pat's famished son, the lout
And his daughter, scrapings of the pot.

Thankless the task, to create
Fine manners on salt and potatoes,
To hatch out the morrow's priest
From father's old waistcoat;

Spelling out for the shockhaired
The wars of Caesar,
Hannibal in the Alps or
The Emperor Nero on the fiddle;

To construct with a slate pencil the town Troy,
Thumbnailing the geography of heroes;
All history from Adam down
To hobble home on bare toes;

With profit and loss and mensuration
Goes towering Agamemnon
And Arius with his heresy
Of Three-in-one and Homousion,

To be lost in little walls and ricks of turf,
Dwindle down at peasant fires,
Huge ghosts in hungry fields
Wandering without memories.

No profit in it, or credit. Boors thrive
But I eat afield with the crows;
No goose gravy for Tom Euclid;
The master feasts on the hedgerows;

Yet, Pallas Athene, your true legionary
In the last earthworks, the lone garrison, still
Arrays himself in the delicate dactyls to ·
Decline you to the barbarian.

Samuel Beckett

(1906–1989)

[EXCERPT FROM]

Malone Dies

Samuel Beckett was born in Dublin in 1906. He is described in Anthony Cronin's biography of him as "a sickly, thin baby who cried constantly." He grew up on the outskirts of the city and went to Trinity College Dublin, where he studied French and was on the tennis team. By the end of the twenties, he had left Dublin for Paris, where he met Joyce. Beckett was deeply influenced by finding this Irish writer who defied categories and who, while obsessively local, was also open to European influence and levels of stylistic innovation neither known nor sanctioned in Irish writing at that time.

Beckett is a comic, lyric, absurdist writer who, as time went on, experimented more and more with style and meaning, burning off detail and explication, leaning more heavily on suggestion and symbol. Finally, the fictions and plays he produced became treasures of mystery and vision. They serve, even today, as a dark and courageous restatement of the artist's purpose and commitment in the twentieth century. In 1969 he received the Nobel Prize for literature. The citation noted that the award was "for his writing, which—in new forms for the novel and drama—in the destitution of modern man acquires its elevation."

His plays include *Eleutheria* (written during the 1940s but published in 1995), *Waiting for Godot* (1952), *Endgame* (1957), *Krapp's Last Tape* (1958), *Happy Days* (1960), *Play* (1963), *Come and Go* (1965), *Breath* (1969), *Not I*

(1972), *That Time* (1975), *Footfalls* (1975), *A Piece of Monologue* (1980),
Rockaby (1981), *Ohio Impromptu* (1981), *Catastrophe* (1982), and *What Where*
(1983). Among his novels are *Murphy* (1938), *Watt* (1945), *Mercier and Camier*
(written in 1946 but not published until 1974), *Molloy* (1951), *Malone Dies*
(1951), *The Unnamable* (1953), and *How It Is* (1961).

Beckett is known today as an artist of stripped-back theater; as a laureate
of gesture, silence, and inference. But he began as an engaged Dubliner, a
writer in the aftermath of a grand literary endeavor and a member of a
community that had been shadowed by revolution: the small Protestant
merchant class, threatened by new ways and a radical political direction.
Something of that—if you look for it—is in the wonderful passage excerpted
below from *Malone Dies*. The portrait of the anxious parents is intimate and
exact. The writing is also—rarely for Beckett—autobiographical in its
depiction of the large-headed, gull-eyed boy. It implies an actual city of Dublin
and a real situation. It also points, as little else in Beckett's work does, to the
youth and imaginative growth of a writer who would leave Ireland—as Joyce
had—only to redefine it.

He was the eldest child of poor and sickly parents. He often heard them talk
of what they ought to do in order to have better health and more money. He
was struck each time by the vagueness of these palavers and not surprised
that they never led to anything. His father was a salesman, in a shop. He used
to say to his wife, I really must find work for the evenings and the Saturday
afternoon. He added, faintly, And the Sunday. His wife would answer, But if
you do any more work you'll fall ill. And Mr. Saposcat had to allow that he
would indeed be ill-advised to forego his Sunday rest. These people at least
are grown up. But his health was not so poor that he could not work in the
evenings of the week and on the Saturday afternoon. At what, said his wife,
work at what? Perhaps secretarial work of some kind, he said. And who will
look after the garden? said his wife. The life of the Saposcats was full of
axioms, of which one at least established the criminal absurdity of a garden

without roses and with its paths and lawns uncared for. I might perhaps grow vegetables, he said. They cost less to buy, said his wife. Sapo marvelled at these conversations. Think of the price of manure, said his mother. And in the silence which followed Mr. Saposcat applied his mind, with the earnestness he brought to everything he did, to the high price of manure which prevented him from supporting his family in greater comfort, while his wife made ready to accuse herself, in her turn, of not doing all she might. But she was easily persuaded that she could not do more without exposing herself to the risk of dying before her time. Think of the doctor's fees we save, said Mr. Saposcat. And the chemist's bills, said his wife. Nothing remained but to envisage a smaller house. But we are cramped as it is, said Mrs. Saposcat. And it was an understood thing that they would be more and more so with every passing year until the day came when, the departure of the first-born compensating the arrival of the new-born, a kind of equilibrium would be attained. Then little by little the house would empty. And at last they would be all alone, with their memories. It would be time enough then to move. He would be pensioned off, she at her last gasp. They would take a cottage in the country where, having no further need of manure, they could afford to buy it in cartloads. And their children, grateful for the sacrifices made on their behalf, would come to their assistance. It was in this atmosphere of unbridled dream that these conferences usually ended. It was as though the Saposcats drew the strength to live from the prospect of their impotence. But sometimes, before reaching that stage, they paused to consider the case of their first-born. What age is he now? asked Mr. Saposcat. His wife provided the information, it being understood that this was of her province. She was always wrong. Mr. Saposcat took over the erroneous figure, murmuring it over and over to himself as though it were a question of the rise in price of some indispensable commodity, such as butcher's meat. And at the same time he sought in the appearance of his son some alleviation of what he had just heard. Was it at least a nice sirloin? Sapo looked at his father's face, sad, astonished, loving, disappointed, confident in spite of all. Was it on the cruel flight of the years he brooded, or on the time it was taking his son to command a salary? Sometimes he stated wearily his regret that his son should not be more eager to make himself useful about the place. It is better for him to prepare his examinations, said his wife. Starting from a given theme their minds laboured in unison. They had no conversation properly speaking. They made use of the spoken word in much the same way as the guard of a train makes use of his flags, or of his lantern. Or else they said, This is where we get down. And their son once signalled, they wondered sadly if it was not the mark of superior minds to fail miserably at the written paper and cover themselves with ridicule at the viva voce. They were not always content to gape in silence at the same landscape. At least his health is good, said Mr. Saposcat. Not all that, said his wife. But no definite disease, said Mr. Saposcat. A nice thing that would be, at his age, said his wife. They did not know why he was committed to a liberal profession. That was yet another thing that went without saying. It was therefore impossible he should be unfitted for it. They thought of him as a doctor for preference. He will look after us when we are old, said Mrs. Saposcat. And her husband replied, I see him rather as a surgeon, as though after a certain age people were inoperable.

What tedium. And I call that playing. I wonder if I am not talking yet again about myself. Shall I be incapable, to the end, of lying on any other subject? I feel the old dark gathering, the solitude preparing, by which I know myself, and the call of that ignorance which might be noble and is mere poltroonery. Already I forget what I have said. That is not how to play. Soon I shall not know where Sapo comes from, nor what he hopes. Perhaps I had better abandon this story and go on to the second, or even the third, the one about the stone. No, it would be the same thing. I must simply be on my guard, reflecting on what I have said before I go on and stopping, each time disaster threatens, to look at myself as I am. That is just what I wanted to avoid. But there seems to be no other solution. After that mud-bath I shall be better able to endure a world unsullied by my presence. What a way to reason. My eyes, I shall open my eyes, look at the little heap of my possessions, give my body the old orders I know it cannot obey, turn to my spirit gone to rack and ruin, spoil my agony the better to live it out, far already from the world that parts at last its labia and lets me go.

I have tried to reflect on the beginning of my story. There are things I do not understand. But nothing to signify. I can go on.

Sapo had no friends — no, that won't do.

Sapo was on good terms with his little friends, though they did not exactly love him. The dolt is seldom solitary. He boxed and wrestled well, was fleet of foot, sneered at his teachers and sometimes even gave them impertinent answers. Fleet of foot? Well well. Pestered with questions one day he cried, Haven't I told you I don't know! Much of his free time he spent confined in school doing impositions and often he did not get home before eight o'clock at night. He submitted with philosophy to these vexations. But he would not let himself be struck. The first time an exasperated master threatened him with a cane, Sapo snatched it from his hand and threw it out of the window, which was closed, for it was winter. This was enough to justify his expulsion. But Sapo was not expelled when he so richly deserved to be. For I want as little as possible of darkness in his story. A little darkness, in itself, at the time, is nothing. You think no more about it and you go on. But I know what darkness is, it accumulates, thickens, then suddenly bursts and drowns everything.

I have not been able to find out why Sapo was not expelled. I shall have to leave this question open. I try not to be glad. I shall make haste to put a safe remove between him and this incomprehensible indulgence. I shall make him live as though he had been punished according to his deserts. We shall turn our backs on this little cloud, but we shall not let it out of our sight. It will not cover the sky without our knowing, we shall not suddenly raise our eyes, far from help, far from shelter, to a sky as black as ink. That is what I have decided. I see no other solution. It is the best I can do.

At the age of fourteen he was a plump rosy boy. His wrists and ankles were thick, which made his mother say that one day he would be even bigger than his father. Curious deduction. But the most striking thing about him was his big round head horrid with flaxen hair as stiff and straight as the bristles of a brush. Even his teachers could not help thinking he had a remarkable head and they were all the more irked by their failure to get anything into it. His father would say, when in good humour, One of these days he will astonish us all. It was thanks to Sapo's skull that he was enabled to hazard this opinion and, in defiance of the facts and against his better judgment, to revert to it from time to time. But he could not endure the look in Sapo's eyes and went out of his way not to meet it. He has your eyes, his wife would say. Then Mr. Saposcat chafed to be alone, in order to inspect his eyes in the mirror. They were palest blue. Just a shade lighter, said Mrs. Saposcat.

Sapo loved nature, took an interest.

This is awful.

Sapo loved nature, took an interest in animals and plants and willingly raised his eyes to the sky, day and night. But he did not know how to look at all these things, the looks he rained upon them taught him nothing about them. He confused the birds with one another, and the trees, and could not tell one crop from another crop. He did not associate the crocus with the spring nor the chrysanthemum with Michaelmas. The sun, the moon, the planets and the stars did not fill him with wonder. He was sometimes tempted by the knowledge of these strange things, sometimes beautiful, that he would have about him all his life. But from his ignorance of them he drew a kind of joy, as from all that went to swell the murmur, You are a simpleton. But he loved the flight of the hawk and could distinguish it from all others. He would stand rapt, gazing at the long pernings, the quivering poise, the wings lifted for the plummet drop, the wild reascent, fascinated by such extremes of need, of pride, of patience and solitude.

Kate O'Brien

(1897–1974)

[EXCERPT FROM]

My Ireland

Kate O'Brien was born in Limerick, the daughter of an extravagant, cheerful father—Tom O'Brien, who bred horses—and a mother who died when she was six. She attended convent school in Limerick and celebrated the experience in her memoir *Presentation Parlour*. In 1915 she went to University College Dublin. Like other first-year arts students, she attended Roger Chauvire's lectures on French literature. In 1962, in an essay called *UCD as I Forget It*, she recalled that experience: "He took literature into cold daylight; he cut it out clearly as an exact and exacting skill. Listening to Chauvire upon French writing in the 17th and 18th century, I grew up."

In the early 1920s O'Brien moved to London. In 1924, for a brief time, she was a wife. In Hampstead Town Hall she married Gustav Renier, who became well known later for his polemical book called *The English, Are They Human?* The marriage ended in less than a year, however. Although never politically or even overtly lesbian, her writing explores with subtlety and courage the stresses on female sexuality in a conventional society. Two of her novels, *Mary Lavelle* (1936) and *The Land of Spices* (1941), deal with homosexual themes. Both were banned in Ireland. These themes continued, although more obliquely, in such novels as *The Flower of May* (1953) and *As Music and Splendour* (1958).

There is a consistent, visionary quality in O'Brien's most assured work.

Despite the Galsworthian influence evident in her first best-selling book
Without My Cloak (1931), her true interests ran deeper than class or generation. It is her preoccupation with sexuality in the Irish context, and with the
fractures between sense and spirit—as well as the struggle to heal and resolve
them—that make her best novels, *Mary Lavelle* (1936) and *The Ante-Room*
(1931), such compelling and essential reading.

Despite her deep love for Limerick, it is rare to see Irish identity or themes
of Irish imagination made explicit in O'Brien's work. Her combination of
visionary Catholicism and dissident sexuality, as well as persuasive style, have
made her a central Irish writer. But it is unusual to see her locate herself in the
literary traditions of her own country. This excerpt from her travel book *My
Ireland* (1962) provides a rare and welcome glimpse of her views of one of her
forebears, Lady Gregory.

Augusta Persse of Roxborough in Galway was born in 1852, and in 1881 she
married an elderly neighbour, Sir William Gregory of Coole Park. Before she
was forty she was a widow, with one child, Robert, and she set herself to
bring him up well and to preserve for him, with planting and good hus-
bandry, the estate of his fathers. The Gregorys, Colonial servants of
England, had usually been good landlords and were respected, and unremarkable. So was their large, bare-faced, Georgian house in great woods by
the Seven Lakes — respected and unremarkable. And that was enough for it
to be, we can imagine, in the view of the sensible, intelligent woman who
governed it in the 1890s for her little son.

Coole Park is gone now. The house is gone, that is. The Irish Land
Commission sold its stones to a knocker about thirty years ago. The surrounding woods are being afforested and administered by the Department
of Lands; the lakes still flow and drain into each other, though the swans
have left them — for Lough Cutra nearby, they say; and the Tree, the beech
tree of Coole in the now desolate garden near the ghost of the house, is
guarded by wire netting, so that those irrepressible illiterates and unknowns

who must carve their petnames or their arrowed hearts, if at all possible, on
the Parthenon or on Cormac's Chapel, may be baulked of mingling their
absurd memorials with the gaily hacked initials of a few great people.

More beautiful houses, richer, grander, flamed and vanished through
Ireland in the early years of this century, in awful causes of war, such as are
common vengeances and offences throughout the world. But Coole had no
enemies and was not burnt, but passed peacefully in its time to the Irish
Government. And it is only by a fluke, by that fluke of fame that Augusta
Gregory, the last Lady Gregory, brought to it in serving Irish literature that
within half of one life-time it changed from an unassuming country house
into a landmark and a national pride. And only just before it died. Like its
own swans, Coole sang before its death.

What happened was this: Augusta Gregory, about her landlord business,
grew interested in the people she met all about between Gort and Kinvara.
Suddenly in middle age she found her mind startled and refreshed by their
idiom and habit, and their turns of thought. Her young son also grew alert to
their speech and wanted to learn it. Douglas Hyde was bicycling about the
west, collecting the Irish language, its stories and poems — the love songs of
Connacht. Lady Gregory listened to him, and to the people he listened to —
and, in order to teach her son, set herself to learn Irish.

That was the small, private beginning.

Next was that the kind widow asked the young poet, William Butler
Yeats, to spend some summer months in her house. It was 1897. Yeats was
unhappy, hopelessly in love — as, for the fertilisation and benefit of English
poetry, he was to remain for some years. His hostess knew this — and probably thought it natural and seasonal in him. But for his health she dragged
him with her in and out of the shops and cottages where she took down stories and tried to learn her Irish. Yeats listened, and half-listened — and went
off in the autumn, back to Woburn Buildings and The Rhymers' Club, and
Lionel Johnson, and *The Countess Cathleen*.

In 1898 he was back again, at Edward Martyn's house nearby, Tulira. His
host had written two plays, *The Heather Field* and *Maeve*, and he had completed *The Countess Cathleen*. And, by chance, on a wet summer day, the two
playwrights and Lady Gregory drinking tea in the house of a neighbour,
Count Florimond de Basterot, Yeats sighed, as he thought irrelevantly, for

his "hopeless plan" of an Irish Theatre. "In a little country house at Duras, on the sea-coast where Galway ends and Clare begins." Lady Gregory had never been interested in the theatre, but the old, sophisticated Count liked the talk of new plays — so it went on, and she listened, and possibilities pressed and dissolved. And before dark she "put up" the Abbey's first £25, and the Irish Theatre was born.

The host to this event was the last of a French émigré family which had taken shelter here rather than in Dublin in 1793, and after restoration of its titles in France had retained Duras House near Kinvara as a summer place. And this last de Basterot, Florimond, who died there in 1904, had finicking, fastidious ideas in regard to race and place. He lived always between Paris, Rome and Duras House — could abide neither London nor Dublin. He was a committed pagan and worldling, and was greatly loved and respected by the quiet people round Kinvara. Arthur Symons wrote of him in *Cities of Italy* that "after a lifetime of disinterested travelling in which he trained his eyes to a perfect susceptibility and his judgment to a perfect impartiality in the noting and comparison of so much of the world's scenery, came finally to a deliberate preference of this scenery about Rome . . ."

The Count was in fact a connoisseur, for only a true connoisseur would be so authoritatively at peace with the Roman landscape. So his summer fidelity to Duras pleases one who knows West Clare and Galway to be proper fields of searching and unsentimental *expertise*. One wonders what his friend Guy de Maupassant thought of the Burren and the seashore when he visited Count Florimond there? Paul Bourget wittily linked the region's spiritual to its physical character when he christened it *Le Rojaume de Pierre*. But the thirteenth-century Cistercian Fathers, building the Abbey of Corcomroe nearby, were ahead of Bourget when they named their foundation *Santa Petra*. For a holy rock it is in its forlornness, nave standing open to the winds, and to distracted spirits, as Yeats thought.

We must go back to Coole. Only briefly, to look enviously down the rides of the seven woods; to taste silence and consider the nettles and fallen stones that Yeats foresaw; and to decipher a few of the carvings on the beech-tree. George Bernard Shaw spared neither trouble nor space for his three letters; probably there are other initials from the great, general world, but I do not recognise them. The important ones, for what was afoot between Coole and

Dublin, are W. B. Y., J. M. S. and A. G. herself. Yeats named the three, "Augusta Gregory and John Synge and I." But Lennox Robinson too indeed, and Sean O'Casey, who loved his hostess truly, and Jack Yeats and George Moore and — they are not easy to decipher from beyond the wire netting, but all of them together are the Irish Literary Movement — and it moved from Coole. For the Old Lady did not say NO, either at the beginning of her groping purpose, or when the road was clear. She taught herself to be an artist and to serve and drive artists — and there is no better thing to do, never mind the mistakes, the rows or the ingratitude.

"She was like a serving maid amongst us," said some old man about the place where she died. She was a serving maid to the Abbey Theatre too.

Sean O'Faolain

(1900–1991)

[EXCERPT FROM]

"The Gaelic Cult"

Sean O'Faolain was born in Cork in 1900, the son of a member of the Royal Irish Constabulary. In his youth he was especially influenced by the plays that came to the Cork Opera House. He wrote of them as bringing into his youth "strange and wonderful news—that writers could also write books and plays about the common everyday reality of Irish life."

O'Faolain's legacy remains historically that of a writer emerging in a new Ireland. His belief in the importance of Irish experience remained central until his death in 1991, but never complacent. His short fiction, visibly inflected by Turgenev and Chekhov, addressed themes of faith and doubt; of sexuality and sin. His work is deeply antiauthoritarian, and he remains a model of writerly dissent—never accepting the relation between the State and the writer as exempt from challenge. O'Faolain's short stories attracted attention early and were later gathered into his *Collected Stories* (1983). His early novels, *A Nest of Simple Folk* (1933) and *Bird Alone* (1936), were similarly successful.

O'Faolain is one of the few self-conscious men of letters to emerge in Irish writing in the twentieth century. He was a master at setting out the challenges for Irish writers in the aftermath of the new state. Often he identified the challenges not just as craft and experiment—although he published a fine critique of form, *The Short Story*, in 1948. More often than not, however, he defined the dangers to the Irish imagination as ones of self-delusion: in article after article, in argument and essay, he portrayed the Irish mind as mired in its wish list of "Irishness"; the complacent identity of a risen people.

In his editorials in his wartime journal *The Bell*, founded with Peadar O'Donnell in 1940, O'Faolain upbraided the fledgling state. Again and again, he took the edge of his wit to the pieties of the new Ireland. In a later generation Benedict Kiely said that the unswerving candor of O'Faolain's polemic had "put Irish writers in his debt forever." This piece below is from his editorial in the December 1944 edition of *The Bell*. It makes an energetic opposition to other arguments on the Irish language in this book. It also continues the emphasis on how crucial and painful that dream of a recovered world was, and would always be, to the Irish writer.

By about 1900, there began to emerge — almost wholly in English, it may be said — a vivid awareness of the existence of an Ireland that had been completely forgotten. That was Gaelic Ireland. What was even more wonderful and exciting, there were still places where men and women told ancient folktales by the fireside, believed in the *sidhe*, held in their rude hands the thin thread of Ariadne back to the forgotten labyrinth. All one needed to get back to that wonder-world was to be able to speak Irish. One could even touch that world without it. Yeats, Lady Gregory, Synge, Colum, all the poets of the Anglo-Irish Revival drank eagerly at the fountain, and handed the winy goblets back to such of the populace as had the wit and heart to gather around them. No young man reading these lines — not even young Gaelic enthusiasts of today — can realise what that discovery of the "ancient mother" meant. Its outward signs were Anglo-Irish Literature and the founding of the Gaelic League in 1893. But let us keep our eyes on the point — there is still no mention of the "Gaelic Nation" as a political ideal.

So far, then, we see the three elements: constitutional politics, in pretty low water after the fall of Parnell, the Separatists now burrowing underground, and this new Gaelic inspiration. Arthur Griffith established Sinn Fein in 1905–1906. (I repeat that there is, so far as I have been able to see, no mention in all his writings of the "Gael.") The first modern politician after

Parnell whom I have found seizing on Gaelic Ireland *as a prototype*, or model, to be reincarnated in a politically free Ireland is, of all people, the Socialist Jim Connolly in his *Labour in Irish History* (1910). Whether it is with him or with somebody else that the grand delusion begins he had it badly. He was apparently under the impression that the antique social order enshrined for those whom he called "our Gaelic forefathers" certain nobly desirable democratic rights and institutions, and that the modern, debased commercialised Irish stood between the people and these admirable traditions. Alas for the glory of Tara's Hall, nothing could have been farther from the truth. He could have saved himself and thousands of others much disappointment and more folly had he done no more than look at the Gaelic preface to the great collection of Gaelic Laws known as the "Senchus Mor," which lists all the awful things that existed before these laws were codified — plagues and disorders of every kind, and, as the crowning-worst, such general anarchy that "even the churl's son dared to consider himself the equal of the son of a king."

Whoever began it, there it is, in one example, already at work: and if some student of our universities should make the whole question a subject of research he would find other examples. I seem to remember that Mr. Sean Milroy (Heaven forgive him) wrote a book, also in praise of the Brehon Laws. Constance Markievicz gave lectures about the subject — an extraordinary medley of Marx, Republicanism, and Gaeldom. The general idea of the "Gaelic Nation" is implicit in the very title of Mr. P. S. O'Hegarty's interesting book *The Indestructible Nation* which, note, was originally given as a series of lectures to the London Gaelic League "in [I quote the author's own words] the first and best decade of Sinn Fein, in 1911–1913."

There one can see the idea of a Revival shake hands with the idea of a Revolution. As we know, the Gaelic League was shattered by that hand-shake. The first President and founder, Dr. Douglas Hyde, now President of Ireland, resigned from it in 1915 when the militant separatists inside the League — they had deliberately gone into it in order to control it politically — insisted on making Independence one of its avowed objects. From that day onward politics infected Gaelic; and the idea of the "Gael" and the "Gaelic Nation" infected politics. It is all summed up in a well-known phrase of Pearse — "Not merely free but Gaelic as well, not merely Gaelic but free as well."

I am afraid that we have become so accustomed to the jargon of this mystique that some, reading that phrase again, will dumbly react to it in a reflex now almost mechanically conditioned by twenty years of propaganda. They may say, "A Gaelic Nation? Well — why not? It sounds all right." It sounds all right. But let us shake off the drug and ask: What did Connolly and Pearse mean? They refer to a period when the people of Ireland possessed and lived by an indigenous culture of their very own — laws, dress, language, social order, and so on: and they refer, simultaneously, to later periods when various Irishmen, finding themselves misgoverned by the British people, propounded the solution of the absolute and unqualified separation of Ireland from Britain as a modern Republic. Two entirely different ideas are there thrown together — one cannot say "mixed" together because they are immiscible. For the antique, Gaels never heard of and would have fought to the death against the idea of a Republic and all it connotes, and the men who first initiated the idea of Republicanism — Tone onward — knew nothing about the antique Gaels and would, whether Davis, Lalor or Jim Connolly, have been appalled by the reality of those days and conditions. If anything other than common-sense were needed to prove that the men of 1916 were, like the men of '48 and '67, not social revolutionaries but romantic insurrectionists, this idea of an Ancient-Modern-Republican-Gaelic-Nation should suffice. It is obvious that nobody could base anything like a social revolution on the lines of this fairy-tale fantasy.

Actually long before 1916 a very real revolution in Ireland had been brought about by the pressure of the Irish Parliamentary Party, or really by Davitt — a true and genuine social reform of the largest kind — when they won the land for the people: so that the most serious social gravamen had already been removed before the political change-over occurred. That marks off Davitt as a man apart in Irish history: one of our very few real revolutionaries, perhaps our only one. It shows us, too, how revolutions occur, on the pressure of actual not imaginary circumstances. The only other big thing waiting to be done after that was perceived clearly by another realistic man, Griffith — the need for autonomy in order to make possible an industrial revolution. So that what is needed, and perhaps alone needed today is not so much a further revolution as a revolutionary *approach* to both land and industry to set the dynamo going full-blast.

We can see, now, why the insurrectionists seized on the Gaelic Nation ideal, absurd and impossible as it was: their hearts were full, but their minds were vacant: into the vacuum there swept the first exciting idea to hand. Far be it from me to assail the memory of brave and noble-hearted men whose courage and idealism we will for ever honour. But we must not imagine that they had all the virtues; and the virtue of political thought they had not. Yet, to this day, their dual theory dominates the minds of our legislators, or of most of them — I find it hard to think that men like Mr. Sean Lemass, for instance, is thus affected — so that all you have to say to them is "Not merely free but Gaelic as well, not merely Gaelic but free as well," and their mouths will begin to water like Pavlov's dogs.

It is an amazing hypnosis. But still more amazing is the manner in which it affects the minds it dominates. For it produces nothing positive. On the contrary its effect is wholly negative and inhibitory; as with some mumbo-jumbo that is feared for its destructive powers and given mere lip-service to keep it quiet. Anything that has been done has been done without reference to it or without any assistance from it — whether it be the Shannon Scheme, or improved rural housing, or the growing of wheat, or migratory schemes to lessen unemployment, or the efficiency of the Army, or the development of Air Transport, or Tourism, etc. Thus all that the more perfervid Gaelic addicts have ever contributed to any of these things is a nark. Why should the Army play rugby! Tourism will ruin the West! Keep the Gaelic migrants inside a kind of Red Indian reservation — as was proposed last month by the Gaelic League at its Annual Conference. This is natural because the mystique is the opponent of all modernisations and improvisations — being by nature, in its constant reference to the middle-ages — terrified of the modern world, afraid of modern life, inbred in thought, and, so, utterly narrow in outlook. All its ideas of life are mediæval. Take even industry which might be thought safe from it. Can we seriously hope to develop a dynamic industrial future with a system of education which is based on an uncritical adoration for Finn MacCool (or Thomas Davis) and which has no interest in encouraging, let alone in producing, young technicians? Look even at the school-readers *in English*. For all the reference they make to the world of science or industry they might have been prepared for Ancient Britons. And does the mystique not affect politics — its politics are shiveringly isolationist; and is not our industrial future close bound to politics, seeing that we can have no

large commercial future unless we look to the wide world as our market? In
culture the mystique is equally fearful and inbred. That should be evident in
our literary censorship alone which strives to keep out anything that savours
of a bold facing-up to modern problems — banning even books by reputable
Catholics abroad, books and pamphlets sanctioned by the most reputable
members of all churches. How utterly different all that is to the magnificent
courage of O'Connell, who said to our people, "There is another world outside. Follow me. I will lead you into it."

But we are not yet finished with the wonders of this hypnosis. We know,
as I have said, the many good things our legislators have done without
thanks to it. That means that when they do anything effective they are, for
that time, free of the Cult and do not really, in their clearer brains, then
dream any longer of harking back to the mediæval myth. Yet, not one single
man of them will admit it. They still imagine that they are carrying out the
Gaelic gospel. They are thus in the delightfully befuddled condition, and
this is the most wonderful wonder of all, of being under the delusion that
they are under a delusion.

Is this just a joke? Simple examples of the result offer themselves fre-
quently. Thus, last month, as I write, the Gaelic half of the delusion was
under the delusion that it was holding an Oireachtas or annual all-Ireland
Festival of Gaelic Culture. Apart from a couple of ceilidhes in the Dublin
Mansion House, and a boxing tournament, there was little sign of a Cultural
Festival at all. Yet, even such hard-bitten businessmen as Mr. Louis Elliman
of the Gaiety Theatre, who is a Jew, and his genial English-born manager, Mr.
Hamlyn Benson, were apparently hypnotised into believing in the pleasant
fancy. They must have been slightly puzzled when, in due course, the curtain
for the Gaelic play *Deamar agus a Bhean* rose on a theatre apparently quite
empty. The Dublin "Evening Mail" reported that it was not, in fact, quite
empty; the Minister for Education with a party of eight held the dress-cir-
cle; and there were also six critics in a bunch; the Gallery was empty; on
searching the highways and by-ways of the Parterre and the rest of the house
14 other devotees were discovered in the darkness. There was also, during
the week, an Exhibition of Paintings, reported by the "Irish Times" as being
mainly reminiscent of South Kensington. Though how a painter, or a boxer

that, for the rest of the year, has been just a painter or a boxer can suddenly become a Gaelic painter or boxer is difficult to understand.

An even more puzzling example of the stultifying effect of being under a double delusion is the political fact. The whole argument of those hypnotised by the ideal of the "Gaelic Nation" is that we are being infected by the English language, by English and American books, by English and American music, by English radio, by English manners and customs. If that be so, it surely seems more than illogical if these people should deliberately decide to go on enjoying all the advantages of political association with the country which is so constantly proclaimed as the source and origin of all these allegedly offensive things. The reason for that is clear, too. For what has happened is that the separatist half of the thing has been quietly dropped, or exchanged for a variety of subterfuges whose final *effect* has been to muddle us completely as to our true relations with Britain and the world. It was dropped, of course, because to be a genuine separatist you have to possess that revolutionary approach which I have mentioned. And whatever else we have got, we have not got that. The whole thing is thus a dead mouse that our leaders go on playing with — possibly because they do not yet realise that the unhappy mouse died about two hundred and fifty years before they discovered it. But the whole thing is very foolish, and rather painful. Though there is something touching about it too. It is all part of the natural tendency of an inexperienced people — without insult and indeed in a certain oblique pride we might call ourselves a primitive people — to go on myth-making long after the age of myths. It would appear in fact that there is a lot of Hans Andersen still left in men like Mr. de Valera. Let us not confuse this political mystique or cult with the specific matter of the Language itself. That is a quite different matter. That is a simple and clear matter. Let us, by all means, learn and read and, when we choose, speak our language. It has its value, it has its pieties. You can, it is true, be free men and not speak a native language: but that is obvious — as the example of America and thousands upon thousands of good Irishmen today can shew. You can speak your native tongue and not even desire to be politically free: as Wales can shew. Yet, if we do not possess our own native language, and what it contains, we are spiritually and intellectually the poorer.

On the other hand, a language is in itself only a noise. It has no mysterious therapeutic value. As many unpleasant people speak Gaelic as English. But the unfounded notion behind the present Gaelic cult is that you can "think" Gaelic: as if, did I choose to write this article in Gaelic, I would think it out to a different conclusion! No — unless a language is a door to a rich store of thought, political thought, social thought, philosophical thought, scientific thought, it can only be a doorway to those indefinable things — often foolish, but always warm, human and precious — that we call our memories. Gaelic will do that for us, but only that, since of all those other kinds of thought the Gaelic world has nothing to offer us. Let us then drop the cult. The course will be simple after that.

Irish should be made the language of instruction in districts where it is the home language, and English the second language taught as a school subject. I would not, at any stage, use English as a medium in such districts. Where English is the home language it must of necessity be the first language in the schools. But I would have a compulsory second language (*voluntarily selected*) satisfied that in five-sixths of the schools it would be Irish. But in all details of their programme, the schools should have autonomy.

That seems a reasonable proposal. Would it satisfy the devotees of the Cult? Would it satisfy Mr. de Valera? I hope so, because with the exception of the two italicised words — inserted solely by way of explanation of his meaning — it is a quotation from Patrick Pearse, and his solution. If it were adopted we would be free of the mental miasma that has resulted from the Cult, free to think out our problems with unconfused minds as a modern people in a modern world.

Conor Cruise O'Brien

(b. 1917)

[EXCERPT FROM]

"Pride in the Language"

Conor Cruise O'Brien was born in Dublin in 1917. His parents and several of his relatives were noted nationalists and activists. He graduated from Trinity College in 1939 and went into foreign affairs, becoming both a diplomat and literary critic. He has been able to gather separate lives of writing, political service, and activism into a rare poise.

After a distinguished career as a diplomat, O'Brien was elected to the Dail (Irish Parliament) in 1969. He served as minister for posts and telegraphs in 1973. His views on Irish nationalism, partially set forth in such books as *States of Ireland* (1972), were blunt and controversial. They were also consistent with his sense of the contribution of Edmund Burke, the eighteenth-century Irish orator and statesman. Burke's perception of tyranny within radicalism led to his defining treatise, *Reflections on the Revolution in France*, published in 1790. O'Brien's important study of Burke, *The Great Melody*, was published in 1992.

Ireland has had relatively few public intellectuals. Conor Cruise O'Brien is one. In his comments and analyses he seeks to resolve spheres of action and language that are often kept separate. He has an acute sense of the theater of events, matched with a subtle appreciation for the way language can alter the perception of them. As a cultural historian in Ireland, he has had few equals, although his views would be contested by several of the writers— living and dead—in this book. Nevertheless, his acute commentary often touches a nerve, and his prose has unique edge and wit. In the process it redefines connections between writers and writing that may be obstructed by—as he sees it—a false historical retrospect; by hypocrisy or even apathy.

This eloquent and abrasive piece, whose occasion is the death of Sean O'Faolain, is an example. It identifies self-deceptions about the language spoken in Ireland. It also continues the charged conversation O'Faolain initiated in *The Bell*, which is taken up by other writers later in this book. It comes from his 1994 essay collection, *Anthology*.

The Cultural Capital of Europe did not distinguish itself last week. On Saturday last, a day of brilliant sunshine, the Memorial Service for Sean O'Faolain was held at St. Joseph's Church, Glasthule.

Sean O'Faolain, who died at the age of 91, could aptly (though not elegantly) be described as the Grand Old Man of Irish Letters. If a writer of comparable distinction, belonging to any other nation, were being commemorated in the national capital, the Memorial Service would have been crowded with representatives of the nation's entire Establishment.

That applies to every other nation in the European Community (with the possible exception of Belgium) and to other European nations, such as Poland, Czechoslovakia, Sweden and Norway. Not so with us.

Let it be recorded here, for the information of posterity that, at the Memorial Service for Sean O'Faolain, on May 4, 1991, there was present not one single member of the Oireachtas, the Parliament of Ireland.

There was, indeed, a degree of official representation: the bare bleak minimum. The President was represented by an aide-de-camp; so was the Taoiseach. I am not reproaching either the President or the Taoiseach with their absence; both may well have had prior commitments.

But the absence of all members of an entire Parliament cannot be similarly explained. What that symbolises is a gaping hole in the heart of our national culture. Dublin, in the 1990s, isn't fit to be the Cultural Capital of anything.

I reflected sadly, during the week, on the meaning of that act of cultural absenteeism, on the part of the elected representatives of the Irish people. That act has to mean something: what does it mean?

I believe that it reflects a skewed relationship, on our collective part, to language and consequently to literature. We speak, read and write one language: English. That was the language in which Sean O'Faolain habitually wrote and through which he became famous. But we feel obscurely that we ought to be speaking, reading and writing a language other than that which we actually do speak, read and write.

We have two official languages: the second is the one we use: the first is the one we think we ought to be using. We don't read — and most of us can't read — the writers who use the first official language, but we have some respect for them, in a vague and perfunctory sort of way.

We do read the writers who write in the language we habitually use, but we don't feel much collective pride in them. Their collective product is denominated "Anglo-Irish Literature." We are unlikely to feel warm towards anything labelled "Anglo-Irish."

The Gaelic Revival movement will be a hundred years old in two years time. It did not succeed. It failed to preserve even what was then left. There were over 600,000 Irish speakers at the turn of the century, and most of these would have been native speakers.

A report published this week shows the number of native speakers is down to 10,000.

The Revival Movement failed to revive, and its only movement was backwards. But it did generate a huge amount of political hypocrisy and — what was worse, because more insidious — a habit of listening to official nonsense, in an approving sort of way, as you might listen to the prattle of an innocent child.

The Gaelic Revival failed to persuade the Irish people to speak Irish. But it did succeed in something. It succeeded in securing the lip-service of the great majority of the elected representatives of the Irish people (in this Republic).

And it succeeded in making the Irish people a little ashamed of the fact that they continue to speak English, and not Irish. The shame is not sufficient to bring about a resolve to learn Irish properly, and use it habitually.

If it were sufficient to do that, that might be a very good thing. But it is sufficient to make us feel permanently ill at ease with the language we actually do speak.

We use it pragmatically, and as a matter of expediency. But we don't love it. We don't take pride in it. We even tend to resent it as something imposed on us by the ancient oppressor.

We forget that our people chose to become English-speakers, of their own free will, at a time when they could have gone on speaking Irish had they chosen to do so.

I don't know whether there is any other people which habitually speaks one language, while feeling that it ought to be speaking another. (Some of the Welsh, perhaps, or some of the Scots.) In any case, it is a curious condition and cannot be a healthy one, psychologically speaking.

And it is that condition, I believe, that accounts for the complete absence of our parliamentarians from the Memorial Service for Sean O'Faolain.

Since we have collectively — and silently — decided to go on speaking English, we must, for the sake of our psychological health, come to terms with that decision. We must learn both to respect and to love the language we actually speak.

We must learn to honour the men and women of our stock who have enriched the literature of that language. As long as we have not learned these things, we shall be lacking in self-respect.

People who have no respect for the language they speak can have no respect for their own selves.

Liam O'Flaherty

(1896–1984)

[EXCERPT FROM]

Two Years

Liam O'Flaherty was born on Gort na gCapall, on Inishmore, the largest of the Aran Islands. He was educated in Galway and went to University College Dublin. He then made the decision to join the British Army. He suffered shell shock in France in 1917, then traveled widely, returning to Ireland in 1920. He was part of the War of Independence and opposed the Treaty with Britain. His Republican politics were interwoven with a strong left-wing stance and support for the labor movement. All of this, later, would become part of his literary work.

O'Flaherty was a melodramatic realist. His masters were in Europe. The shadows across his work are those of Zola and Balzac—of writers who heightened the reality they selected. He was one of the first Irish writers to apply the dramatic lighting of this technique to Irish historical subject matter. His masterly short story "Going into Exile" as well as his pathbreaking novel *Famine* (published in 1937) are radically enabled by this technique. His other novels include *Thy Neighbour's Wife* (1923); *The Black Soul* (1924); *The Informer* (1925), which was made into a film of the same name by John Ford; *The Assassin* (1928); *Skerret* (1932); and *Shame the Devil* (1934). His short story collections include *The Short Stories of Liam O'Flaherty* (1937), *Two Lovely Beasts and Other Stories* (1948), *Dúil* (1953), and *The Pedlar's Revenge and Other Stories* (1976). He also published *The Life of Tim Healy* (1927).

For a new generation of Irish writers, Ireland was no longer so local, nor so welcoming. O'Flaherty's intellectual curiosity, international outreach, and impatience with his own country would become the standard kit of new Irish writers. In the piece excerpted below, from an autobiographical book called *Two Years* (1930), he describes his decision to return to Ireland. It is a watershed in his young writing life: He has traveled. He has been away. But, finally, despite it all, it is his own country that calls him back. This, too, would become a familiar story.

I RETURN HOME

I was beginning to see myself. I did not yet see myself, nor was I destined to do so for another two years. But this sudden fit of laughter was a sign of the inner madness that was growing on me, forcing me to retire within the walls of my mind, and to abandon active contact with a world in which I was but a straw blown by contrary winds, now hither, now thither, now soaring high on the bosom of a frivolous gust, only to fall limp through a vacuum, and remain stuck on a mud clod, until a horse's hoof and the sun made me pliant to another breeze. Ignorant, without belief, without will to forge the scattered and diverse fragments of my material intellect into such a homogenous substance as would give me power over my fellows, I was beginning to see that I must remain a wreck, that it was not the war which had made me a wreck but nature, which had destined me for other things. Greater or less? That mattered nothing. The important thing was to know and to accept.

What, then, was the world revolution to me, who was fit to be no better than a drummer in its wars or the holder of a stirrup for some brass-brained boor to put his foot therein? Now I saw the world and its laws, its wars, its prophets, and the quickly changing countenance of its philosophy as a drama filmed on a globe beyond my being, but turning to my hand and subject for the exercise of my observant vision. Shrinking with a coward's fear from the magnificence of the world's tumult, that arena where strong men battle for power, where gods and the various sciences of government are like pieces of chess in a game played by men whose nerves are steeled by the greatness of their ambitions, I took refuge in the delicately fashioned world of my imagination. Hidden there from observation, I could build my own castles, and mime the outer strength I lacked with wordy subtlety.

Where? What place could be more remote than the place of my nativity? A rock forgotten by the world. On its bleak rocks I would make my soul dance and rock my songs on the cradle of the great ocean winds that blow against its cliffs, and then set forth into the world armed with a wiser weapon than my hands could wield.

Next morning I went down to the wharves of New York, and was lucky enough to find an English ship that needed a few hands. I signed on as a fireman. The ship was bound first for Rio de Janeiro, and then, after having called along the coast to Buenos Aires, she was going back to Europe.

Elizabeth Bowen

(1899–1973)

[EXCERPT FROM]

The Mulberry Tree

Elizabeth Bowen was born in Dublin in 1899. She was the child of Anglo-Irish parents. She was deeply aware of her Irish roots, although equally conscious of the complexity of them. She wrote eloquently of divided cultural and imaginative loyalties. Following her father's mental breakdown, she and her mother moved to London. She was educated at Downe House and went briefly to art school. In 1923 she married Alan Cameron, an educator and broadcaster with the BBC. She also began her association and friendship with such Bloomsbury writers as Rose Macaulay. The end of the 1920s found Bowen corresponding with Virginia Woolf.

In some ways Bowen can be seen as a Bloomsbury stylist. Her cool, forensic prose opened those themes of failure, erotic disappointment, and childhood hurt that fill her novels. It is to Bloomsbury also that she owes the acute sense of violated place that allowed her to write with such authority on wartime London, particularly in *The Heat of the Day* (1949). Some of her novels are *The Hotel* (1927), *The Last September* (1929), *Friends and Relations* (1931), *To the North* (1932), *The Death of the Heart* (1936), *The Little Girls* (1964), and *Eva Trout* (1968).

No Irish writer was clearer than Bowen about the tensions between the English and Irish imagination. She once described them as "a mixture of showing-off and suspicion, nearly as bad as sex." Her own divided identity was a constant theme in her work. In the piece below, published in a posthumous volume of essays called *The Mulberry Tree* (1999), she skirts the issue. The tone, as always, is civil and engaged, as if the divisions could be managed by reason and review. In fact, these were areas requiring a tense imaginative vigilance from Bowen; and she knew it. Her affinities to Ireland ran deep. She appreciated its landscape, people, and literature. She allowed herself, to a considerable degree, to be owned by them. But she is candid in this piece that England made her a writer. If she is not comfortable with the contradiction, she is honest and resolute about it.

Here she chronicles the old arts of Ascendancy belligerence—the fighting, the challenges, the pride. Literature followed later when, in her words, they "interchanged sword-play for word-play." This excerpt is a rare and revealing glimpse into a phenomenon of twentieth-century writing in Ireland: the energy and tension of the Anglo-Irish imagination.

My belligerence, to a degree given an outlet, to a degree neutralised by school life, was inborn, a derivative of race. Irish and Anglo-Irish have it in common. It stood out, possibly, more strongly in the placidity of England. At times a tiresome trait, it is not a detestable one, being poles apart from aggressiveness — which as we know is engendered by some grudge, spite or bias against the rest of the world. Your belligerent person has no chip on his shoulder, and tends to sail through life in excellent spirits. He likes fighting. He distinguishes between a fight and a quarrel, on these grounds: a fight, soon over, purifies the air and leaves no one the worse (unless they are dead), whereas a quarrel, unlikely to be ever wholly resolved, not only fouls the surrounding air but may set up a festering trail of lifelong bitterness. That distinction has always been clear to me. I would go miles out of my way to avoid a quarrel.

Sir Jonah Barrington, to whose *Personal Sketches of His Own Times* I owe as all-round an account as I hope to find of the manners, tenets and general outlook on life of my ancestors, his compatriots and contemporaries, witnessed the regrettable decline of duelling in Ireland — where, as a manly practice, it had survived its all but extinction across the water. Cease to be lawful it might: a blind eye was turned to it. It was in the tradition, generic to that society which gave Sir Jonah and my relatives birth: the Ascendancy, with its passion for virtuosity of all kinds, not least sword-play or mastery with a pistol. In the best days, apparently, almost everyone fought:

> Earl Clare, Lord Chancellor of Ireland, fought the Master of the Rolls, the Right Honourable John Philpot Curran, with twelve-inch pistols. The Earl of Clonmel, Chief Justice of the King's Bench, fought Lord Tyrawly, about his wife, and the Earl of Landaff, about his sister; and others, with sword or pistol, on miscellaneous subjects. The Judge of the County of Dublin, Egan, fought the Master of the Rolls, Roger Barrett, and three others; one with swords. The Chancellor of the Exchequer, the Right Honourable Isaac Corry, fought the Right Honourable Henry Grattan, a privy counsellor, and the chancellor was hit. He also exchanged shots or thrusts with *two* other gentlemen. A baron of the exchequer, Baron Medge, fought his brother-in-law and two others — a hit. . . . The Judge of Prerogative Court, Doctor Duigenan, fought *one* barrister and frightened *another* on the ground. The latter was a very curious case. . . . The Provost of the University of Dublin, the Right Honourable Hely Hutchinson, fought Mr. Doyle, Master in Chancery: they went to the plains of Minden to fight. . . . The Right Honourable George Ogle, the Orange Chieftain, fought Barny Coyle, a whisky distiller, because he was a *papist.* They fired eight shots without stop or stay, and no hit occurred: but Mr. Ogle's second broke his own arm by tumbling into a potato-trench. . . .

Sir Jonah abridges, he says, "this dignified list," which, even so, takes up two of his pages: and I have further abridged it — his point is made. His attitude is, if nostalgic, reflective also: "It is nearly incredible what a singular passion the Irish gentlemen (though in general excellent tempered fellows) had for fighting each other and immediately becoming friends again." Actually (we have it on his authority) a duel frequently served to cement a friendship. And why not? Did not the prestige date back to the chivalric tradition, to knightly jousting? — not really more honourable, and (should you not care for that sort of thing) just as futile? Semi-sacredness came to attach to family weapons: "Each family had its case of hereditary pistols, which descended as an heirloom." The Barringtons were "included in the armoury of our ancient castle of Ballynakill in the reign of Elizabeth (the stocks, locks and hair-triggers were, however, modern). . . . One of them was named '*sweet lips*' the other '*the darling*.' " (One must not allow Sir Jonah to grate on one.) Sheridan, loosing Sir Lucius O'Trigger, in *The Rivals,* on to the modish — but in the Irish baronet's view, half-hearted — society of Bath, adds credibility to the Barrington jottings. Heiress-hunting (another national sport) does not occupy all Sir Lucius's time: he is masterminding Bob Acres into a duel. He is, however, riled by technical hitches —"I don't know what's the reason," he cries aloud, "but in England, if a thing of this kind gets wind, people make such a pother that a gentleman can never fight in peace and quietness."

Horsemanship apart, the Anglo-Irish, together with what was left of the indigenous autocrats, would subsequently have been in a poor way were it not for writing. To that we have taken like ducks to water. Accommodating ourselves to a tamer day, we interchanged sword-play for word-play. Repartee, with its thrusts, opened alternative possibilities of mastery. Given rein to, creative imagination ran to the tensed-up, to extreme situations, to confrontations. Bravado characterizes much Irish, all Anglo-Irish writing: gloriously it is sublimated by Yeats. Nationally, we have an undertow to the showy. It follows that primarily we have produced dramatists, the novel being too life-like, humdrum, to do us justice. We do not do badly with the short story, "that, in a spleen, unfolds both heaven and earth" — or should. There is this about us: to most of the rest of the world we are semi-strangers, for whom existence has something of the trance-like quality of a spectacle. As beings, we are at once brilliant and limited; our unbeatables, up to now, accordingly, have been those who best profited by that: Goldsmith, Sheridan, Wilde, Shaw, Beckett. Art is for us inseparable from artifice: of that, the theatre is the home.

Possibly, it was England made me a novelist. At an early though conscious age, I was transplanted. I arrived, young, into a different mythology — in fact, into one totally alien to that of my forefathers, none of whom had resided anywhere but in Ireland for some centuries, and some of whom may never have been in England at all: the Bowens were Welsh. From now on there was to be (as for any immigrant) a cleft between my heredity and my environment — the former remaining, in my case, the more powerful. Submerged, the mythology of this "other" land could be felt at work in the ways, manners and views of its people, round me: those, because I disliked being at a disadvantage, it became necessary to probe. It cannot be said that a child of seven was analytic; more, with a blend of characteristic guile and uncharacteristic patience I took note — which, though I had at that time no thought of my future art, is, after all, one of the main activities of the novelist. At the outset, the denizens of England and their goings-on inspired me with what a hymn epitomises as "scornful wonder" — protective mechanism? — but I was not a disagreeable child, so any initial hostility wore off. Lacking that stimulus, my attention wandered: society not being by nature interesting, or for long interesting, to the very young, I transferred my gaze from it to its geographical setting. Thereafter, England affected me more in a scenic way than in any other — and still does. It was the lie of the land, with that cool, clear light falling upon it, which was extraordinary.

Frank O'Connor

(1903–1966)

[EXCERPT FROM]

An Only Child

Frank O'Connor was born Michael O'Donovan in Cork in 1903. His parents were hard-pressed; they struggled in the harsh economic climate of the time. His mother, Minnie, about whom he wrote lovingly in his memoir *An Only Child* (1961), worked as a maid to help provide for the family's survival. His father was alcoholic. Themes of family dislocation, of strong women and weak men, would become constants in O'Connor's fiction.

In 1918 he joined the Irish Republican Army (IRA). He was briefly imprisoned after the civil war, from 1922 to 1923. His later disillusionment with civil strife and the rigidity of Irish nationalism echoed for a long time in his work. It is the engine of his compelling short story *Guests of the Nation*. O'Connor worked as a librarian after the civil war. His first book of stories, *Guests of the Nation*, was published in 1929. He was a prolific writer, publishing novellas, short stories, translations of Irish poetry, and essays over the next decades. He also became a director of the Abbey Theatre, retiring from the post in 1939.

O'Connor was a masterful and realistic storyteller. He believed the short story was particularly suited to the Irish experience: it was a form, he argued, hospitable to "submerged population groups." "There is in the short story at its most characteristic," he wrote in his critical study *The Lonely Voice* (1962), "something we do not often find in the novel—an intense awareness of human loneliness." His stories are based on hypnotic speech rhythms, sharp turns of narrative. In later years he was criticized for formulaic writing, but his literary emergence in the thirties gave the Irish literary world a voice determined to craft a truly Irish narrative and yet in tune with the values of the Irish Revival.

But for all his respect for William Yeats—about which he is eloquent in his autobiographical writing—there were other voices in O'Connor's ear. Like his contemporary Sean O'Faolain, he was deeply influenced by the opposing cultural nationalism of Daniel Corkery. He became friends with Corkery as a young man. This brief, loving portrait of Corkery from *An Only Child* gives a picture of the closed, charged world of provincial Ireland after the revival— the dreams, the energies, the angers, and the disappointments.

I haunted the streets for Corkery till I finally trapped him one day by the Scots Church at the foot of Summerhill and casually showed him the cutting from the *Sunday Independent*. He asked if I had the translation with me, and curiously I had that too. He read it carefully with one eye half closed, not commenting too much on the grammar, which was probably invisible through the typographical errors, and said judicially that it *was* a beautiful translation. At any rate, he apparently decided that, since what could not be cured must be endured, he had to admit me to his own little group. After all, I was now a published author.

He lived in a small suburban house on Gardiner's Hill with his mother and sister, surrounded by books and pictures. Over the mantelpiece was large watercolour of his own of a man with a scythe on Fair Hill, overlooking the great panorama of the river valley. Inside the door of the living room was a bust of him by his friend, Joe Higgins, which — if my memory of it is correct — is the only likeness of him that captures all his charm. He presided over his little group from a huge Morris chair with a detachable desk that he had made for himself (he was an excellent craftsman, having been brought up to the trade, and once told me in his oracular way that "nobody had ever met a stupid carpenter," which I later found to be untrue).

He had a good deal of the harshness and puritanism of the provincial intellectual which I share. As those brought up to wealth and rank tend to under-rate them, people accustomed from childhood to an intellectual atmosphere can take classical standards lightly and permit themselves to be entertained by mere facility; not those who have had to buy them dear. Once, when I was working on the railway, and had spent a whole week's pocket money on Wilde's *Intentions*, I met Corkery and he glanced at the book and shook his head. "It'll ruin whatever style you have," he said, and even the suggestion that I might have a style did not make up to me for the realization that once again I had backed the wrong horse.

Most of his friends belonged to a little group that had worked with him when he ran a tiny theatre in Queen Street. The most faithful visitor was Denis Breen, a schoolteacher like himself, who had provided the music and married one of the actresses. He was a big, emotional man with a fat, sun-coloured face, clear, childish blue eyes, and a red moustache that he apparently cultivated for the sole purpose of eating it — a face Franz Hals would have loved. At Gaelic League meetings he roared down patriotic souls who decried English music and talked of the greatness of Byrd, Dowland, and Purcell, whom none of us had ever heard of. He also professed to be an atheist, which was rather like proclaiming yourself a Christian in modern China, and the defensiveness this had induced in him was reflected in everything he did and said. He had a great contempt for our little colony of German musicians, whom he spoke of as though they were Catholic priests, as "bleddy eejits." They, more objectively, spoke of him as a genius without musical training. It might be fairer to say that his temperament was too immoderate for the precise and delicate work of the artist — the very opposite of Corkery's. The two men were always arguing, Corkery gently and inquiringly, Breen uproariously and authoritatively, something like this. "Well, on the other hand, would it not be possible to say . . . ?" "Me dear man, it's possible to say anything, if you're fool enough." I listened in shame for the whole human race to think that anyone could be so presumptuous as to disagree with Corkery.

I did not like Breen. I was connected with him through two coincidences: one that he had taught me for a couple of days before I left Blarney Lane for good, and even in that short time he had beaten me (Irish teachers, like American policemen, never having learned that to go about armed is not the best way of securing obedience and respect); the other was that my mother and his mother, who kept a little sweet shop at the gate of the University, had been friends. *His* mother had told *my* mother that even when he was a small boy no one could control him. He would get hungry at night, go down to the shop for biscuits, sample every tin and leave them all open, so that by morning her stock was ruined. Even when I knew him he would begin his tea by eating all the sweet cakes in case anyone else took a fancy to them. He was greedy with a child's greed, shouted everyone down with what he thought "funny" stories or denunciations of the "bleddy eejits" who ran the country or its music, and battered a Beethoven sonata to death with his red eyebrows reverently raised, believing himself to be a man of perfect manners, liberal ideas, and perfect taste. All of which, of course, he was, as I learned later when we became friends, for though his wife and my mother would look blank while he ate all the confectionery and then shouted for more; and though afterwards he hammered Wolf's *An Die Geliebte* unconscious; he struck out the last chords as only a man who loved music could do it, scowling and muttering: "Now listen to the bloody stars!" He quarrelled bitterly with me after the first performance of a play called *The Invincibles* because he had convinced himself that I had caricatured him in the part of Joe Brady, the leader of the assassins — a brave and simple man driven mad by injustice — and though at the time I was disturbed because such an idea had never occurred to me, it seems to me now that the characters in whom we think we recognize ourselves are infinitely more revealing of our real personalities than those in which someone actually attempts to portray us.

Molly Keane
(1904–1996)

[EXCERPT FROM]

"Elizabeth of Bowen's Court"

Molly Keane was born in Ballyrankin, County Kildare, in 1904. Her real name was Mary Nesta Skrine. Her father originally came from a Somerset family and her mother was the author, Moira O'Neill. She once described them as "a rather serious Hunting and Fishing Church-going family." During the 1930s Keane wrote under the pseudonym of M. J. Farrell, a name said to have been adopted from a Wexford public house. She married into the Keane family, but her husband died at the young age of thirty-six. She was left to raise two daughters on her own.

As a young writer she was prolific. Her early novels, written under the Farrell pseudonym, were *Young Entry* (1928), *Taking Chances* (1930), *Mad Puppetstown* (1934), *Devoted Ladies* (1934), *Conversation Piece* (1937), *Full House* (1937), *Rising Tide* (1937), and *Two Days in Aragon* (1941). They are united with the later identity of Molly Keane by a similar turn toward the comedy of manners, with an edge and sharpness of dialogue. In 1981, after an absence from writing, she published *Good Behaviour* under her married name. It became an acclaimed comedy of manners.

In trying to define the relation of Irish writers to the writing of their own country, there are moments of clarity. Times when the traffic of literary influence—the connections between Irish writers and Irish writing—is plainspoken and personal. So it is here. Molly Keane met Elizabeth Bowen

and knew her in Cork. They shared some family connections and some profound historical alignments. Both were Anglo-Irish; both felt deep ties to an
Ireland their ancestors colonized. Both wrote of the decay of the Big House,
the erosion of confidence of a ruling class, as well as their own ambivalence
over the loss of power that attended the loss of privilege. Both writers, to
some extent, sought to heal moral complexities with gestures of style and wit.

As this piece below makes clear, Molly Keane recognized the essence of
Elizabeth Bowen and valued her friendship. But she also suggests the isolation
that went with the Anglo-Irish inheritance. The excerpt is a testament of
affection, written after Bowen's death. In this brief, anecdotal, treasurable
account Keane opens a window into those challenges of writing and identity
that the wit and vision of both Bowen and Keane helped to clarify.

What I would most like to express, to make *live* (as Mark Bence-Jones has
the house, with its 38 windows, full of changing light, and its silvery stone),
is the immense quality of attraction that Elizabeth possessed in such a high
degree. Her looks, like the looks of the house, were elusive. I always thought
she had the air of an aristocratic Elizabethan adventurer — home from the
sea with a rich prize, when she had finished a book, setting out on a voyage
of discovery when she was starting one. She wasn't beautiful, strictly speaking, but she dressed as remarkably as any beauty dares to, and with a careless
distinction. When she came into a room the atmosphere changed. Even
should one have a companion with his interest nailed and focused (one
hoped!) his eyes wandered. Attention failed. He wanted to be near Elizabeth.

It was the same with young and old, with literary men, or solid country
gentlemen. Once in *her* orbit, the enchantment held them.

I remember a *very* non-literary country gentleman saying to me: "I was
rather *bovvered* what to talk about at lunch. But *she* was so easy I could have
been talking to another member of White's!" I think that was a charming
tribute to her versatility. But it was no special effort for her: she loved men.
And men's company and love were necessary to her. So were good food, and

drink, and good talk, and jokes with friends. She entered into every enterprise, whether she was looking at a fairy shoe found in the mountains, or the winner of the 2,000 Guineas (owned by her great friend, Ursula Vernon), she was equally involved, and never shy of asking questions.

One loved having a drink with Elizabeth: her wits absolutely flamed, whether the drink was just before a grand dinner party at Bowen's Court — and they could be very grand and formal parties — or in a dingy roadside bar, a magic sense of the absolute importance of *enjoyment* was equally present.

She was marvellous to her woman friends, generous, forgiving, tolerant even of their youngest children. I know my children loved and relied on her: I remember her sweeping through the Shelbourne Hotel one evening, wearing a big yellow straw hat on her then blonde hair, and stopping to talk with us. After she had gone, my daughter Sally, aged 5, asked: "Who was the lady who looked like a lovely summer evening?" I suppose it was partly Elizabeth's large, happy assurance that evoked such a comparison from one so young.

The big yellow hat was typical of her sense of the importance of clothes. Elizabeth's junk jewellery, chosen and worn with some daring, was a tremendous build-up and facade on the fortress of her looks — her ears shrank behind beautiful and preposterous earrings. That sense of importance never left her.

The last time I saw her, we were having dinner with Stephen and Ursula Vernon in a restaurant in Kinsale. It was summer time, and she was wearing a stiff, white, silk coat, faintly reminiscent of old Vienna and Strauss waltzes and white uniforms. Next year she died. But that evening we discussed seriously the question of really good expensive "wiggies," and how much time they might save at the hairdressers. She planned to buy herself one as soon as she got back to London. I expect she did, and wore it to enormous effect, in the same way that junk jewellery seemed right and enhancing on her. Only Angus MacBean, the great photographer, ever did her style proper justice.

Apart from her genius for people and her love of giving or taking entertainment of all sorts and kinds, Elizabeth had a strongly disciplined religious side. On Sunday mornings she came into the hall just before eleven o'clock, wearing definitely less country, but not exaggeratedly London clothes. She had clipped on less vibrant ear-rings and as she talked pulled leather gloves with long wrinkling wrists on to her hands. She often walked down the drive to the little church, built by her family, at the gates. She never pressed any guest to go with her. She prayed. She sang. She listened with polite attention to any sermon. Then, back to the library and pink gins before lunch — those unforgettable martinis or pink gins in those stemless, goldfish-bowl sized glasses.

After Elizabeth's death the church was abandoned, rain coming through the roof, and dead birds in the aisle.

The chief instigator in the church's restoration — a tribute and memorial from her friends — is the Rev. Dr. Robert McCarthy. Derek Hill is another friend deeply concerned with the project. With the support of Desmond Guinness and the Georgian Society, they have achieved a memorial in which, because of its strength and its beauty, above all because of its escape from gloom, we have a fitting and perpetual testimony to Elizabeth.

It was Derek Hill who produced her untypically straightforward Nativity play in Derry Cathedral — an adventurous Ecumenical event to undertake in war-ravaged Ulster; crowds came to see it there, and so did the strangely diverse audience of her fox-hunting, racing and literary friends when Stephen Vernon directed the cast — drawn from the above classes — at the play's first presentation in Limerick.

Elizabeth died far too young — and if she had lived to a hundred, she would still have been too young to die. Sometimes overworked and over-stressed, she was never lonely or alone in her life, and I imagine that, if she still endures, though she is beyond her living friends, she is never short of a companion her equal in wits and stature. She is not wandering companion-less among the stars that have a different birth. Companionless? Never — in this, or any, life.

John Hewitt

(1907–1987)

"An Irishman in Coventry"

John Hewitt was born in Belfast in 1907. His father was a teacher who became principal of Agnes Street Mixed School, near the Shankill Road. Hewitt went to Methodist College and the Queen's University in Belfast. From the start he was a liberal socialist who supported progressive causes. He was also a local historian, treasuring Ulster customs and speech. He believed deeply in regional energies, writing that "meaning and significance might be sought in a limited region, with its local history and traditions and special characteristics." He also had a sophisticated sense of the doomed traditions that often constitute the hidden history of a people, such as the Rhyming Weavers in England, about whom he wrote.

His publications include *Conacre* (1943), *No Rebel Word* (1948), *The Lint Pulling* (1948), *Collected Poems, 1932–1967* (1968), *An Ulster Reckoning* (1971), *Time Enough: Poems New and Revised* (1976), *The Rain Dance: Poems New and Revised* (1978), *Kites in Spring: A Belfast Boyhood* (1980), *The Selected John Hewitt* (1981), *Freehold and Other Poems* (1986), *The Collected Poems of John Hewitt* (edited by Frank Ormsby, 1991), and *Ancestral Voices: The Selected Prose of John Hewitt* (edited by Tom Clyde, 1987).

Hewitt's work becomes easier to locate and understand once it is seen as reflecting his empathy with dissent, which in turn reflects the dissenting quality of his own imagination. Nevertheless, in a nationalist island and in a

troubled time, Hewitt's position as a poet was often isolated and misunderstood. For this reason—given the courage and individualism it required—
much of his work, in retrospect, looks both prescient and durable.

Hewitt was also well aware of the difficulty of making an imaginative
construct out of a moral ambiguity such as colony. Yet he knew that without
the attempt, a very real part of the Irish experience—that of the planter—
would remain unvoiced. This important, moving Irish poem, reprinted below,
is part of that attempt. It is a complex address to a history that forgave almost
no one. Written when he was in the English city of Coventry, Hewitt builds a
strenuous, passionate poem from a dark margin of the Irish imagination. It
registers—in deeply instructive ways—the circumstance of his isolation
becoming the source of his imagination.

A full year since, I took this eager city,
the tolerance that laced its blatant roar,
its famous steeples and its web of girders,
as image of the state hope argued for,
and scarcely flung a bitter thought behind me
on all that flaws the glory and the grace
which ribbons through the sick, guilt-clotted legend
of my creed-haunted, Godforsaken race.
My rhetoric swung round from steel's high promise
to the precision of the well-gauged tool,
tracing the logic in the vast glass headlands,
the clockwork horse, the comprehensive school.

Then, sudden, by occasion's chance concerted,
in enclave of my nation, but apart,
the jigging dances and the lilting fiddle
stirred the old rage and pity in my heart.
The faces and the voices blurring round me,
the strong hands long familiar with the spade,

the whiskey-tinctured breath, the pious buttons,
called up a people endlessly betrayed
by our own weakness, by the wrongs we suffered
in that long twilight over bog and glen,
by force, by famine and by glittering fables
which gave us martyrs when we needed men,
by faith which had no charity to offer,
by poisoned memory and by ready wit,
with poverty corroded into malice
to hit and run and howl when it is hit.

This is our fate: eight hundred years' disaster
crazily tangled as the Book of Kells,
the dream's distortion and the land's division,
the midnight raiders and the prison cells.
Yet like Lir's children banished to the waters
our hearts still listen for the landward bells.

Louis MacNeice

(1907–1963)

"Dublin"

Louis MacNeice was born in Belfast, the youngest son of parents—John and Lily MacNeice—who came from the west of Ireland. John MacNeice became Rector of St. Clement's, and in 1908 he was appointed to the church of St. Nicholas in Carrickfergus, where the family was to remain. Louis MacNeice was educated in England, at Sherborne. After that he went to Oxford University.

In poetic terms MacNeice belonged most visibly to the thirties generation of poets in Britain—W. H. Auden, Stephen Spender, and C. Day Lewis. Left-leaning, prescient about the approach of fascism, and committed to the political poem, these poets were broadly popular and in touch with their audience. *Letters from Iceland*, co-authored by Auden and MacNeice in 1937, is an instance of this. A racy Byronic journalism imbues their craft; the poetic strategy is unabashedly populist. This was his second book. His first, *Poems*, was published in 1935.

Although associated with British poetry of the thirties, MacNeice was also consciously and self-reflectively Irish. In 1939 he published *Autumn Journal*—widely regarded as his best work. It is a poem of twenty-four sections, each of them shifting through a wide range of topics. The work showed the richness of his divided heritage and the subtlety of the inward questioning it caused him. He continued publishing throughout the forties and fifties. *Collected Poems, 1925–1948*, came out in 1949. His *Selected Poems* was edited in 1964 by Auden. Another volume of *Selected Poems* was edited in 1988 by Michael Longley.

The tradition of the outsider in Irish literature—or, to use another term, *the internal exile*—runs deep. In terms of Irish writing, MacNeice defined himself as much by what he was not as by what he was. He brought an astringent eye to the enclosure of Irish history; he positioned himself on margins he himself delimited. This marginal stance is crucial to his aesthetic; his cool refusal to belong to any preset literary orthodoxy made him a powerful and necessary exemplar for later Northern Irish writing. His stance is exemplified below in the celebrated poem "Dublin," in which MacNeice shows himself to be a laureate of anti-place—an underexplored category in Irish literature. Here he excludes himself imaginatively from the magic and enclosure of Dublin as cultural capital, while defining the qualities of the city as sharply and accurately as anyone ever has.

Grey brick upon brick,
Declamatory bronze
On somber pedestals —
O'Connell, Grattan, Moore —
And the brewery tugs and the swans
On the balustraded stream
And the bare bones of a fanlight
Over a hungry door
And the air soft on the cheek
And porter running from the taps
With a head of yellow cream
And Nelson on his pillar
Watching his world collapse.

This was never my town,
I was not born or bred
Nor schooled here and she will not
Have me alive or dead
But yet she holds my mind

With her seedy elegance,
With her gentle veils of rain
And all her ghosts that walk
And all that hide behind
Her Georgian facades —
The catcalls and the pain,
The glamour of her squalor,
The bravado of her talk.

The lights jig in the river
With a concertina movement
And the sun comes up in the morning
Like barley-sugar on the water
And the mist on the Wicklow hills
Is close, as close
As the peasantry were to the landlord,
As the Irish to the Anglo-Irish,
As the killer is close one moment
To the man he kills,
Or as the moment itself
Is close to the next moment.

She is not an Irish town
And she is not English,
Historic with guns and vermin
And the cold renown
Of a fragment of Church Latin,
Of an oratorical phrase.
But oh the days are soft,
Soft enough to forget
The lesson better learnt,
The bullet on the wet
Streets, the crooked deal,
The steel behind the laugh,
The Four Courts burnt.

Fort of the Dane,
Garrison of the Saxon,
Augustan capital
Of a Gaelic nation,
Appropriating all
The alien brought,
You give me time for thought
And by a juggler's trick
You poise the toppling hour —
O greyness run to flower,
Grey stone, grey water,
And brick upon grey brick.

Myles na Gopaleen

(1911–1966)

[EXCERPT FROM]

"Waama, etc."

Myles na Gopaleen was born in Tyrone in Northern Ireland in 1911, the fifth of twelve children. His name, Myles na Gopaleen, its variant Myles na gCopaleen, and Flann O'Brien are all pen names of Brian O'Nolan, the Irish novelist, essayist, journalist, and incomparable satirist. "Myles na Gopaleen" is drawn from a minor character created by the nineteenth-century novelist Gerald Griffin. It comes from his book *The Collegians*.

Na Gopaleen had a brilliant career as an undergraduate at University College Dublin, where he edited a magazine called *Blather*. On graduating, he joined the Irish Civil Service and over many years rose to a senior position, although few detected in him any real enthusiasm for the job. He remained in Dublin for the rest of his life.

There is a range and brilliance, an almost Bardic invective to na Gopaleen's style that is hard to convey. His work left behind a unique legend in Irish life and writing. Some might say that na Gopaleen, with his crooked wit and unswerving satire, is the true and accurate inversion of the Irish public intellectual. He was satiric in proportion as he felt Irish society to be oppressive. The literary community was not spared. In time it became a prime target for his savage humor. No writer was exempt, and certainly no contemporary.

In a letter written to the *Irish Times* in the forties he commented on a poem published there by Patrick Kavanagh: "I think Mr Kavanaugh [*sic*] is on the right track here. . . . Perhaps the *Irish Times*, timeless champion of our peasantry, will oblige us with a series in this strain covering such rural complexities as inflamed goat-udders, warble-pocked shorthorn, contagious abortion, non-ovoid oviducts and nervous disorders among the gentlemen who pay the rent." Among na Gopaleen's publications are *At Swim-Two-Birds* (1939; reprinted in 1960), *An Béal Bocht* (1941), *The Dalkey Archive* (1964), *The Third Policeman* (1967), and *The Hard Life* (1973).

From early in his writing career, Myles na Gopaleen amplified the tradition of experimental Irish writers, such as Joyce and Beckett, who were skeptical of what they felt to be the conservatism of the Irish Revival. Na Gopaleen's sense of interior exile from the Irish writing world was intense. Literary life in Dublin never had a more scalding or perceptive satirist. He could be, as this extract from his *Irish Times* column shows, superbly dark and funny, dealing in the currency of Irish speech even while mercilessly lampooning it.

I have received by post a number of papers inviting me to become a member of the Irish Writers, Actors, Artists, Musicians Association, and to pay part of my money to the people who run this company. I am also invited to attend a meeting in Jury's Hotel on Sunday week. Foot I will not set inside that door; act, hand or part I will not have with that party.

At one of the preliminary meetings of this organisation, I bought a few minor novelists at five bob a skull and persuaded them to propose me for the presidency. Then I rose myself and said that if it was the unanimous wish of the company, etc., quite unworthy, etc., signal honour, etc., serve to the best of my ability, etc., prior claims of other persons, etc., if humble talents of any service, etc., delighted to place knowledge of literary world at disposal of, etc., undoubted need for organisation, etc.

To my astonishment, instead of accepting my offer with loud and sustained applause, the wretched intellectuals broke up into frightened groups and started whispering together in great agitation. From where I sat in my mood of Homeric detachment I could distinctly hear snatches of talk like "never sober," "literary corner-boy," "pay nobody," "Stubbs every week," "running round with a TD's wife," "skip with the Association's assets," "great man for going to Paris," "sell his mother for sixpence," "belly full of brandy and unfortunate children without a rag," "summoned for putting in plate glass window in Santry," "pity unfortunate wife," "half the stuff cogged from other people," "sneer at us behind our backs," "use Association's name," "what would people think," "only inviting attention of Guards," "who asked him here," "believe he was born in Manchester," "probably fly-boy," "cool calculated cheek": and so on, I regret to say. Subsequently a man with glasses got up and mumbled something about best thanks of all concerned, proposal somewhat premature, society not yet wholly formed, bring proposal forward at later date, certain that choice would be a popular one, with permission of company pass on to next business, disgraceful sweat rates paid by broadcasting station . . . I thought this was fair enough, but think of my feelings a few days afterwards on hearing that Mr. Sean O'Faolain had been elevated to the same Presidency. One shrinks from gratuitous comparisons, but man for man, novels for novels, plays for plays, services to imperishable Irish nation for services to i. I. n., popularity as drawingroom raconteur for p. as d. r., which was the better choice? I leave the answer not only to my readers but also to a betrayed posterity who may yet decide that Dermot Mac-Murrough was not the worst.

QUESTIONABLE AIMS

In any event, I was completely opposed to some of this organisation's aims. For instance, it is proposed to secure "improved rates for all literary work." This simply means an even heavier deluge of unpardonable "poetry," more articles entitled "Big John: A Sketch," and a premium on mediocrity generally. It is also sought to have "concerted agreement on copyrights, contracts, etc." What sort of an agreement is a "concerted agreement," or is there such a thing as a unconcerted, disconcerted, or misconcerted agreement? "Special rates for radio scripts." Why? They all bore even my thick wife. Reduce the rates and you'll get less of them making a clack in your ear. "Free legal advice." This will disemploy several worthy solicitors, a fiery Celtic breed that I admire. "Recovery of fees." Yes, but minus ten percent. Get your money in your hand before you put pen to paper, that's what I say.

Also, having regard to the categories mentioned, membership seems to be open to every man, woman and child in Ireland. Even my wife could claim to be a "commentator" (whatever they mean by that word) and everybody knows that all these organisations are really formed in order to give people a pretext for getting away from their families. So what's the use?

Furthermore

This is the land of Ireland and now that WAAMA is in existence and in active operation, it is time that a "split" was organised and a rival body formed. Would any person who thinks that he or she has not had a fair deal from WAAMA please communicate with me at this office? We will form our own organisation, with better aims and heavier annual dinners. Pretty girls will be admitted free and nobody will be bored with guff about Sigrid Undset or James Joyce Cabell. How about it, lads? I am determined to be president of something before I die — of Ireland itself, if need be.

My suggestion the other day that the lines to be spoken in a new play at the Abbey should be displayed on banners suspended from the balcony and read off by the players as they go along, has won me golden opinions from the acting clique in WAAMA. They say that they are frequently asked to perform in very bad plays, and that no torment is so terrible as that of being compelled to commit muck to memory. An authoritative spokesman in official circles also stated last night that there appeared to be "no objection" to my plan. That, of course, pleases me. Had his reaction been otherwise, I should have been compelled to "view" his pronouncement "with concern."

Yes, the plan is a good one. There would be no necessity to tell the actors beforehand what play they are appearing in. They just come out on the stage, peer into the auditorium, and then come out with some dreadful remark about "Old John," or "Brigid, his wife."

My plan has another great advantage in these nights of rushing for last 'buses. Supposing it is a case of missing the end of the play or missing your 'bus. Being possessed of reason, you are damned if you'll miss your 'bus. But neither is it necessary to go home wondering what happened. You simply turn round and peer up at the balcony. Admittedly, it would look queer near the end of the play to have half the audience sitting with their backs to the stage and spelling out in loud whispers what the actors are going to say when they get a chance. Anything, however, is better than walking home in the rain. In an extreme case the entire audience might agree to take the rest of the play "as read," and clear out *en masse* in the middle of the last act, thus releasing the tired actors and giving them a chance of getting a lift home also. For the actors are human, too. Each had a mother.

Mary Lavin

(1912–1996)

[EXCERPT FROM]

"The Will"

Mary Lavin was born in East Walpole, Massachusetts, in 1912. At ten she returned with her mother to Galway, making her homes between Meath and Dublin. From then on she lived and published in Ireland. Her short stories constitute a major reworking of the direction of Irish writing. She is a crucial part of the refashioning of Irish Revival literature into a modern corpus of writing—challenging, probing, and deeply contemporary in its chronicling of the lives and motives of ordinary people in the new Ireland.

Lavin went to University College Dublin and published her first story in *The Dublin Magazine* in 1938. She married William Walsh in 1942 and was widowed in 1954, left as the provider for three young daughters. Her fiction draws a bleak, powerful line through the disappointments and realities of forties and fifties Ireland. Anti-intellectualism and repression are highlighted in her work. But Lavin is also uniquely capable in her management of the delicate balance between individual conscience and the customs of a society. In extended short fiction like *The Becker Wives* (1946), she takes a fresh, un-expected view of their relation, never romanticizing the tensions between them.

Her published work includes *Tales from Bective Bridge* (1942), *The Long Ago* (1944), *The Becker Wives* (1946), *At Sallygap* (1947), *A Single Lady* (1956), *The Patriot Son* (1956), *A Likely Story* (1957), *Selected Stories* (1959), *The Great*

Wave (1961), *The Stories of Mary Lavin*, vol. 1 (1964), *In the Middle of the Fields* (1967), *Collected Stories* (1971), *The Second Best Children in the World* (1972), *A Memory* (1972), *The Stories of Mary Lavin*, vol. 2 (1973), *The Shrine* (1977), *Selected Stories* (1981), *A Family Likeness* (1985), and *The Stories of Mary Lavin*, vol. 3 (1985). She also wrote two novels: *The House in Clewe Street* (1945) and *Mary O'Grady* (1950).

In the extract below, from her celebrated story "The Will," the central character, Lally, falls deeper and deeper into religious fantasy. She wants a mass said for her mother, who has died without reconciling with Lally. The story provides a glimpse of the scarred and sacred terrain of Irish faith, complete with lurid images of hell flame and destruction. It is also a shrewd canvassing of the relation between those images and the strengths and weaknesses of Irish imagination. And like John McGahern's testimony on the Church, it is a wrenching and eloquent critique of an Ireland that is fast disappearing from view.

The housekeeper went across the hall and opened a door on the left. She closed it after her, but the lock did not catch and the door slid open again. Lally heard the conversation distinctly, but with indifference, as she sat down on the polished mahogany chair in the hall. Because nothing was going to thwart her from her purpose.

"There's a woman outside who insists on seeing you, Father."

"Who is she?" said the priest, his voice muffled, as if he was wiping a serviette across his mouth.

"She gave her name as Conroy," said the woman, "and she has a look of Matthew Conroy, but I never saw her before and she looks as poor as a pauper."

"I did see a strange woman at the graveside with the family but I wasn't speaking to her." The priest's voice was slow and meditative. "I heard that there was another sister, but there was a sad story about her; I forget what it was exactly. I'll see her," he said. The sound of a chair scraped the floor and soon his feet rang on the polished wood as he crossed the room towards the hall.

Lally was sitting on the stiff chair at the fire, shielding her face from the heat of the flames that dragged themselves like serpents along the logs in the fireplace, but she sprang up as the priest approached. He was going to see her. In her mind she heard the train whistle once more, it was still far off, but it was instilling its presence on the country evening.

Lally was insistent. "I'm in a hurry, Father. I'm going away on this train. I'm sorry to have to disturb you. I only wanted to ask a favour." Her voice was uncontrollable as the flames leaping in the grave. "My name is Lally Conroy."

"Sit down, sit down." The priest took out a watch from under the cape of his soutane. "You have six minutes yet," he said.

"No, no, no," said Lally, "I mustn't miss the train. I wanted to know if you will say a Mass for my mother first thing in the morning. I'll send you the money for the offering the minute I get back to the city. I'll post it tonight, from the GPO, there's a collection at midnight. Will you do that, Father? Will you?" As if the interview was over she stood up and began to go backwards, moving to the door. Without waiting for an answer she repeated her urgent question. "Will you? Will you do that, Father? First thing in the morning!"

The priest looked down at the shabby boots and the thick stockings. "There's no need to worry about Masses being said. Your mother was a good woman," he said. "And I understand that she herself left a large sum in her will for Masses to be said for her after her death."

"Oh, Father, it's not the same thing for people to leave money for Masses to be said for their own souls, it's the Masses that other people have said for them that count." Lally's thoughts leapt ahead in her excitement. "I want a Mass said for her with my money. I want three Masses said. But I want the first one to be said at once, the seven-thirty Mass. And it has to be said with my money. My money!" Lally emphasised.

The priest leaned forward with an ungovernable curiosity, "Why must it be your money?"

"I'm afraid," said Lally, "I'm afraid she might suffer. I'm afraid for her soul." The eyes that stared into the flaming heart of the fire were indeed filled with fear, and as a coal fell, revealing gaping abyss of flaming fire, her eyes filled with absolute horror at the heaving reflection of her idea in the red flames of the fire. "She was very bitter." Lally Conroy broke down for the first time since she had news of her mother's death. "She was very bitter against me for twenty or thirty years, and she died without forgiving me. I'm afraid for her soul." She looked up at the priest. "You'll say them as soon as ever you can, Father?"

"I'll say them," said the priest. "But don't worry about the money. I'll offer them from myself."

"That's not what I want," Lally cried hastily. "I want them to be paid for with my money. That is what will count most, that they are paid for out of my money."

Humbly the priest accepted the dictates of the bedraggled woman in front of him.

"I will do as you wish," he said. "Is there anything else troubling you?"

"The train! The train!" Lally cried, and she fumbled with the catch of the door.

The priest took out his watch again.

"You'll just have time to catch it," he said, "if you hurry." And he opened the door. Lally ran out into the dark street again.

For a moment she felt peace at the thought of what she had done, and running down the wet gravelly drive with the cold rain beating on her flushed face, she was able to occupy her mind with practical thoughts about the journey home. But when she got into the hot and stuffy carriage of the train, the tears began to stream down her face again, and she began to wonder if she had made herself clear to the priest. She put her head out of the carriage window as the train began to leave the platform and she called out to a porter who stood with a green flag in his hand.

"What time does this train arrive in the city?" she asked, but the porter could not hear her. He put his hand to his ear but just then the train rushed into the darkness under the railway bridge. Lally let the window up and sat back in the seat.

If the train got in after midnight, she would ring the night bell at the Franciscan Friary and ask for a Mass to be said there and then for her mother's soul. She had heard that Masses were said night and day in the friary. She tried to remember where she had heard that, and who had told her, but her mind was in great disorder. She leaned her head back against the cushions as the train roared into the night, and she feverishly began to add up the prices that were due to her from the tenants in the top rooms. She then subtracted from the total the amount that would be needed to buy food for the children for the week. She would have exactly two pounds ten. She could have six Masses said at least for that much. There might even be money over to light some lamps at the Convent of Perpetual Reparation. She tried to comfort herself by these calculations, but as the train rushed through the night she sat more upright on the red-carpeted seats that smelled of dust, and clenched her hands tightly as she thought of the torments of Purgatory. When flakes of soot from the engine flew past the carriage window, she began to pray silently, with rapid unformed words that jostled themselves in her mind with the sheaves of burning sparks.

Brendan Behan

(1923–1964)

Confessions of an Irish Rebel

Brendan Behan was born in Dublin in 1923. He came from a cultured, musical family in Dublin's inner city. His uncle, Peadar Kearney, wrote the Irish national anthem. His brother, Dominic, was a noted song writer. In his 1958 work *Borstal Boy* he writes of his Dublin childhood: "All our mothers had all done the pawn-pledging on Monday, releasing on Saturday. We all knew the chip shop and the picture house and the fourpenny rush of a Saturday afternoon, and the summer swimming in the canal." Behan became an active Republican and was sentenced to Borstal in England for two years in 1939. In 1942 in Dublin he was sentenced to fourteen years in prison for the murder of two detectives. He served four of them in Mountjoy and the Curragh. These prison experiences were central to his later writing.

Behan is sometimes represented as defending the constituency and tradition of Dublin working-class life. Certainly he resisted reflexive nationalism. He spoke of it having "practically killed the old ballads of Dublin forty years ago with the rise of the Gaelic League." Nevertheless, he had a far more subtle, complicated reaction to the weave of nationalism and literature. His real constituency, like the old Dublin ballads, was a powerful and vital vernacular: dramatic, living speech. Where it was constrained by the new conventions of Irish culture and literature, he resisted.

Behan's plays are built on this speech. In 1954 *The Quare Fellow* was

produced. Its anarchic cadences brought a new energy to theater. His experi-
mental play, *The Hostage*, followed the next year. Some of his prose books are
Borstal Boy (1958), *Brendan Behan's Island* (1962), *Hold Your Hour and Have
Another* (1963), *Brendan Behan's New York* (1964), and *Confessions of an Irish
Rebel* (1965). Below is an excerpt from this last work. It describes the young
Behan visiting the magisterial editor of the *Irish Times*, Robert Smiley. His
comments and references, whether to William Yeats or to Dublin, are entirely
irreverent. Through the exuberant disrespect comes something more serious,
however: the fascinating sight of the literary revival being put to the test by a
rigorous and challenging new Irish writer.

It was late afternoon before I had recovered sufficiently enough to mosey
round to the *Irish Times* office in Westmoreland Street to see Robert Smiley.
I had decided, after I'd a few glasses of whiskey in me, to tell him the truth,
for in the main I only told lies in the way of business — to get a drink and a
feed or the price of my keep — to humble and simple souls, and Robert
Smiley was neither of these.

"You'll kill yourself more with the drink than ever you will with the
I.R.A., Brendan," he said, as I walked into the room. I respected him greatly
for this and the matter was discussed no further. Instead we fell to talking
about a certain respectable member of the aristocracy who had spent a week
trying to persuade W. B. Yeats to get out and fight in Easter Week, 1916.
Legend had it that Yeats asked her what did she take him for, said he was too
delicate a man, and threw her down the stairs two days after the fall of the
General Post Office because he was going to write a poem about it.

At one time she had been on the Committee of International Red Aid,
and she always insisted on giving this organisation its full name, in case it
would be mistaken for the Irish Republican Army. She had fallen out with
the I.R.A. in 1934 on the general question of the day-to-day struggle, and the
particular one of their refusal to spare a dozen twelve-ounce sticks of gelig-
nite for a parcel to be sent to the Secretary of the Employers' Federation
during the coal strike.

Described by many as "a champion of the downtrodden in every land, a fiery preacher for every good cause in her native land — the breaking-up of the big estates, the revival of the Irish language, and birth control — a splendid figure of revolting womanhood," she was believed to have been instrumental in getting Frank Harris and Charlie Chaplin to visit Jim Larkin in Sing Sing. She certainly used her influence with Governor Al Smith to get him out. Smith had an almost feudal regard for her on account of her family having evicted his family out of their cottage in County Cavan back in the old days.

"I suppose you wouldn't know those parts, Brendan?" said Smiley.

I knew them well and have friends there and I knew Bally-jamesduff, and if I didn't know Lappanduff mountains I knew the song about it and heard it first sung in a bar on the Falls Road in Belfast.

> . . . on Cavan's mountain, Lappanduff,
> One fought with bravery,
> Until the English soldiers shot
> Brave Sean MacCartney . . .

Cavan of the little hills. For Cavan, the man said, you turn right at Navan. This happens to be true. I've done it.

We left the office together in the height of good humour and by way of no harm we called in at Michael's for a drink. But Smiley, ever an abstemious man, flew on the one wing and after a half of stout was off home. At the door, he turned and handed me an envelope.

I went into the "jacks" and opened it. Inside was a blue ten-pound note and I put it in my pocket. Good man, I said to myself, but aloud, "Now aren't you the great sport, Robert Marie Smiley!"

I went back to the bar.

"The same again, Michael," said I, "and a drink for yourself."

"Thanks," said Michael.

I threw down the tenner.

"A blue one, be Jaysus!" said Michael. "You're blood's worth bottling."

And there was great respect going on in the bar that evening for Brendan Behan. Doctor Crippen made room for me on the one side and McIntaggart the other side of me. Beside them I stood, like Christ between the two thieves.

McIntaggart's name in Irish was "Mac an tsagairt," or "son of the priest." Some tease from Connemara told him this, and since then he'd gone round the gullible public with the tale that he was the son of a bloody priest. Not that anyone in this public house would believe the Lord's Prayer from his mouth. If you asked McIntaggart the time you'd check it on the telephone if you wanted the right time.

Doctor Crippen's real name I did not know. He got his nickname from the time he was a barman in a Free State Army canteen and was said to have poisoned the soldiers with bad drink. It was said that the man killed more that way than the I.R.A. whom they were fighting at the time.

Crippen in his day was a sergeant-major in the Free State Army and played Gaelic football for the Army Metro who were drawn from the barracks of the Dublin Metropolitan Garrison. Michael, the publican, respected him greatly for his former glory on the football field but Crippen did not know this. He was a gentle person and the only thing I knew him to boast about was his association with a literary magazine and his friendship with the associate editor.

The editor was a little left wing Republican from an island in the Atlantic Ocean off the coast of West Cork. He began writing when he came out of gaol in the "twenties and Ireland had still the vogue amongst the English writing and reading class, on account of the Black and Tans putting Ireland on the Liberal conscience." Like all the other peasant writers he was an ex-schoolmaster and wrote lovingly about simple folk of his native place. I could make neither head nor tail of anything he wrote and this editor suspected as much. He did not like me for it, nor any of my bits of short stories would he publish.

But the associate editor, a big, hardy boy that boxed for Trinity College, was one of the gentlest people that I have ever met. He was a Protestant clergyman's son and had a mania for backing horses. This was shared by Crippen, who adored him, and Crippen was forever recalling the memory of his friend, now working for the B.B.C. in London.

As I had just come back from England, he asked me, as I knew he would, how his friend was ever since? I told the assembled company my story and for the most part I told the truth, at the same time giving good account of myself. Hours later, blinking into the night, I directed my gaze towards my kip, and as I made the long journey home, I fell to thinking that it was not every day in these weeks I get a bit of respect in this town. It might never happen again. A change is as good as a rest.

At this stage of the game, what readies I had, and there was not a deal of them, came from my bits of articles, short stories, poems and radio scripts. I originally wrote *The Quare Fellow* under the title *Casadh Sugdin Eile* (The Twisting of Another Rope) after Douglas Hyde's play, *The Twisting of the Rope*, and it was first written as a radio script. Later I turned it into a one-act play and submitted it to the Abbey Theatre who rejected it, saying that one day I might write a play. God damnit, you might as well be out of this world as out of the fashion, for didn't Joyce and O'Casey have their plays rejected one time? I extended it to three acts and wrote the same play in English, for although I didn't agree with him I remember a screw from Cork telling me in Liverpool that to read and speak Irish would not do you a deal of good in these times.

"What good is it anywhere outside a few in Ireland?" he said.

In English or Irish I knew I'd wait years to be read in Dublin, but I sent it back to the Abbey and this time the manager suggested that I meet the producer to see if it would be possible to make it stageable. He explained that as I had based the play on the twenty-four hours preceding the execution of a man for carving up his brother, any one of the warders up in Mountjoy might choose to recognise himself and bring a libel action.

Fugh the producer, I said in my own mind, we don't speak the same language; I took it back, waited a few weeks, and submitted it again. Back like a shot it came, and prompt with it too. Like Joyce, I put it aside and went on with my other writing. By now I was well known in the writing game and as the Irish have great *meas* for the traveller, I decided to write a detective story about Dublin's underworld, but using my knowledge of France, which was by now considerable, as the background. I wrote it under the phoney name of Emmet Street, which is the name of the street opposite the one I was reared in North Dublin, partly because around the fashionable area of Grafton Street the Dublin intelligentsia still regarded me as a writer of pornography and partly because the district around Emmet Street is famous for another reason.

Beside Emmet Street is Rutland Street where formerly lived a man who was later President of the Irish Republic, Sean T. Kelly. But he lived in a whole Georgian house whereas the rest of the street was mostly tenements. In a back room in one of these lived Matt Talbot, and after his death there was a move on to make him a saint. But Sean O'Casey, who came from that area and lived only a couple of hundred yards from him, refers to him as "Mad Talbot." Not only in matters of the theatre, but also in matters appertaining to Dublin, do I bow to the expert.

Máire Mhac an tSaoi
(b. 1922)

[EXCERPT FROM]

The Same Age as the State

Máire Mhac an tSaoi was born in 1922, the daughter of a Belfast IRA leader and a political activist mother. She grew up in a household of intense literary and political debate. Her mother's brother, Pádraig de Brún, was a celebrated scholar of the Irish language and is a central figure in the piece reprinted below. As an Irish poet of defining distinction and importance, she has also been an advocate for the centrality of the Irish language. She has warned, in articles and essays and interviews, that in the modern state that Ireland has become, there is always a risk of not simply forgetting, but also disowning an imaginative heritage. Not least because that heritage, and the language oppressed by its correlative history, implies the pain of defeat.

In this glowing account of Irish as a familial and national inheritance, the opposite becomes true: the hopes and future of a language are outlined and are claimed as inseparable from the identity and future of a people. She states boldly that her family, at the time of the establishment of the State, believed passionately in the "restoration of Irish to its rightful dignity as the national language of Ireland." This account continues the charged and crucial conversation, included through the contributions of various writers in this volume, between Irish writers and the reality of the Irish language and its future.

Máire Mhac an tSaoi doesn't turn away from the complications that followed for her. For example, in a 2000 interview in Berkeley for the

Conversations with History series, she said: "Writing in a minority language is fraught with difficulties. The Irish that I write is the Irish that people spoke more than fifty years ago. All the generations for whom ideally I write are dead." Her career as a writer, her collaborations with her husband, Conor Cruise O'Brien—she easily and gracefully transits between her maiden and married name as a writer—and her life as a civil servant have all confirmed her steadfast commitment to the language.

Her Irish language collections include *Margadh na saoire* (1956), *Codladh an ghaiscígh agus véarsaí eile* (1973), *An galar dubhach* (1980), *An cion go dtí seo* (1987), and *Shoa agus dánta eile* (1999). She also published a book of translations in 1959 called *A Heart Full of Thought*.

Her memoir, *The Same Age as the State*, published in 2003 under her married name, Máire Cruise O'Brien, is an essential account of the subtle imaginative navigations of a woman, poet, and linguist among the complications of a new history.

PART I:
ALTERNATIVE LIFESTYLE

I must now set down my personal memories of the 1920s and 1930s and, in particular, of the part played by the Irish language in the life of Ireland at that time, and I must admit to a feeling of some discomfort at the task. If I have understood its nature correctly, it is a peculiarly difficult one. It involves bringing to life a period of the past beyond the reach of memory for a substantial part of my readership, on the one hand, and yet too recent to have become fashionable, on the other. It involves doing this on a basis of personal recollections from childhood and early youth; this is a positive minefield of booby traps. Like all people whose talent it is to exploit their emotions, I prefer to do so under a decent veil of literary convention, and not in any immediate capacity as witness, or advocate. Yet this is the double role I am now called upon to assume. I may say that so profound was the conditioning in ancestral piety through which I, like all my generation, passed, that I can in no way refuse to take on this function, which has fallen to me through the ineluctable processes of time. I must grapple with it as best I can, and I must ask the reader to bear with me in the process. The era for which I speak was no mean era, and the people who inhabited it no mean people. Perhaps they deserve a better chronicler.

By now you will want to know what all this soul-searching has to do with the Irish language and its celebration; I will explain. My parents and their circle, at the time of the foundation of the Republic, believed absolutely and unapologetically in the restoration of Irish to its rightful dignity as the national language of Ireland, and they believed in its preservation and restoration as a living language. This was on their part no joyless and xeno-phobic enterprise, but a great, life-enhancing undertaking that permeated and enriched their entire experience and was, without exaggeration, an influential factor in every quotidian decision they were called upon to take. They were part of that body of young people throughout the country, in their late twenties and early thirties — an intellectual leaven — many of them exceptionally gifted and imbued with a love of and an enthusiasm for art and culture in all their forms, a love and enthusiasm that (alas!) could only appear simplistic and naive today. They were, above all, incandescent with fun and hope and self-confidence, which perhaps burnt all the brighter in that they were emerging from times of discouragement and very real grief.

The central inspirational figure of this group, as you will perhaps have gathered, was undoubtedly my mother's brother, Paddy, a linguist, classicist and humanist in the great tradition of Erasmus and More. As is so often the case in rural Ireland, the bond between brother and sister was very close. Their parents, as we saw, belonged to the last generation of native speakers in the Tipperary of Kickham and *Knocknagow*, and the triumphant estab-lishment of Irish as an academic subject during their schooldays did the rest: I have never known any two people more effortlessly and completely bilin-gual. My father, on the other hand, was a theoretical revivalist only. He learnt Irish as an adult as he learnt German, but never spoke any language other than English with any ease. In this he was typical of his Northern, urban cul-ture, which did not produce linguists, for want of the facility, essential to that end, for making a fool of oneself. His Irish, however, infiltrated his poetry, as it did all that generation's.

Those students who had the good fortune to attend my mother's lectures on the *Dánta Grá* (classical Irish love poetry), in University College, Dublin, will remember the extraordinary phenomenon of a warm and witty twentieth-century, middle-aged, middle-class Irish lady entering completely into the mind of the medieval Gaelic poet in his lighter moments, and communicating her understanding and her enjoyment to her hearers. Here were two highly sophisticated and idiosyncratic cultures complementing and illuminating each other. That symbiosis has been a part of my life as far back as I can remember. People who experienced it still talk of it. Our present parish priest in Howth remembers her saying, "You must not look at the seventeenth century through the spectacles of the present day."

In the troubled circumstances of those times, which I have tried to convey in the last chapter, my father was much away from home and his place was taken by my Uncle Paddy. Every Friday he came from Maynooth to stay the night and I went with him on the crossbar of his bicycle to his Mass on Saturday mornings in Loreto Hall. Our spare room was known as Pabu's room. "Pabu" was my early realisation of Paddy Browne, which stuck to him for life. The two men, Paddy and my father, were very different in temperament but identical in ideals. Their friendship was profound and enduring, founded on trust, respect and mutual generosity. A lesser man than my father might have resented his children's education being taken over by his brother-in-law; a lesser man than my uncle might have insinuated into that education some disenchantment with the realities of pragmatic politics. It did not happen.

It is said that a too perfect childhood unfits you for life, but I would not barter my golden childhood for any possible alternative. The theory of the time was that if one adult in a household spoke consistently to the children only in a given language, the children would grow up speaking that language, irrespective of what other languages they might also learn. In our household my Uncle Paddy constituted himself that adult, and he never spoke to us except in Irish. He did this so successfully that, for a long time, I believed him to know no other tongue. I was an incurious, self-centred, unobservant child, a lot of whose life went on inside her head, but sometime after my First Communion, when I was interpreting for my uncle to a petrol-pump attendant on the road from Dublin to the Dingle Peninsula, it dawned on me that the exercise might not be entirely necessary; the adults were smiling in a peculiar way.

It was thanks to the constant presence of my Uncle Paddy that all my knowledge of the world of art and letters was mediated through Irish. At the age of four I played the boy that leads the blind prophet Tiresias on stage in my uncle's translation of the *Antigone* of Sophocles — performed in Loreto Hall by the students — and I was deeply conversant with the story, although in my secret heart I thought Antigone was too big a girl to be altogether interesting. At ten I created the part of Joas in the first production in Irish of Racine's *Athalie* — Pabu's translation again — and identified completely with the boy-king in his breathtaking exchange with the terrible queen. There is a part of my mind that still thinks of *Treasure Island* as a novel written in Irish because my uncle read it to us in Irish, translating at sight from the English as he went along. It was the kind of party-piece, polymath that he was, that he could always perform with panache, and that we took for granted. He taught me my first Latin (through Irish) at six, my first, indeed my only Greek at ten. He taught my brother maths and physics, also through Irish — we never spoke any other language with him. He spoke English only to my father in the family. He taught my little sister to play Bridge; my lack of card sense he deplored. With him we read and memorised and recited reams of poetry in several languages; he himself retained from boyhood the wonderful, verbal memory of the Irish rural illiterate, now a thing of the past. We read omnivorously; the big eighteen-inch by twelve-inch edition of Shakespeare's historical plays was too heavy for us to handle and we crawled all over it on the floor. For many years afterwards I believed a "bastard" to be an official of the English Royal Court, something like a *poursuivant*. Some of us, I'm afraid, also scribbled on some of the pages. We have that same book here in our house in Howth yet. These are trivial juvenile memories: I list them only to establish my credentials as a witness to an extraordinary experiment in what would now be called alternative lifestyles; to bear witness to its influence and effects at the time, or to its lack of them, then and thereafter.

Benedict Kiely

(b. 1919)

[EXCERPT FROM]

The Waves Behind Us

Benedict Kiely was born in Drumskinny, County Fermanagh. When he was an infant, the family moved to the Gallows Hill area of Omagh, where he spent his childhood. His youth and a fledgling vocation in the Jesuits were cut short by illness. In 1938 he moved to Dublin, where he worked as a freelance journalist. In 1941 he graduated from University College Dublin.

Heinrich Böll once described Kiely as "the Irish Balzac." The reasons for this label are not hard to find. A substantial career of journalism and publishing fiction and essays has produced a vivid, humane body of work. Like Balzac, Kiely is a regional writer who is also a national one. Again like the French writer, in his work anecdote is in the service of narrative. The exuberant continuum of his fiction—its curiosity and color alike—has given delight to many readers.

His short story volumes include *A Journey to the Seven Streams* (1963), *A Ball of Malt and Madame Butterfly* (1973), *A Cow in the House* (1978), *The State of Ireland: A Novella and Seven Short Stories* (1981), *A Letter to Peachtree* (1987), *The Trout in the Turnhole* (1996), and *The Collected Stories of Benedict Kiely* (2001). Among his novels are *Countries of Contention* (1945), *Poor Scholar* (1947), *The Captain with the Whiskers* (1960), *Dogs Enjoy the Morning* (1968), and *Proxopera: A Tale of Modern Ireland* (1977). In 1999 he published *Benedict Kiely: A Raid into Dark Corners and Other Essays*.

Apart from his other distinctions, Kiely has occasionally served as an almost Boswellian witness to the quirks and eccentricities of Irish literary life. Beneath the humour of his approach, however, is a vivid and affectionate literary sensibility. In the account below of Patrick Kavanagh, whose work he admired, Kiely describes seeing him for the first time in the old Radio Eireann offices on Henry Street. There is delight and regret—and even a small awe for the apparition of demigods—in this description of the Monaghan poet, ensconced in a studio in the middle of Dublin "roaring at Ireland."

Backstage in Radio Eireann was a little different. But also memorable. A friend of mine, married to a relation of mine, knew an important official in the radio station who had promised that some night he would show my friend and his wife around. It was located in the most historic General Post Office, from the attic (upper floor) of which all our broadcasting was then done. So I went with them and, for the very first time, stepped in at that side door from Henry Street and, using the stairs — because the elevator was, as it so often was, out of order — ascended to look down and walk along that longest corridor in Ireland. Come to that, I don't recollect having seen a longer corridor anywhere else. But I'm not much of a travelled man and there may well be many longer corridors in Russia or in China Herself.

Perhaps my thoughts as I walked along that corridor were on the shouting and burning and destruction of 1916 and on the possibility that there might still be a few ghosts there. The corridor was very quiet: not at all as I was to see it many times afterwards, busy with people darting like rabbits out of one office and into another, or with cultured groups standing at doorways and talking of everything on the earth, or, as became them and their vocations, on the air. Then up the narrow stairs and into a large room, with a large table and chairs, and a grand piano and idle music stands, and we were left there to sit looking through glass at the poet, Patrick Kavanagh.

He was, although you would never have thought it to look at him, reviewing books: he looked more like Cuchulain warring with the relentless waves. He was, I think, quite unaware that he had spectators. But not an audience, because the sound was not coming through to us. He waved his arms. He shuffled his shoulders. He roared at Ireland. To look at him in that glass cage one would never have thought, as I was afterwards to discover, that he could be gentle, childlike, amiable, understanding, even if few men ever worked harder to disguise their virtues than he did. He was a variable man.

Frequently you'll remember people as you first saw them and, for me, Paddy Kavanagh is still in a glass box. Not as he was when he used to sit punditising serenely in the office of the *Standard* in Peter O'Curry's days at the corner of Pearse Street and Tara Street. He owed a lot to Peter and acknowledged that in a dedication. For Peter had written the first news story ever about Paddy: in the *Irish Press* in late 1936 or early 1937. And I had read it in Omagh post office where I was then a sorting clerk and telegraphist.

Not as he was on the day when, with the expression of a schoolboy timidly presenting an essay to a censoring teacher, he handed me a sheet of paper and said: "Could we sing that to the air of 'The Dawning of the Day.'"

And I read, written in pencil:

On Raglan Road on an autumn day I saw her first and knew
That her dark hair would weave a snare that I might some day
rue. . . .

We raised our voices in splendid cacophony. It gives me an odd feeling still to think that, after the poet himself, I may have been the first person ever to see that song written down. At that time I was also in college with the beautiful young woman who had inspired the words. Like the poet, we all worshipped from a distance.

Nor even as he was the night a crowd of us toured a series of pubs boldly trying to sell a pair of sandals the poet had cobbled for himself. But cobbled them too big even for his feet, and he had a fine foot. Tomas Ò Duinn, an eminent Gaelic journalist, was of the party, and Kevin B. Nowlan, small in stature but a gigantic historian, and a soldier called Connolly from Boston, and a man called Canito, from Marseilles. No man did we find with feet to fill the sandals. But as we turned the corner at Vincent's Hospital a man, God rest him, dropped dead and, as we carried him into the hospital, we could not help noticing that he had the biggest feet any of us had ever seen.

No: because of my first visit to Radio Eireann, Patrick Kavanagh, the poet, sits for me for ever in a glass box, a saint in a shrine, waving his arms, roaring at Ireland. . . .

Richard Murphy

(b. 1927)

"Wellington Testimonial"

Richard Murphy was born in County Mayo in 1927, the son of a former governor of the Bahamas. Although he was educated in England, Murphy has always felt imaginatively close to his Irish heritage. Of his background he once wrote: "My mother belonged to a family who owned estates in Mayo as beautiful and as bankrupt as Coole: but my father was Irish by race, as our name declares—some say it means 'sea-fighter'—and he was educated in Ireland by winning scholarships all the way from an impoverished rectory seven miles from where I have lived for the past fifteen years."

While Murphy is not an overtly political poet, his work is eloquently grounded in the cultural divisions of Irish history. He has explored his own feelings of exclusion, of being on a historical margin, both in poems (such as his long poem *The Battle of Aughrim*) and in his autobiographical memoir *The Kick* (2004). *The Battle of Aughrim* addresses deep fissures in Irish history. In a piece written in 1975 he states: "I suggest that the division of Ireland is not just in our country, but in every Irishman's blood; and has to be resolved individually, before the conflict can be settled as a whole. One should not falsify the ancient and current Irish equation with passionate simplicities, but try to clarify by defusing some of the explosive credal myths. Ultimately our divisive legends, some of which I explore in the long poem, turn out . . . to be grounded in error and ignorance."

His published work includes *The Archaeology of Love* (1955), *Sailing to an Island* (1963), *The Battle of Aughrim* (1968), *High Island* (1974), *High Island: New and Selected Poems* (1975), *Selected Poems* (1979), *The Price of Stone* (1985), *New Selected Poems* (1989), *The Mirror Wall* (1989), and *In the Heart of the Country: Collected Poems* (2000). Murphy's poems, not unlike John Hewitt's, often register degrees of exclusion. Occasionally, however, through wit and irony he uncovers a different history as well as a separate state of mind. This voicing of the Wellington monument in Dublin—an aftermath of British rule—is such a piece.

Needling my native sky over Phoenix Park
I obelize the victory of wit
That let my polished Anglo-Irish mark
Be made by Smirke, as a colossal spit.

Properly dressed for an obsolete parade,
Devoid of mystery, no winding stair
Threading my unvermiculated head,
I've kept my feet, but lost my nosy flair.

My life was work: my work was taking life
To be a monument. The dead have won
Capital headlines. Look at Ireland rife
With maxims: need you ask what good I've done?

My sole point in this evergreen oak aisle
Is to maintain a clean laconic style.

John B. Keane

(1928–2002)

[EXCERPT FROM]

Self-Portrait

John B. Keane was born in Listowel, County Kerry, in 1928. He lived his entire
life there, running a popular public house from 1955 on. His powerful,
eloquent plays draw on the history, speech, and reality of the people of North
Kerry. Many of Keane's plays are among the most noted and frequently
performed in the Irish repertory. Among his most celebrated plays are *Sive*
(first staged 1959), *Sharon's Grave* (1960), *The Highest House on the Mountain*
(1961), *No More in Dust* (1961), *Many Young Men of Twenty* (1961), *Hut 42*
(1962), *The Man from Clare* (1962), *Seven Irish Plays* (1967), *The Year of the
Hiker* (1972), *The Field* (1965, adapted later as a film of the same name), and
Big Maggie (1969).

His plays gave voice to many issues of rural Ireland that had not previously found their way into currency or acceptance. He writes forcefully about
emigration, poverty, and the brutality of forced marriages. His characters
are often bound by relationships—either human or historical—they did
not choose. And they barely survive between extremes of inarticulacy and
eloquence.

Although the Abbey Theatre was committed to the Irish repertory from
its foundation by William Yeats and Lady Augusta Gregory, the connection
with new Irish dramatists was not always smooth. John B. Keane—populist,
democratic, and independent—was not likely to show too much deference to

the canon makers of Irish theater, however well draped in the mantle of historical authority.

In the piece below, excerpted from his 1964 *Self-Portrait*, Keane leaves a fascinating account of the trials of trying to put his play *Sive* into production in the late fifties. Revealingly, he outlines the tension between local, rural drama groups and a metropolitan theater culture. It is an unexpected glimpse of the new structures of theater in that era. *Sive*, after some ordeal, did get produced. It has since, in the Druid Revival, been reevaluated as one of the most important contemporary Irish plays.

Chapter VII

I wrote a three-act play in a few months and I called it "Barbara Shearing."

I submitted it to Radio Eireann and it was accepted, subject to a certain amount of re-writing. It was then adapted for radio and it proved a highly successful diversion, but it was only a diversion and it lacked depth.

Before it was heard over the Radio, however, I went one night with Mary to see the Listowel Drama Group in "All Souls' Night" by Joseph Tomelty. I was impressed and, as far as I can remember, it was the first full-length play of consequence I had seen up till then. When I came home that night I was impatient and full of ideas. I sent Mary to bed and filled a pint. I sat by the fire for a while and after a quarter of an hour I reached for my copy-book and pencil.

I started to write and six hours later, or precisely at 6:30 A.M., I had written the first scene of "Sive."

I didn't think a whole lot of what I had written and I very nearly crumpled the crammed sheets and tossed them into the fire. Lucky for me, I didn't. About a fortnight later I had completed the first draft of "Sive." I showed it to a few people I knew and their opinion was the same. It wouldn't work. For one thing, the names of the characters were nothing short of ludicrous, the theme was outworn and the language too flowery.

I went through the play a second time, and submitted it to the Abbey

Theatre. About five weeks later it was returned to me without a word of any kind. I left it lying dead for a few weeks and would have forgotten about it but for a conversation I had with Billy Kearney of the Listowel Drama Group. He suggested that I give it to him to read. I did and he liked it.

Listowel Drama Group were interested. They planned two plays for the following season, and mine was to be one. Bill Kearney sent the play to Mícheál Ó hAodha of Radio Eireann. He wrote back immediately and stated that he would do it over the radio. He made a few sensible suggestions and wrote that if the Listowel Drama Group produced "Sive" it would be the greatest thing that ever happened to amateur drama in Ireland. Frankly, I didn't think so. Neither did anybody else, although we had a certain amount of faith in the play.

Brendan Carroll of Listowel was the producer. He certainly worked hard on the production and anybody who has seen the Listowel Drama Group in Brendan Carroll's production will never forget it.

I am deeply indebted to the Listowel players. They were the first English-speaking amateur group to appear on the Abbey stage. They packed the Abbey for a week, during a heat wave. They were a credit to Listowel and to the amateur drama movement. In a sense they made history and they deserve a special place in the history of Irish theatre.

"Sive" goes on in New York soon and I have been invited to help with its production and to make a few television appearances to assist the publicity end. I haven't made up my mind whether I'll go or not. If I want the play to succeed I must go, but I am not keen on an enforced absence from home. My limit is a weekend in Dublin. Even Belfast gives me the willies and anyway, from what I gather, it is extremely difficult to come across a good pint in New York.

Hugh Leonard
(b. 1926)

[EXCERPT FROM]

Home Before Night

Hugh Leonard was born as John Keyes Byrne in Dublin in 1926. He once said, "My mother was passionate. She was stubborn, the dominant one in the family. She dominated my father." His drama, fiction, and journalism have celebrated strong characters and explored the power and hurt of the lives lived by them. He is a prolific playwright and has written two auto-biographical studies: *Home Before Night* (1979) and *Out After Dark* (1989). His widely successful play *Da* (1973), a study of a father, is a classic of the Irish theater.

His other plays include *The Big Birthday Suit* (1956), *A Leap in the Dark* (1957), *Stephen D* (1962, an adaptation of James Joyce's *Portrait of the Artist as a Young Man* and *Stephen Hero*), *The Poker Session* (1964), *Mick and Mick* (1966), *The Late Arrival of Incoming Aircraft* (1968), *The Patrick Pearse Motel* (1971), *Da* (1973), *The Au Pair Man* (1974), *Time Was* (1980), *A Life* (1981), *Suburb of Babylon* (1983), *Pizazz* (1986), *Selected Plays of Hugh Leonard* (1992), and *Moving* (1994). He has published one novel, *Parnell and the Englishwoman* (1992), and several volumes of essays, including *Leonard's Last Book* (1978).

Although Leonard brings a dark, mordant wit to puncturing the myriad postures of Irish life, including the literary ones, he is also eloquent and affirmative about the reach of imagination and the consequent power of language in Ireland. His debt to writers like Sean O'Casey is plain and acknowledged. The excerpt reprinted below takes up the story of his hero, Jack, in his autobiographical account of a Dublin childhood, *Home Before Night*, at the point where Jack goes to work for the Land Commission. As the central character of the book, Jack is described as young and disaffected. Yet in this passage his assumption that all avenues of imaginative life are now closed off to him is turned aside by one experience: He learns about Sean O'Casey, the dramatist of Dublin's working life.

Jack goes to see *The Plough and the Stars* at the Abbey. To his surprise and delight, he discovers that the play speaks for his own life. He even finds his own people, his own immediate relatives, mirrored and celebrated there. In the process Jack understands there might be a future for him in such an enterprise. The passage is a poignant example of the way Irish writing passed from generation to generation. The excerpt also attests to the fact that Irish literature by the 1950s had a broad, powerful appeal across cultures and expectations. And that, at last, it was beginning to issue imaginative permissions to a wide variety of younger Irish writers.

Every morning when you came in, you signed the attendance book, and Mr. Drumm would carry it off to his own table to mark the names of the latecomers in red ink. One day, he made to pick up the book, then looked closely at it. "Come here and sign your name, Mr. Kennedy," he said.

"Oh, I signed me name," Mr. Kennedy said without budging from his chair, and sure enough Jack had seen him bending over the book with a pencil in his hand.

"You did not sign your name," Mr. Drumm said. "You will come here and do so now."

"Oh, I signed it right enough," Mr. Kennedy said happily.

A redness was spreading into Mr. Drumm's face. "And I tell you you did not. Now sign this book or be marked absent."

Mr. Kennedy just grinned as if he was too cute to fall for an old trick the like of that. Mr. Drumm's finger stabbed at the book like the needle of a sewing machine. His voice was hoarse with rage.

"Do as I say!"

There was a hush in the room as Mr. Kennedy got up from his table, taking with him the magnifying glass he used for reading. He was bent over the book for a long time, and when he straightened up his face threw a pink, happy light on Mr. Drumm.

"Ah," he said, "did you rub it out on me?"

At first Jack had thought that the people around him were mummies that needed burying, but before long he realized that he was in an orchestra of head cases, with Mr. Drumm as the conductor. He could never be as unhappy again as he had been on that first day, but more than ever he longed to be free of the place. He had been there for six months when a man named Paddy Malone remarked to him: "A great ending to a great play."

"What is?"

"That tune you were whistling: 'Keep the Home Fires Burning.' It comes in at the end of *The Plough and the Stars*. You know: by O'Casey."

He shook his head.

"You what? You call yourself a Dublinman and you never heard tell of O'Casey?"

"Well, yeah, I heard of him, but —"

"Lord God. I'm from Cork where they eat their young, yet I know him backwards. And you the fellow with his nose forever stuck in a book. What are you reading there, anyway?" He picked up a book from Jack's table. "The Garden by L. A. G. Strong." He grunted. He had air hair, turning iron grey. His mouth was set in a pretended disgust. "Are you having me on or what? You never heard of *The Plough and the Stars*?"

"No."

"And you're the man who wants to write books?"

Someone had been spreading yarns. "I never said I —"

"Listen to me. It's on at the Abbey, so would you ever go down there and see it and not be making a holy show of yourself."

He winked and strolled away, singing "Keep the Home Fires Burning" in a Cork tenor that made Mr. Drumm's eyes swing around like searchlights.

That evening Jack went to the Abbey Theatre. He had never seen a play before, except for *The Colleen Bawn* on Dalkey town hall, where the girl was thrown off the rock into the lakes of Killarney, and all the hard chaws had stood up to see her land on a mattress. Now he saw an actor named McCormick, who was as real as Mr. Quirk in Kalafat Lane had been, or Jack's uncle Sonny, or any of the old lads who stood spitting at Gilbey's corner or the harbour wall: a foxy-faced jackeen in a hard hat, who would look to gut you one minute and be a decent skin the next. And there was a younger actor named Cusack who was the Young Covey, and when he changed out of his working clothes and remembered to take the packet of Woodbines from his overall pocket, the people nudged one another and whispered: "Oh, that's very good." But it was more than the acting that made Jack stand outside the theatre afterwards, looking towards the rooftops for the red glow of Dublin burning that he had seen through the window of Bessie Burgess's attic room. The life that roared through the play itself had spilled over from the stage, sweeping him with it so that he knew he would never again be content just to sit and watch and applaud with the rest of them. The thought burned him like fever.

He went along Marlborough Street to the quays, and from the dark of the river the east wind leaped at him like a robber. He held his coat collar shut, and his hand shook with cold. He went trotting past the row of hansom cabs and the snorting horses, racing the lights of the last train as it crossed the loop line bridge to Tara Street. The guard held the door of the last compartment open for him, and he sat down opposite a young man and a girl. The man looked sulkily at him: by interloping Jack had spoiled his chance of a coort.

The pair of them could strip to their skins for all he cared. He looked away from them through the window and saw his reflection in the dark glass. It was amazing how calm he looked. His breath in the unheated compartment threw a mist upon the glass, but even then he could see, as if it was out there by the tracks, the door he would escape through.

Anthony Cronin

(b. 1928)

Dead as Doornails

Anthony Cronin was born in County Wexford in 1928. He is a distinguished poet and novelist as well as a prolific journalist and biographer. He is also the author of one of the true classics of Irish memoir, *Dead as Doornails*. Cronin's poetry collections include *Poems* (1958), *Collected Poems, 1950–73* (1973), *Reductionist Poem* (1980), *RMS Titanic* (1981), *41 Sonnet Poems* (1982), *New and Selected Poems* (1982), *The End of the Modern World* (1989), *Relationships* (1992), and *Minotaur* (1999).

In 1996, Cronin published the noted biography *Samuel Beckett: The Last Modernist*. He followed it in 2003 with *No Laughing Matter: The Life and Times of Flann O'Brien*, a book John Banville called "a fascinating, dispiriting, and unflinchingly candid portrait." As these studies suggest, as well as the title of his critical volume, *A Question of Modernity* (1966), Cronin has been a modernist from the start, an advocate of experimental poetry and fiction in a post-Yeatsian culture that showed little interest in either. He championed the innovation of Irish poets like Denis Devlin and Thomas McGreevy, who were listening stations for European influences. As an associate editor of *The Bell* and literary editor of *Time and Tide*, he was able to exercise his sense of a broader discourse.

Cronin—as editor, poet, and novelist—befriended many of the writers of the 1950s; Patrick Kavanagh, Myles na Gopaleen, and Brendan Behan kept his

company and tried his patience. At that time Dublin was a notably unstruc-
tured literary environment—a place of hard drinking and harsh economic
want. After their deaths, in 1976, he published *Dead as Doornails*. It is a
unique memoir of literary friendship, a subtle elegy for fulfilled talents and
unfulfilled lives. Few books on the writing life are as funny or tenderhearted;
few are as profoundly sad. In this excerpt the comedy is uppermost. Nevertheless, the antic behavior of Behan and Kavanagh provides a spectacular and
not-to-be-doubted insight into Irish writing as it was then.

It was Christmas, and we came out of McDaid's about nine o'clock to find
that it was raining. The Christmas lights were on in Grafton Street, there
were more people than usual about, and a bunch of carol singers was standing
at the corner with coat collars turned up, still sweetening the damp night air.

They carried placards advertising their charitable intent — something to
do with the St. Vincent de Paul Society, or the Legion of Mary or the Morning
Star hostel for down-and-outs. As we stood in the rain deliberating the next
move, Brendan began to mutter. As I have said, he had in those days a fero-
cious hatred of the Catholic Church in all its manifestations. We decided to
go to Keogh's, which is in Anne Street, and moved towards the corner. The
carol singers were still hard at it, tenor and alto, bass and treble, but as we
passed them Brendan suddenly seized one of the placards and proceeded to
tear up the cardboard and smash the lath while roaring "Chairman Mao
TseTung will soon put a stop to your fucking gallop, ye creepin' Jesus's ye."
The singing ended on various notes while he flung the fragments across the
road towards Mooney's, bellowing away. There was a moment's hiatus, everybody, including myself, being taken by surprise, and then a couple of by-
standers rushed him. He was off like a hare, up Grafton Street and towards
Stephen's Green, with about four fellows after him. Fear lends wings to the
feet and Brendan kept his distance. At the top of the street he dashed into the
roadway and succeeded in gaining the far side well ahead, the others having
followed with more respect for the traffic, I crossed over too, but with even
more circumspection. Brendan pounded on towards the Harcourt Street end.

The inner side of Stephen's Green was in those days lit by ordinary street lamps and there were pools of light with intervals of darkness in between. The pursuers ran on until suddenly it was evident that there was no quarry in front, then stopped unevenly, regrouped and began to argue among themselves. I stopped too. It was, as Brendan would say, the best of my play. After peering into the bushes inside the railings, they began to straggle back and, hoping not to be identified as the companion of the atheistic communist, I went on and even met them, walking as casually as I could, though of course in fear and trembling. They were still hotly debating and occasionally peering, so I passed unrecognised, whistling a little tune.

I had almost reached the far corner when I heard my name called. It was Brendan, crouching inside under a dripping laurel bush.

"Did you climb those railings?" I asked in surprise.

"Of course I did. Why wouldn't I? Didn't I fucking paint them?" he answered petulantly.

I had to be content with the logic, though it was an astonishing feat to have swung himself over in a dark interval and in the time available.

"Well you'd better climb out again now," I said, "because I badly need a drink."

He climbed over, this time with, it seemed, immense difficulty, and blowing like a grampus. I watched, powerless to aid or hinder, until at last he dropped down beside me. We had both forgotten by then about the outraged populace.

Suddenly there was a rush of feet from quite close by and a shout of "There he is, the rotten bastard." Brendan was off again, this time towards the Russell Hotel, but they caught us in the middle of the road. There was nothing for it but to turn and fight.

Whether it was the shock of our sudden *volte face* or not, after a few rather ineffectual punches were exchanged they gave ground before us, and I learned again what a little determination will do in a fight, a thing an intellectual is always, alas, inclined to forget. In the confusion we got up the steps of the Russell and burst into the lobby on top of a startled porter and some guests.

"There's a mob out there," shouted Brendan, already beginning to bolt the glass panelled door. The surprised porter came over to have a look for himself. There were in fact four fellows standing outside on the pavement, gesticulating and shouting, but apparently regarding the hotel as some sort of sanctuary, and uncertain as to what to do next.

"Get the rozzers," said Brendan in tones of command. "I'm a Dubbelin man. I'm a citizen of no mean city and I'll show these bogmen that there's law and order in this town."

By the time a police-car arrived the mob of four had apparently given up hope of getting us and drifted off. Brendan told the sergeant he had been attacked for no reason at all in the streets of his own city by a crowd of murderous countrymen he didn't know but suspected to be members of a rural-based organisation of fascist tendencies.

Unimpressed, but equally incurious, the police drove us round the Green and dropped us at the corner of Merrion Row. We went to O'Neill's. Brendan expressed no word of apology, remorse or regret, but he seemed a bit shifty, and at one stage he flattered me by saying "You're handy with your dukes," which, like all successful flattery, attributed to the opposite party an aptitude he did not possess but would like to.

He stayed that night in Hatch Street and the following morning we found ourselves, not for the first time, broke on Christmas day. We made one or two fruitless visits and then decided to call on a friend who lived in Waterloo Road. After a long wait in the cold, we got on a number ten bus and there, sunk in gloom, we found a solitary Patrick Kavanagh. Such was his degree of self-pity that he even failed to get upset at the sight of Brendan. "I woke up this morning," he said. "And what morning was it? It was Christmas morning, the morning of joy, the birthday of the Prince of Peace. 'No war, nor battle's sound, was heard the world around, The idle spear and shield were high up hung.' And what had I in the house? I had a stale herring from yesterday, a stale uneatable herring. But there was the telephone, fully connected, and ready, you would surely to God and in the name of the Prince of Peace think, to ring. But was there one person in the whole wide city of Dublin who would ring me up to ask me how I was making out and maybe ask me to spend the holy Christmastide with them? There was not. I waited there on my lonesome in the cold for hours and eventually I had to get on the blower myself to a blackguard I know. On this day of all days it's essential to drown your sorrows. I know what I'm in for. It's the worst day in the year and it brings out the bollocks in everybody. But I'll risk it for the sake of a drink."

William Trevor

(b. 1928)

Excursions in the Real World

William Trevor was born William Trevor Cox in Mitchelstown, County Cork, in 1928. His mother was raised in the North, his father in the South. "I feel that writers of fiction do belong in a no man's land some place," he has said. "I certainly feel I do." To some extent, these elements of a self-conscious displacement are the same ones that have given his fiction the power and delicacy of an outsider's art. His first job was as a sculptor. In a BBC interview he described his disengagement from visual art: "I lost interest in it because it was abstract. I think I was perhaps losing people. I missed the people I had once carved as it were, and I just stopped." After his marriage in 1952 he emigrated to England, where he worked several jobs. With his choice of fiction writing, he went back to art by a different route: he returned to carving people.

Trevor's early work is largely set in England. Later he turned more to Ireland and the Irish Troubles. Some of his most notable books are *The Ballroom of Romance and Other Stories* (1972), *Angels at the Ritz and Other Stories* (1975), *Fools of Fortune Bodley Head* (1983), *Excursions in the Real World* (1993), *Felicia's Journey* (1994), and *The Story of Lucy Gault* (2002). Although he has not defined himself as an Irish writer, he is considered one. Locating Trevor, however, is difficult: although he belongs at first sight to the realistic tradition of short fiction in Ireland—with Sean O'Faolain and Frank

O'Connor—a closer look tells another story. The Ireland Trevor describes is plastic, surreal, and elusive; the real nation is never in view. The darkly comic strategies he deploys place him nearer to Samuel Beckett than to Frank O'Connor. He is a deceptively experimental writer.

Trevor is also affectionate about the Irish past. For many Irish writers the definition of imagination begins with the naming of origin. So it is here. In the piece below, from *Excursions in the Real World*, Trevor struggles to evoke an idyll of Munster, with memories of "a provincial world, limited and claustrophobic." "All memory," he writes, "is grist to the fiction-writer's mill."

A Dream of Munster's Arcadia

All memory is grist to the fiction-writer's mill. The pleasure and the pain experienced by any storyteller's characters, the euphoria of happiness, the ache of grief, must of course be the storyteller's own. It cannot be otherwise, and in that sense all fiction has its autobiographical roots, spreading through — in my case — a provincial world, limited and claustrophobic.

I grew up in what John Betjeman called "the small towns of Ireland" — in my case, Mitchelstown, cut down to size by the towering Galtee mountains and the Knockmealdowns, Youghal by the sea, Skibbereen lost somewhere in the back of beyond.

There were others besides, but to these three in County Cork I return most frequently. Mitchelstown is still famous for its martyrs and its processed cheese, a squat little town, looking as though someone has sat on it. A good business town, my father used to say.

Youghal, smartly elegant in my memory, is tatty on a wet afternoon. An earful of German tourists crawls along the seafront, the misty beach is empty. Once, people pointed here and remarked: I listened and my eavesdroppings told of an afternoon love affair conducted on that brief promenade, he a married doctor, she a lady in disgrace. I see them now as I made them in my fascination: she is thin, and dressed in red, laughing, with pale long hair; he is Ronald Coleman with a greyer moustache. They smile at one another; defiantly he touches her hand. They are breathtaking in their sinning, and all their conversation is beautiful; they are the world's most exciting people.

I walk away from their romance, not wanting to tell myself that they were not like that. On the sands where old seaside artists sprinkled garish colours the rain is chilly. Pierrots performed here, and the man and woman who rode the Wall of Death sunned themselves at midday. From the Loreto Convent we trooped down here to run the end-of-term races, Sister Therese in charge. The sands haven't changed, nor have the concrete facades of the holiday boarding-houses, nor the Protestant church with its holes for lepers to peer through. But Horgan's Picture House is not at all as it was. It has two screens now and a different name, and there are sexual fantasies instead of Jack Hulbert in Round the Washtub.

In Youghal there was a man who shot himself in a henhouse. Life had been hell for this man, the voices whispered, and the henhouse, quite near the back of our garden, developed an eeriness that the chatter of birds made even more sinister. The henhouse isn't there any more, but even so as I stand where it was I shudder, and remember other deaths.

Youghal itself died in a way, for yellow furniture vans — Nat Ross of Cork — carted our possessions off, through Cork itself, westward through the town that people call Clonakilty God Help Us, to Skibbereen, at the back of beyond.

Memory focuses here, the images are clearer. Horses and carts in the narrow streets, with milk churns for the creamery. On fair-days farmers with sticks standing by their animals, their shirts clean for the occasion, without collar or tie. A smell of whiskey, and sawdust and stout and dung. Pots of geraniums among chops and ribs in the small windows of butchers' shops. A sun-burnt poster advertising the arrival of Duffy's Circus a year ago.

It was a mile and a half, the journey to school through the town, past Driscoll's sweetshop and Murphy's Medical Hall and Power's drapery, where you could buy oilcloth as well as dresses. In Shannon's grocery there was a man who bred smooth-haired fox-terriers. He gave us one once, a strange animal, infatuated by our cat.

In the town's approximate centre, where four streets meet, a grey woman still stands, a statue of the Maid of Erin. E O'Donovan, undertaker, still sells ice-cream and chocolate. The brass plate of Redmond O'Regan, solicitor, once awkwardly high, is now below eye-level. In the grocers' shops the big-jawed West Cork women buy bread and sausages and tins of plums, but no longer wear the heavy black cloaks that made them seem like figures from another century. They still speak in the same West Cork lisp, a swift voice, difficult for strangers. I ask one if she could tell me the way to a house I half remember. "Ah, I could tell you grand," she replies. "It's dead and buried, sir."

The door beside the Methodist church, once green, is purple. The church, small and red-brick, stands behind high iron railings and gates, with gravel in front of it. Beyond the door that used to be green is the dank passage that leads to Miss Willoughby's schoolroom, where first I learnt that the world is not an easy-going place. Miss Willoughby was stern and young, in love with the cashier from the Provincial Bank.

On the gravel in front of the red-brick church I vividly recall Miss Willoughby. Terribly, she appears. Severe and beautiful, she pedals against the wind on her huge black bicycle. "Someone laughed during prayers," she accuses, and you feel at once that it was you although you know it wasn't. "V poor" she writes in your headline book when you've done your best to reproduce, four times, perfectly, "Pride goeth before destruction." As I stand on the gravel, her evangelical eyes seem again to dart over me without pleasure. Once I took the valves out of the tyres of her bicycle. Once I looked in her answer book.

I am late, I am stupid. I cannot write 20 sentences on A Day in the Life of an Old Shoe. I cannot do simple arithmetic or geography. I am always fighting with Jasper Swanton. I move swiftly on the gravel, out on to the street and into the bar of the Eldon Hotel: in spectral form or otherwise, Miss Willoughby will not be there.

Illusions fall fast in the narrow streets of Skibbereen, as elsewhere they have fallen. Yet for me, once there was something more enduring, nicest thing of all. Going to Cork it was called, 52 miles in the old Renault, 30 miles an hour because my mother wouldn't permit speed. On St. Stephen's Day to the pantomime in the Opera House, and on some other occasion to see the White Horse Inn, which my father had heard was good. In Cork my appendix was removed because Cork's surgical skill was second to none. In Cork my tongue was cut to rid me of my incoherent manner of speaking. *To* Cork, every day of my childhood, I planned to run away.

Twice a year perhaps, on Saturday afternoons, there was going to Cork to the pictures. Clark Gable and Myrna Loy in *Too Hot to Handle*. *Mr. Deeds Goes to Town*. No experience in my whole childhood, and no memory, has remained as deeply etched as these escapes to the paradise that was Cork. Nothing was more lovely or more wondrous than Cork itself, with its magnificent array of cinemas, the Pavilion, the Savoy, the Palace, the Ritz, the Lee, and the Hadji Bey's Turkish Delight factory. Tea in the Pavilion or the Savoy, the waitresses with silver-plated teapots and buttered bread and cakes, and other people eating fried eggs with rashers and chipped potatoes at half-past four in the afternoon. The sheer sophistication of the Pavilion or the Savoy could never be adequately conveyed to a friend in Skibbereen who had not had the good fortune to experience it. The gentleman's lavatory in the Victoria Hotel had to be seen to be believed, the Munster Arcade left you gasping. For ever and for ever you could sit in the middle stalls of the Pavilion watching Claudette Colbert, or Spencer Tracy as a priest, and the earthquake in San Francisco. And for ever afterwards you could sit while a green-clad waitress carried the silver-plated teapot to you, with cakes and buttered bread. All around you was the clatter of life and of the city, and men of the world conversing and girls' laughter tinkling. Happiness was everywhere.

Thomas Kinsella

(b. 1928)

Prologue

Thomas Kinsella was born in Dublin in 1928. He is a poet, translator, and publisher. He has continued some of the traditions of the Cuala Press in his own small printing house, Peppercanister Press. He has published widely and his translations from the Irish have been influential. His 1969 translation of the *Táin Bó Cúailnge* was an important event. His poems have appeared in both limited and collected editions. His darkly challenging, modernist-inflected later work has been a continuous and strong presence in contemporary Irish poetry.

He graduated from University College Dublin in 1946 and joined the Irish Civil Service while still a student, switching to night courses. The poems that appeared in his first two full collections, *Another September* (1958) and *Downstream* (1960) (he published *Poems* in 1956), were followed by *Wormwood* (1966) and the long poem *Nightwalker* (1967). These were followed again by *Notes from the Land of the Dead and Other Poems* (1973), *One and Other Poems* (1979), *Peppercanister Poems 1972–1978* (1979), *St Catherine's Clock* (1987), *Poems from City Centre* (1990), *Madonna and Other Poems* (1991). In 1981 he published *An Duanaire: 1600–1900: Poems of the Dispossessed*. His critical work includes *The Dual Tradition: An Essay on Poetry and Politics in Ireland* (1995); and *Readings in Poetry* (2006).

In later years, Kinsella's poetry has followed a path of experiment, marked by disruptive syntax and dark lyricism. But his early work—from which the piece below comes –tracks a new Ireland in the freshest and most dissident way possible.

The post-Republic Ireland of bus stops, suburban gardens, commuter schedules and mortgages was a fascinating and broken place to which he became a faithful laureate in his first volumes. The superb poems of *Downstream* (1960) are prefaced by this witty and edgy *ars poetica* which is plainly in a spirited conversation with the earlier and oracular exhortations of Yeats: *Irish poets learn your trade.*

The poem here promises a different trade and a new Irish poet—one more in tune with the new state and ready to provide, even tongue-in-cheek, a new version of the Irish imagination. It is a humane and delightful moment in Irish literature.

I wonder whether one expects
Flowing tie or expert sex
Or even absent-mindedness
Of poets any longer. Less
Candour than the average,
Less confidence, a ready rage,
Alertness when it comes to beer,
An affectation that their ear
For music is a little weak,
These are the attributes we seek;
But surely not the morning train,
The office lunch, the look of pain
Down the blotched suburban grass,
Not the weekly trance at Mass . . .
Drawing on my sober dress
These, alas, I must confess.

I pat my wallet pocket, thinking
I can spare an evening drinking;
Humming as I catch the bus
Something by Sibelius,
Suddenly — or as I lend
A hand about the house, or bend
Low above an onion bed —
Memory stumbles in the head;
The sunlight flickers once upon
The massive shafts of Babylon
And ragged phrases in a flock
Settle softly, shock by shock.

And so my bored menagerie
Once more emerges: Energy,
Blinking, only half awake,
Gives its tiny frame a shake;
Fouling itself, a giantess,
The bloodshot bulk of Laziness
Obscures the vision; Discipline
Limps after them with jutting chin,
Bleeding badly from the calf:
Old Jaws-of-Death gives laugh for laugh
With Error as they amble past,
And there as usual, lying last,
Helped along by blind Routine,
Futility flogs a tambourine . . .

Brian Friel

(b. 1929)

In Interview with
Des Hickey and Gus Smith

Brian Friel was born in Omagh, County Tyrone, in 1929. His father was a school principal. When Friel was an infant, they moved to Derry. Summer holidays were spent with his mother's people in the Glenties in County Donegal.

Friel's plays have been concerned, from the beginning, with peculiarly Irish issues—emigration, language, memory. They have unfolded in a time when each of these themes has come under intense and often painful scrutiny in Ireland. Friel's subtlety of characterization and dialogue rarely allows audiences to align easily with this belief or the other. In addition, there is often a dark lyricism, a pessimism in his view of history.

Some of his plays include *Philadelphia Here I Come!* (1964), *Lovers* (1967), *Crystal and Fox* (1968), *The Freedom of the City* (1973), *Volunteers* (1975), *Living Quarters* (1977), *Aristocrats* (1979), *Faith Healer* (1979), *Translations* (1980), *Making History* (1989), *Dancing at Lughnasa* (1990), *Wonderful Tennessee* (1993), *Molly Sweeney* (1995), *Give Me Your Answer, Do!* (1997), and *The Home Place* (2004). He has adapted Turgenev and Chekhov for the stage. His plays are central texts of twentieth-century Irish literature.

The interview below was conducted in 1972. The violence in the North was taking hold. Friel was concerned about his own work and the state of Irish writing in general. Ironically, even as he spoke, he was on the threshold of the most productive and affirming time of his own creativity. But his speculation about Ireland's distance from the work of earlier writers, such as William Yeats and Lady Gregory, provides a fascinating insight into an Irish playwright's sense of legacy from the Irish Revival. Friel's continuation of the Irish repertory has been central to modern Irish literature. His contribution recalls one of his own phrases: in a preface to Turgenev's *A Month in the Country* in 1992, Friel wrote of the relation between Chekhov and Turgenev: "So they gave life to each other."

1972

... I began writing when I was about nineteen. I know that after *Philadelphia* it was said that I was a born writer, but I don't know what a born writer is. The craft of writing is something you learn painfully and slowly. There was no background of writing in my family and I don't know how much of my talent is indigenous. I don't think there were many other writers in Derry. Some people feel that if you are a writer or painter you must live in a colony, but I find writing a very private and personal existence and I was aware of no sense of loss at being the only writer in Derry. I was a full-time writer from 1960, writing mostly short stories in those days. I had been a teacher until then.

I began *Philadelphia* in 1962 or '63. It was a play about an area of Irish life that I had been closely associated with in County Donegal. Our neighbours and our friends there have all been affected by emigration, but I don't think the play specifically concerns the questions of emigration. *Philadelphia* was an analysis of a kind of love: the love between a father and a son and between a son and his birthplace. This is a theme I have tried to explore in three or four plays. *Cass McGuire*, *Lovers*, and *Crystal and Fox* were all attempts at analysing different kinds of love. A writer does not look at his work on a vertical scale. He doesn't say that one play was better than another. In four plays I attempted to analyse a concept of love. In *Crystal and Fox* I reached a conclusion from my point of view; in other words, I had mined this vein to the end, and perhaps the vein was not rich enough. At any rate I reached a kind of completion and left this area to write a play in a completely new direction, *The Mundy Scheme*.

Other European countries have been warm and generous towards my plays, but not England. I think the English are unsympathetic to anything Irish. I don't mean this to be a chauvinistic comment; I believe the English refuse to take the Irish seriously on any issue. On the other hand, my respect for and interest in Broadway is nil. To me Broadway is an enormous warehouse in which dramatic merchandise is bought and sold at the highest possible profit. Occasionally good things happen there, but by and large it has nothing to do with the art of theatre.

People ask why I have not written a play about the civil rights movement. One answer is that I have no objectivity in this situation; I am too much involved emotionally to view it with any calm. Again, I don't think there is the stuff of drama in the situation. To have a conflict in drama you must have a conflict of equals or at least near equals. There is no drama in Rhodesia or South Africa and similarly there is no drama in the North of Ireland. In a lengthy address I gave about the Theatre of Hope and Despair, I made the point that American and European plays were nihilistic and concerned with the destruction of man's psyche. But I don't think this is true any longer. Many of the young English dramatists are vitally concerned with resurgent and hopeful man. I think the Theatre of Hope exists in this sense. Writers like Osborne, Wesker and [Henry] Livings are optimistic people who happen to use black canvases. When you discuss the theatre in Ireland you talk of O'Casey and the discussion ends. But the world has become much smaller and we should now view ourselves not in an insular but in a world context. An Irish dramatist need not handle his material differently. The canvas can be as small as you wish, but the more accurately you write and the more truthful you are the more validity your play will have for the world.

It was Lady Gregory who said of the Abbey Theatre's tour of America that the Abbey had won much praise for itself and raised the dignity of Ireland. What the Abbey achieved in its early years was enormous; today its role must change. It cannot keep doing the same thing year after year, decade after decade. What it must now do is what the English National Theatre and any first-rate repertory can do — put on the plays of the country. The Abbey has a measure of financial security in its subsidies and can take risks as no commercial management can. This should be its new strength, and no one should expect it to do today what it did at its inauguration. It is a strange situation in which the Abbey's proud boast is that it plays to ninety-five percent houses. That is the kind of boast the Windmill Theatre might have made. A better claim would be that they have put on ten plays, nine of which were terrible but one of which was good. The Abbey directors rejected my play *The Mundy Scheme* by three votes to one. When I submitted the play I stipulated that if it were accepted for production I would require Donal Donnelly as director and Godfrey Quigley to play the leading role of the Taoiseach. I asked for a decision within one week. Let me say that I submitted the play with the gravest misgivings and little enthusiasm. One week later Alan Simpson, who was the Abbey's Artistic Adviser, rang Donal Donnelly to say that the play had been rejected. I was not disillusioned. I have never seen myself writing for any particular theatre group or any particular actor or director. When I have written a play I look for the best possible interpretation from a director and actors, and after that my responsibility ends.

I am uneasy about the future of the writer in Ireland. Ireland is becoming a shabby imitation of a third-rate American state. This is what *The Mundy Scheme* is about. We are rapidly losing our identity as a people and because of this that special quality an Irish writer should have will be lost. A writer is the voice of his people and if the people are no longer individuals I cannot see that the writer will have much currency. We are losing the specific national identity which has not been lost by the Dutch or the Belgians or the French or Italians. We are no longer even West Britons; we are East Americans. A writer cannot exist financially in Ireland unless his work is read or performed in Europe or America. An Irish writer can, of course, write serials for television or radio, but I think we would be as well off working in a solicitor's office.

I abandoned short-story writing before I grew tired of it and now that I am becoming disenchanted with the theatre the chances are that I will go back to writing stories. Walter Macken once said to me that he had taken to novel writing because there were too many middlemen in the theatre. All theatre is a kind of compromise. When you write a play you have the ideal actors in mind, but you never get them; you have the ideal director in mind, but you never get him. In one way the Irish writer works under difficult conditions because of our damned Gaelic introspection. In another way he works under better conditions than if he were living in Paris, London, or New York. If you write a mediocre play in Dublin you will get it staged and it will be staged reasonably well and receive a responsible reaction. If you write a mediocre play in a big city [abroad] the chances of having it staged are minimal. But if a young Dubliner writes a play it will be seen, and isn't this what he wants? Unfortunately, we look at this little island, which is so tiny, and imagine that the people who live ten streets away are different to ourselves. We are obsessed with ourselves and cannot see ourselves in a global context. One of our great misconceptions is that Ireland can be ruled only by its government and that the best government is composed of businessmen. This is a fallacy. I see no reason why Ireland should not be ruled by its poets and dramatists. Tyrone Guthrie has said that if Yeats and Lady Gregory were alive today they would be unimportant people. This is the way it is going to be, I am afraid.

John Montague

(b. 1929)

"A Grafted Tongue"

John Montague was born in Brooklyn in 1929. His father was a former Irish Volunteer who fled to the United States after the Troubles. His family returned to Ireland when John was a young child, and he was raised in Garvaghey. He was educated in Armagh and Dublin.

He has lived in Paris, in the United States, and for many years in Cork, where he taught at University College Cork.

His first book, *Forms of Exile*, was published in 1958. Since then, he has addressed a number of distinct and powerful themes: the dispossession of lands and language; the power of poetry to be an agent of resistance; his own search for a private identity in a public time. His long poem "The Rough Field" (1971) is a central achievement in Irish poetry.

Montague's books of poetry and prose include *Forms of Exile* (1958), *Poisoned Lands* (1961), *A Chosen Light* (1967), *Tides* (1971), *The Rough Field* (1972), *The Great Cloak* (1978), *The Dead Kingdom* (1984), *The Collected Poems* (1995), *Company: A Chosen Life* (2001), and *Drunken Sailor* (2004).

The poem below, *A Grafted Tongue,* adds its voice to other considerations of the Irish language in this book. In this case it shows the loss of Irish not in terms of culture or politics alone—although these are implied— but in the deeper context of the private suffering caused by impaired access to a language.

(Dumb,
bloodied, the severed
head now chokes to
speak another tongue —

  As in
a long suppressed dream,
some stuttering garb-
led ordeal of my own)

  An Irish
child weeps at school
repeating its English
After each mistake

  The master
gouges another mark
on the tally stick
hung about its neck

  Like a bell
on a cow, a hobble
on a straying goat.
To slur and stumble

  In shame
the altered syllables
of your own name;
to stray sadly home

  And find
the turf-cured width
of your parents' hearth
growing slowly alien:

    In cabin
and field, they still
speak the old tongue.
You may greet no one.

    To grow
a second tongue, as
harsh a humiliation
as twice to be born.

    Decades later
that child's grandchild's
speech stumbles over lost
syllables of an old order.

Jennifer Johnston
(b. 1930)

Introduction to
Selected Short Plays

Jennifer Johnston was born in Dublin in 1930. Like Elizabeth Bowen and Molly Keane, she writes of the decay of the Big House. Her first novel, *The Captains and the Kings* (1972), addressed this theme directly. It tells the story of an army officer, a Protestant widower, living out his days in the loneliness of an ambiguous space. In that sense the panic and purposelessness that pervade some of her plots can serve as a small biography of a dying class. She has a subtle and poignant sense of the relationship—often an elusive one— between the private and historical vulnerability of her characters.

Her novels include *The Captains and the Kings* (1972), *The Gates* (1973), *How Many Miles to Babylon?* (1974), *Shadows on Our Skin* (1977), *The Illusionist* (1995), *Two Moons* (1998), *The Gingerbread Woman* (2000), *This Is Not a Novel* (2002), and *Grace and Truth* (2005). She has lived in Northern Ireland for many years. In novels like *The Gingerbread Woman* she confronts the Troubles obliquely; in *Shadows on our Skin* more directly. Her writing is skeptical of gesture and rhetoric, of traditional histories. In an interview in 2000 she said: "We have fed on this story of ourselves as lonely heroes—both men and women—for a long time."

The modest and eloquent introduction to her *Selected Short Plays*, which came out in 2003, describes a rare process in Irish writing: a novelist turned playwright. Her views on characterization, on dramatic tension, allow an insight into an Irish writer working in two forms. The book is dedicated to "all the men, women and children who have been victims of violence and intolerance for so long in this country, Ireland."

I enjoy these pieces. I think I should explain that statement, as most writers are presumed to like what they write, that not, however, being the same thing as enjoying what they write. I enjoyed writing each piece. I sat down each day feeling energetic, enthusiastic and full of vim, not my usual state at all.

Usually I loll in my chair, I write letters to people, I make cups of tea, I fiddle with my computer, anything except write. I groan and moan, tear my hair and bite my nails. Disgusting you may say; I would agree. So, you see, enjoyment doesn't come into it. But these pieces I really enjoyed writing.

O Ananias, Azarias and Miseal (re-titled *Christine* by a director who couldn't cope with my title), crept uninvited into my head. I had some years before written my only book set in Northern Ireland, *Shadows on Our Skin*. I had been seriously aware that the rhythms in this book were those of the south rather than those of the north: I had not yet attuned my ear to the way people spoke here and used the default mode, a sort of stage-Dublinesque. Pretty grim, really, and it annoyed the inside of my head for years. I must have been mulling such thoughts in my mind when Christine spoke to me; quite intimately, she spoke, like some bewildered kindly woman who had just popped in for a cup of tea. I listened for a while before I settled at my writing machine and then it was as if she inhabited me; she spoke the words and my fingers translated the sound of her voice into writing. The whole piece was finished in about four days.

> O ye humble and holy men of heart, bless the
> Lord: praise Him and magnify Him forever.
> O Ananias, Azarias and Miseal, bless ye the
> Lord: praise Him and magnify Him forever.

I was so glad that this wonderful canticle had also been a favourite of Christine, as it had been of mine when I had been a God-fearing girl, many, many years before.

Oh ye spirits and souls of the righteous, bless ye
the Lord; praise Him and magnify Him forever.

Having written the piece I was then faced with the problem: what is this?
A short story? A radio play? A play? Or maybe nothing at all?

I hadn't the foggiest idea.

I sent it to director Caroline FitzGerald, and she rang me to say it was a
play as far as she could see and she would like to direct it. It was in the
process of production that I realised how true and interesting the character
of Christine was, and I also discovered my northern rhythm.

It went from the Peacock Theatre in Dublin to the BBC. However before
they would put on the play they asked me to write more so that listeners in
England might have the nooks and crannies filled in and be able to understand Christine better.

"We need to know more," were the words they used, I think perhaps hoping that I would pad and prod at Christine, explaining things I didn't want
to explain, shining lights in murky corners. I resisted doing this, and was
more or less resigned to the fact that they wouldn't give her air space, when
suddenly her dead husband Billy resurrected himself in my head. A simple
Protestant farmer who was in love with Grace Kelly and believed implicitly
in the holy names: James Stewart, Gary Cooper, Randolph Scott, General
Custer, Billy the Kid, and Billy the King.

"The holy names keep you safe."

His words. He was wrong.

I was charmed by him into writing *Mustn't Forget High Noon*. The BBC
liked it and both pieces were broadcast in 1989. Each play illuminated the
other.

Christine, without any padding or prodding, won a prize. Now that was
good; good for me and good for her.

Moonlight and Music, written many years later, was definitely a play; by this
time I had written a couple of plays, neither of which had achieved great success. They had been performed and had had moderately good reviews, but it
was clear to me that I was not a playwright. I was able to write parts for
actors, but not plays.

A bit dispiriting. But then, why should it be? I am after all a novelist. I was
invited by Jim Culleton to write a short play for a millennium season of short

plays. "Cheap," I was told. You can't get much cheaper than one person! So I sat down and tried and gradually this poor, sad, hard-drinking woman came into my head. I liked her obsession with words and her love for the sad, smoky songs of Ella Fitzgerald. I would have loved someone to come along and rescue her, but there's no room for that sort of thing in a cheap one-person play.

The Nightingale and Not the Lark was the first play that I wrote. The major problem about it was that everyone thought I had written it about my mother. My mother also thought that I had written it about her; this led to grievous complications. It's not a bad little play and it was done in the Peacock Theatre. Lots of people went to see it to see what I was saying about my mother. It was also done by Druid a few months after, and I was able to see that I, as I had thought, had not written a play about my mother at all. I had merely, as all writers do, stolen a thing or two from her life and personality. I forgave myself.

I felt I knew these people: I felt a great sense of achievement when I saw actors take my words and add their own flavour and their own wisdom, flesh them out. I think that is why I continue to struggle to write plays; it is the interaction between the writer, director and the actor that I find so seductive; it's hard to tell whether you've succeeded in breathing true life into your characters when they are still scattered letters on a page, but you know for sure that you did get it right when you lose all sense of ownership and sit in a theatre believing profoundly in what you are seeing on the stage.

I have enjoyed every aspect of these pieces and so, I think, have the actors who have been involved with them, and now I hope that readers will also get pleasure from reading them; a little laughter, a little sadness, a little knowledge, passed from one person to another.

Thomas Kilroy

(b. 1934)

Foreword to Mary Lavin's
In a Café

Thomas Kilroy was born in County Kilkenny in 1934. A prolific playwright and author, he is also a thoughtful commentator on Irish writing. The piece excerpted below, about the influence of Mary Lavin on his own youth and work, is a case in point. About his start as a writer, he has said in an interview: "I think that writing comes out of reading and that writers are in the first place readers. There was also the fact that as a schoolboy I was a scribbler. I went to boarding school and I remember, with some degree of amusement now, at the age of fourteen or fifteen passing around chapter by chapter a thriller that I was writing in the study to distract my friends from their work. I do think that writers are scribblers from a very early age."

His plays include *The Death and Resurrection of Mr. Roche* (1968), *The O'Neill* (1969), *Tea and Sex and Shakespeare* (1976), *Talbot's Box* (1977), *Double Cross* (1986), *The Madame MacAdam Travelling Theatre* (1991), and *The Secret Fall of Constance Wilde* (1997). He is also the author of a novel, *The Big Chapel* (1971). He has adapted Chekhov for the theater.

His piece below comes from a foreword he wrote to Mary Lavin's stories. His reference to her view that "language creates its own world" shows how far Irish writing had come since the Irish Revival: issues of craft and the shapeliness of a piece of writing were now more dominant than those of subject matter or national influence. In defining the impression her work left, he also makes an important remark about new horizons of influence and affinity. "Mary Lavin," he writes, "is one of a generation of Irish writers who looked in the most natural fashion imaginable to the great European canon for examples to write by. There are younger writers, John McGahern and John Banville, for instance, who do so too. But I say this now because it is a connection that is being lost."

This account is a deft and generous uniting of a writer and her achievement. It describes the storyteller's challenges and rewards. It is also a rare perspective, for Irish writing anyway, by a young male writer on an Irish woman writer of an earlier generation.

When I was a young man interested in writing, Mary Lavin became an important presence in my life. It was in the fifties when Tom MacIntyre and I rang her up in Bective and contrived an invitation for ourselves to the Abbey Farm where she was living with the three girls, the first visit of many. I had seen Mary once before when she came to read to the English Society of University College Dublin at Newman House, a young widow in black, long black hair pulled back in a bun, eyes bright as buttons. What I remember most of that reading was an astonishing freshness in the description of flowers.

It was an education in books as well as a meeting with someone who became a dear friend. Which books? This is important, I think, in saying something about the kind of writer that she is and where she rests, securely, in our literary history.

I no longer have the copies of Turgenev's books nor of Flaubert's *Trois Contes* that she pressed upon me — lost, all lost in the migrations and the borrowings. But I can still recall how she talked about the death of poor Felicité in "Un Coeur Simple" and the great parrot in the half-open heavens above her head. And I do have the copy of Tolstoy's *The Kreutzer Sonata*, still in its old yellow World's Classics wrappers, with its inscription from Mary, May 1960. This, she had told me, was a story that had profoundly influenced her when she had first started to write.

It was as if she had instinctively understood the inadequacies of the UCD degree in English of the day as a foundation for someone who wished to write. She was dead right, of course. What she was saying, too, in giving me those much-loved stories was: This is where I come from, these are my models. Mary Lavin is one of a generation of Irish writers who looked in the most natural fashion imaginable to the great European canon for examples to write by. There are younger writers, John McGahern and John Banville, for instance, who do so too. But I say this now because it is a connection that is being lost. There is an impatience among many writers now with anything that doesn't have the immediacy of today's newspaper or television.

Her addiction to storytelling, though, also has to be seen as part of her make-up as a person, a huge curiosity about people, strangers, casual acquaintances and close friends alike. For her the stories they have to tell inscribe some profound truth about their lives. It is as natural for her as chatting in Grafton Street or in The Mews on Lad Lane, as natural as a glass of water. But she also carries these lessons from the masters, which gives her a great regard for the artifice of fiction, how the experience can be shaped by form and in this way how the rhythms of the ordinary can be not only preserved but enhanced.

She once said to me that she felt a story often grew out of an opening sentence. Simply sticking to her first volume, *Tales from Bective Bridge*, you can believe that she means this literally. "Sarah had a bit of a bad name." Or "She was one of the most beautiful women they had ever seen and so they hated her." Or "The cat decided Miss Holland." These are sentences that are already hatching. The hook is in place from the word go. But such sentences are not only beguiling in their promises, they also establish a particular tone, a way of telling that is at least as important as what is being told. That characteristic Lavin tone is at once sympathetic and demanding, highly moral in the way it negotiates human conduct but entirely flexible in its acceptance of the vagaries of experience.

I think she is also getting at something else here in her remark about first sentences. She is talking about the way language creates its own world, and its own readers too, in the process. This reverence for the act of writing is exemplified everywhere in her work. She has even written stories about the nature of fiction, stories "with a pattern" like "The Widow's Son." On another occasion I remember asking her, with that callow courage that you only have at a certain stage of your life, which story she would choose as the finest expression of her art. She said "The Will." Reading it again now I can see why. It is one of a body of stories — "The Little Prince," "Frail Vessel" and that remarkable novella *The Becker Wives* are others — in which she explores, as no other Irish writer has done quite as well, a particular Irish setting, small town, genteel, familial, under threat from the forces of life's anarchy. It would be true to say that her high, early reputation was based upon this body of work.

The stories are always about a family, although the name, Conroy, Grimes, Becker, may change from fiction to fiction. The recurrent antagonism is that between a conniving, cold pursuit of material prosperity on the one hand and a flame-like spirit of passion on the other. The typical battlefield exists between sisters. In the language of the stories, one side is associated with darkness and heavy, clumsy movement, the other with mobility, adventuresomeness, even to the point of destruction. What these stories unveil is the mysterious, deadly antagonism in the world towards creatures of light and air, like Lally Conroy in "The Will."

There are, of course, many other kinds of Lavin stories. Indeed, when you get the chance to look at a selection like this one, that is precisely what emerges, variety.

For example, she has written with generosity about Irish Catholicism, but with her own implacable eye on its worst deformations. She can move from the very gentle irony of "Chamois Gloves," one of the most delicate fictional treatments of girlhood in the nets of religious scruple, to the more hard-edged social dimension of religion on this island in "The Convert," and on to the primal in *The Great Wave*, where religion collides with the forces of nature itself. There is a great range in these stories and they are clearly the work of a spiritual, if iconoclastic, writer.

My own favourite stories, and this obviously has to do with my own relationship with Mary, are those of widowhood, the first of which, I believe, was "In a Café," from the early nineteen sixties. Quite simply, I know the territory of these stories as well as anything else in my life. I know the people who walk in them as I know kin, although everything here is fiction. In these stories she has looked into herself, but never in a limited, solipsistic way. Everything is shaped, subjected to a high degree of formal construction. To effect this kind of distancing upon one's own experience requires an immense inner strength on the part of the writer.

"In the Middle of the Fields," perhaps the greatest of these stories, begins with a passage of great resonance, a lyrical prelude that already contains the movements of emotion that are worked out in the story that follows. The passage is also a fine example, incidentally, of Mary Lavin's mature style.

In one sense it is a simple story, as great stories often are. A widow is alone, lonely in a house within the fields. A neighbour, a widower, comes to the house at night to talk about cutting the grass, but also to reveal his own broken feelings. What happens between them is one of those moments of total revelation, one of those awkward moments between men and women who have nothing in common except a need to be loved. The need is an unconscious one and as unconscious needs often do, it betrays itself in mistakes, misjudgements.

That is why the opening of the story is so apt, so beautifully appropriate in its suggestiveness, its elusiveness. The two characters are surrounded by ghosts in the night, ghosts out of the fields, strange influences beyond their control to which the growing grass of the fields is a constant witness, cyclical as the individual human life can never be. "In the Middle of the Fields" is one of those works that achieve a harmony of all its parts that cannot be conveyed by mere analysis. It is both a highly personal work and at the same time one in which you can observe the artist moulding the material with consummate skill. I love this work because in it Mary Lavin the writer and Mary Lavin the person that I know, have become one.

John McGahern

(1934–2006)

"God and Me"

John McGahern was born in Dublin in 1934. He grew up in Roscommon. The world of his fiction is a still, deep pool of manners, obsessions, and relationships, superbly noted and often lyrically rendered. "Ireland is a peculiar society," he once said, "in the sense that it was a nineteenth-century society up to about 1970 and then it almost bypassed the twentieth century."

Among his novels are *The Barracks* (1963), *The Dark* (1965), *The Leavetaking* (1975), *The Pornographer* (1980), *Amongst Women* (1990), and *That They May Face the Rising Sun* (2001).His short story collections are *Nightlines* (1970) and *High Ground* (1985); they were collected as *The Collected Stories* (1992). His last book was *Memoir* (2005). *The Dark* was banned in 1965, in one of the last and most controversial enactments of the Censorship of Publications Act.

In "God and Me," written for *Granta* in 2005, John McGahern addresses one of the sources and irritants of much Irish writing in the twentieth century: the Catholic Church. It was a settled preoccupation in his work. "I belong to the middle class that grew up very influenced by the Catholic church," he said in one interview.

In a later piece in this book, Joseph O'Connor writes about the space cleared for Irish writers by the intensity and courage of McGahern's themes. He writes of him as a "man who knew . . . that in art there will always be two kinds of simplicity. The simplicity of going away and the simplicity of coming back." This piece shows what was inescapable for McGahern, as indeed for Joyce: systems of faith into which were coded the narratives and myths of a people, and for whose toxic narrowness the only remedy was the power of imagination and the rigor and grace of language.

I grew up in what was a theocracy in all but name. Hell and heaven and purgatory were places real and certain we would go to after death, dependent on the Judgement. Churches in my part of Ireland were so crowded that children and old people who were fasting to receive Communion would regularly pass out in the bad air and have to be carried outside. Not to attend Sunday Mass was to court social ostracism, to be seen as mad or consorting with the devil, or, at best, to be seriously eccentric. I had a genuinely eccentric school-teaching cousin who was fond of declaring that she saw God regularly in the bushes, and this provoked an uncomfortable nodding awe instead of laughter. In those depressed, God-ridden times, laughter was seen as dangerous and highly contagious. The stolidity of the long empty grave face was the height of decorum and profundity. Work stopped each day in shop and office and street and field when the bell for the Angelus rang out, as in the Millet painting. The Rosary, celebrating the Mysteries, closed each day. The story of Christ and how He redeemed us ran through our year as a parallel world to the solid world of our daily lives: the feasts of saints, Lent and Advent, the great festivals of Christmas and Easter, all the week of Whit, when it was dangerous to go out on water; on All Souls' Night, the dead rose and walked as shadows among the living.

Gradually, belief in these sacred stories and mysteries fell away without my noticing, until one day I awoke, like a character in a Gaelic poem, and realized I was no longer dreaming. The way I view that whole world now is expressed in Freud's essay "The Future of an Illusion." I did not know that the ordinary farming people I grew up among secretly viewed the world in much the same terms. They saw this version of Roman Catholicism as just another ideological habit they were forced to wear like all the others they had worn since the time of the Druids, observing its compulsory rituals cynically, turning to it only in illness or desperation. Yet none of this is simple.

Before the printed word, churches have been described as the Bibles of the poor, and the Church was my first book. In an impoverished time, it was my introduction to ceremony, to grace and sacrament, to symbol and ritual, even to luxury. I remember vividly the plain flat brown cardboard boxes in which tulips for the altar, red and white and yellow, came on the bus in winter when there were no flowers anywhere.

In 1903, Proust wrote to his friend George de Lauris:

"I can tell you at Illiers, the small community where two days ago my father presided at the awarding of the school prizes, the curé is no longer invited to the distribution of the prizes since the passage of the Ferry laws. The pupils are trained to consider the people who associate with him as socially undesirable, and, in their way, quite as much as the other, they are working to split France in two. And when I remember this little village so subject to the miserly earth, itself the foster-mother of miserliness; when I remember the curé who taught me Latin and the names of the flowers in his garden; when, above all, I know the mentality of my father's brother-in-law — town magistrate down there and anticlerical; when I think of all this, it doesn't seem to me right that the old curé should no longer be invited to the distribution of the prizes, as representative of something in the village more difficult to define than the social function symbolized by the pharmacist, the retired tobacco-inspector, and the optician, but something which is, nevertheless, not unworthy of respect, were it only for the perception of the meaning of the spiritualized beauty of the church spire — pointing upward into the sunset where it loses itself so lovingly in the rose-coloured clouds; and which, all the same, at first sight, to a stranger alighting in the village, looks somehow better, nobler, more dignified, with more meaning behind it, and with, what we all need, more love than the other buildings, however sanctioned they may be under the latest laws."

When a long abuse of power is corrected, it is generally replaced by an opposite violence. In the new dispensations, all that was good in what went before is tarred indiscriminately with the bad. This is, to some extent, what is happening in Ireland. The most dramatic change in my lifetime has been the collapse of the Church's absolute power. This has brought freedom and sanity in certain areas of human behaviour after a long suppression — as well as a new intolerance.

The religious instinct is so ingrained in human nature that it is never likely to disappear, even when it is derided or suppressed. In *The Greeks and the Irrational*, E. R. Dodds proposes this lucid definition and distinction: "Religion grows out of man's relationship to his total environment, morals out of his relations to his fellow man."

For many years Dodds was a sceptical member of the British Society for Psychical Research. He distinguishes between two approaches to the occult, though he admits they are often mixed in individual minds. The psychic researcher he describes as wishing to abolish the occult in the clear light of day, while the occultist seeks experience rather than explanation. If the true religious instinct as described by Dodds — our relationship to our total environment — will not go away, neither will its popular equivalent seeking signs and manifestations and help in an uncertain and terrifying world.

Not very many years ago, a particularly wet summer in Ireland became known as the Summer of the Moving Statues. Rumours circulated that statues of the Virgin Mary in grottos all around the country were seen to move and had given signs that they were about to speak. Many of the grottos were constructed during the Marian Year of 1954, when no housing estate or factory was built without a grotto of the Virgin and a blessing by a bishop; and there were also grottos from much older times, often set in a rock-face with dripping water, or by a holy well that was once a place of pilgrimage. Crowds gathered in the rain to stare at the statues. There were pictures on TV, reports on the radio and in newspapers. The journalist Dick Walsh decided to travel around Ireland to investigate this phenomenon. He saw many small groups gathered in all weathers staring at the statues as if willing them to move and speak. When he returned, he reported that the statues looked steady enough but he was less certain about the people.

Whether it be these humble manifestations or the great soaring spires of the Gothic churches, they both grew out of a human need. This can be alleviated by material ease and scientific advancement but never abolished.

Still sings the ghost, "What then?"

Tom Murphy

(b. 1935)

An Interview by Maria Kurdi

Tom Murphy was born in Tuam, County Galway, in 1935. He was the youngest of ten children in a Catholic family. An innovative and pathbreaking drama-tist, his plays have been performed nationally and internationally. In addition, he has been associated with some of the most important theaters and theater companies in Ireland, from the Abbey to Druid. He is perceived as one of the most influential, unswerving, and antiromantic voices in Irish writing.

He wrote his first play, *On the Outside* (1959), for the Tuam Little Theatre Guild. *A Whistle in the Dark* (1960) was rejected by the Abbey. In 1962 he emigrated to London and remained there for some years. Among his involve-ments and productions, he was Writer-in-Association with the Druid Theatre Company in Galway from 1983 to 1985. In 1983 he wrote the *Gigli Concert*, which was performed at the Dublin Theatre Festival. In 1985 came the premiere of *Bailegangaire* with the Druid Theatre Company; the play trans-ferred to Dublin and London in 1986. The Abbey produced *The Wake* in 1998 and *The House* in 2000. In October 2001 a festival at the Abbey celebrated the entirety of Murphy's work.

The excerpt below from an interview with Murphy—published in *Irish Studies* in 2004—discusses his sense of theme and form and serves as a series of sharp reminders. There were silences, painful gaps in the 1950s that remain deeply influential on Irish writers today. The silence of emigration, for instance—and the hypocrisy of a society that allowed it—led to the fruitful angers of some of Murphy's early work. "Some commentators," he says in another part of this interview, "have dubbed me a chronicler of the second half of nineteenth-century Ireland. . . . Really, I am interested in the emotional truth above all else."

Murphy's vision can be both harsh and corrective; his scrutiny of failed relationships in a modern Ireland is often disturbing. Although his work does not stand as an addition to the early idealization of the Irish Literary Revival, but more often as a savage corrective, nevertheless there are parallels. He is not a realist. His relish for the theatrical, the melodramatic is foremost. His profound stylizations of suffering and failure are at times comparable to J. M. Synge's alternate and heightened world of language, motive, and character. Above all, Murphy's view of form is painstaking and accurate. As he says in this interview, "I know when the play starts to tell me things."

KURDI: During four decades of creative writing for the theatre you have produced a remarkable diversity of plays. Bearing in mind that the perspectives employed vary considerably, can you identify certain thematic strands across your dramatic oeuvre?

MURPHY: In recent times I noticed that the recurring theme seems to be the search for home. What that "home" means, I am not sure. It used to appear in the plays in the literal, geographical way that we understand the term. Now, I see it more as a search for the self, for peace, for harmony.

KURDI: Looking back to the beginning of your career, did the experience of the contradictions underlying the Irish society of the 1950s and 1960s have a part in turning your dramatic imagination toward the admittedly public genre of drama?

MURPHY: The simple answer is no. I think that we still are as a people quite politically naive. We are corrupt — which is sophisticated, isn't it? — but we are politically naive. For instance, I made many Hungarian friends in my lifetime, particularly in the years when I lived in London, and Czech friends, mid-Europeans, and French people and Spaniards and so on. And in comparison with them, I was very, very self-conscious of how politically unaware I was. You pinpoint the 1950s, which was a stagnant decade here. There was then a great celebration of insularity, we were sufficient unto ourselves, we even had songs which had lines like "Thank God, we are surrounded by water." That, of course, had meanings to do with the tradition of hundreds of years of history with England. But at the same time there was a smugness and a complacency in it that was saying we were purer than others. When in fact, I think, we were naive at best, and we were celebrating a type of ignorance. There is a lot of anger in the early plays. I wouldn't then have been able to articulate what I was angry at, what I was reacting to, but everything Irish was a pain to me. I think that this was an emotional response to the repression of Irish Catholicism and the primitive type of politics that were happening. I come from a small town called Tuam, and it still surprises me that there was such a degree of cynicism — in my circle of friends — about the messages that the Church was offering, and, without our being able to discuss them, or debate them, we had jokes about it all. My reaction was an instinctive one rather than a cerebral one.

KURDI: Did you find the central Europeans whom you met in London more politically conscious than Irish people?

MURPHY: Oh, yes. We basically knew three isms. They were Catholicism, Communism, and Protestantism. We knew them from the slanted view of the Catholic Church. Hungarian or Czech friends knew the *reality*. They were politically involved and repressed by either Nazism or Communism. They had read Marx, they knew Engels, they knew something of political philosophy, rather than just a history as stories. They had endured the Second World War, occupation by foreign powers; some of them would have been militant students who had reacted physically and mentally because of political beliefs, and wrongs, political and social, that were happening. We here, by contrast, were remarkably passive. To cite a true story by way of example: when I was fourteen, a child of my age stole the equivalent of ten cents, or five cents; he was taken in by the police and interrogated, and more interrogations were forthcoming. The same child then stole a tin of rat poison from a shop, ate it and died. That is shocking. But more shocking is that there was only one person in that town of six thousand people who complained to the authorities about the death of this child. And that person, incidentally, was a woman, not a man.

KURDI: I find that the early play *A Whistle in the Dark* offers some parallels with Arthur Miller's *Death of a Salesman* (1949): the father tries to be proud of who he thinks he is in spite of his obvious failure, he is unable to change, and even his theft of an overcoat that he then throws away echoes his son Biff's theft of the millionaire's pen. Are the self-destructive behaviour and illusions of Dada rooted in some post-independence Irish Dream about equal rights and opportunity?

MURPHY: I was twenty-four or twenty-five when I wrote that play. I wasn't thinking as a commentator on the political situation that prevailed. (Incidentally, Miller is not my favourite playwright; I would infinitely prefer Tennessee Williams.) Everybody, as far as I know, has written father figures, from Sean O'Casey to Eugene O'Neill to be "Big Daddy," to, as you say, Willy Loman. Dada in *A Whistle in the Dark* was the character I thought would be totally incredible to anybody who would dream of reading the play or putting it on. Now I think that through whatever talent I had I managed to key or clue into something in him. Because he is the character that most people tell me that they found they knew. He was like their father or an uncle or they knew somebody who was like that. And, indeed, at this vantage point, I could say that he is like a Hitler in microcosm, who created a little army of the children that he brainwashed into monsters to fight a battle for his own real or imagined wrongs and his own shortcomings, weaknesses and so on. But those kinds of thoughts were not consciously in my mind at the time of writing. At that time, there was some kind of rage within me and I discovered writing: it allowed me to express myself and my emotions. And it was therapeutic.

KURDI: Dada in *A Whistle in the Dark* strikes the audience as a stage Irishman character. Do you think that Irish writing should challenge and revise such (often expected) stereotypes rather than try to avoid them?

MURPHY: Perhaps he is a stage Irishman. I rather like melodrama. It is a genre that is looked down on to a degree, and I think it is a great loss to theatre. I do not mean cheap melodrama, where there is no motivation, development, no psychology, no fully formed figures. I don't like the type of drama where somebody says "pass the salt darling," which means "I hate you." I like big colours, I like to paint in big colours. I suppose in the nature of the background that I had in theatre, melodrama would have been the type of play that I would have experienced as a child.

KURDI: How do you see the function of form in drama; when did you start to think consciously about form in your career?

MURPHY: I suppose when I emigrated, went to live in London and lived there practically for the whole decade of the 1960s, and I started to read plays and watch plays. Yet I still find form difficult. I don't think I am ever going to change; it is very unlikely at this stage. I like to discover the play as I go along. Discovery in the process of doing. And that to me would suggest, that if I start thinking about form early on then I will not discover whatever it is that is trying to get out and what I am trying to express. So, in terms of form, I don't really have a system for writing. I know when I am tapping into something; I know when the play starts to tell me things. I guess it is a common enough experience that characters start to tell the writer things, or a piece refuses to move because the piece itself does not want to go in that direction. One has to be patient. One has to respect the piece itself. The play must have its say. The writer's imposing form or structure too early will impede this. Form happens or is imposed at a late or later stage.

Edna O'Brien

(b. 1930)

"Dear Mr. Joyce"

Edna O'Brien was born in Tuamgraney, County Clare, in 1930 and educated at the Convent of Mercy in Loughrea. The year before her birth, the new Irish Free State passed the Censorship of Publications Act. Its stated purpose was "to make provision for the prohibition of the sale and distribution of un-wholesome literature." O'Brien, whose early novels set the individual choices of women against the repressive Irish society of the time, would become one of its chief targets.

"We are each of us the result of our past," she once stated in an interview. "This is not a question of nostalgia or looking backwards, it is the emotional, political, cultural, and spiritual effects on us of both our subjective and ancestral experience." In this respect, her work has been a fever chart of change: a suppressed narrative of the customs and evasions of sexual and social history in Ireland. A history, moreover, that stands in contrast, and sometimes as a critique, of the idealizations and simplifications of women in traditional Irish literature.

In 1954 she married the writer Ernest Gebler. Together with their two sons they went to live in London, where she has remained. In 1960 she published *The Country Girls*, her first novel. The lyrical evocation of a young Irish girl discovering an erotic and instinctive freedom against the odds was an immediate success. With *The Lonely Girls* in 1962 and *Girls in Their Married*

Bliss in 1964, the books formed a persuasive and eloquent trilogy. All three were banned in Ireland, as were several of the works that followed.

O'Brien's style is lyrical and evocative. Her work has not stood in the main line of Irish realist influence. Rather, her prose is impressionistic. The situations she portrays can have a quality of dream to which she brings a surprising measure of experiment, as in her superb novel of location, *A Pagan Place* (1971). She is more often compared to the French writer Colette than to any Irish equivalent.

In 1999, however, when O'Brien published a biography of James Joyce, she revealed a wellspring of Irish inspiration. She writes about him in an earlier piece below. It is neither a conventional nor reverent account of influence, but rather an eye-level view of a source and resource: an idiosyncratic, eloquent journey of tribute and affinity.

Was he garrulous? Did he wear a topcoat? Did he hanker after an estate? Did he play chess or cribbage? Once at evening time was he observed to step out, get into a carriage and immediately and for some mystifying reason get out again and disappear into the house? In short, was he a neurotic? Such questions we always ask about the deceased great, trying in our forlorn way to identify with them, to find some point of contact, some malady, some caprice that brings us and them nearer. Such questions are not satisfactorily answered in works of fiction (writers being by necessity conjurors), nor in the testimonies of friends because friends are prone to lie in the interests of love, hate, stupidity or venom. Ex-lovers are equally unreliable being for ever besotted or irredeemably wounded. But letters tell. Letters are like the lines on a face, testimonial. In this case they are the access to the man that encased the mind that was the genius of James Joyce, Aquarian, Dubliner.

He started to study medicine three times. No two occupations are closer than that of doctor and novelist. Both are trying to arrive at a diagnosis of some kind and hence a metamorphosis. Had he qualified he was bound to have gone on and been a gynæcologist, he with his obsession with womb-

fruit and the bloodflow "chiding the childless." In his youth he was suspi-
cious, contemptuous, unaccommodating. He saw his countrymen as being
made up of yahoos, adulterous priests, and sly deceitful women. He classed
it as "the venereal condition of the Irish." Like the wild geese he had a mind
to go elsewhere, it was not to follow an alien king but to commence a revolution in words. He wanted to be continentalised. He liked the vineyards. He
had a dream of Paris. He likened it to a lantern in the wood of the world for
lovers. He had a craze for languages.

In literature his heroes were Cardinal Newman and Henrik Ibsen. To
Ibsen he wrote, "Your work on earth draws to a close and you are near the
silence. It is growing dark for you." He was nineteen at that time. Young men
do not usually know such things unless there is already on them the shadow
of their future. There was on him. He descended into blindness. The eyes are
the nearest to the brain. He was beset by glaucoma, cataract, iris complaint,
dissolution of the retina. His nerves were like the twitterings of wrens. His
brain pandemoniacal. The sirens were always on. He was having to take
aspirin, iodine, scopolamine. It had its funny side, this daily harassment of
his. His eye doctor had a bet with him that if the front wall of the lens of his
eye was removed would a cataract decide to form itself on the back wall. He
admitted that with such cryptic wit a man like that could have written *Ulysses*.
He was prone to betting. He wagered a pound of dried apricots with his
friend Ezra Pound that his play *Exiles* would not be produced although at the
time there was a management in an agreeable tiz about it. A pound of apricots, a pound of chops, plum pudding, Mass and canticles. Religious motifs
may have dogged him and Latin words and Hades and Potsdam and melan-
colores and Atrahora and the Portuguese for Devil but he remained a plainspoken man. In a tart and almost vulnerable rejoinder he was driven to point
out to his aunt that receiving a copy of *Ulysses* was not like receiving a pound
of chops and he urged her to give cognisance to that fact and get it back from
whatever hooligan had swizzled her out of it, under the name of borrowing.
His mind was forever computing. In the next letter, or the letter following, he
plied her with questions. Had such and such a house ivy on its seafront wall,
how many steps were there down to the sea, could a man climb over a certain
railing into Eccles Street. To him words were not literature but numerals, dig-
its, things that when he strung them together in his wild, prodigious way, took

on another light, another lustre, and were the litany of his lapsed Catholic soul. He liked hymnbooks and tittle-tattle and all tongues to be welded in together. The English he strove for was pidgin, Cockney, Irish, Bowery and biblical. To avoid being cloying, to run no risk of being literary, he always prefaced or postscripted his incandescent phrases with a joke. When asking Italo Svevo to collect a briefcase, he first described it with fiendish accuracy, its oilskin cloth, the approximate weight, the approximate measurement and the protrusion which struck him as having a likeness to a nun's belly. Then he said, "In this briefcase I placed the written symbols of the languid lights which occasionally flashed across my soul." Only by giving a pedestrian complexion to the whole thing could he communicate his real feeling, rather like having to make a declaration of love on a banana skin.

Love. Love as we practise it makes dotards of us all. Blackmailers. Infants. It is a solace to know that he sublimely fell into those traps. No detachment, no grand phrases but raging boiling lust and suspiciousness and doubt. His love object, and a lasting one, was from Galway, the city of his tribal name. Are such things total chance? She had reddish-brown hair and he wanted that she had fuller breasts and fat thighs. To achieve that he urged that she drink cocoa. Back in Dublin without her, where he was on the ludicrous mission of helping to have cinemas opened, he was racked with thoughts of their youth, their courtship, her absence. Was his son really his son? Was not the bloodstain the first time rather slight? Could he be smacked by her? Or better still flogged? Could he be her child? Could she be his mother? The brown stains on her girlish drawers sent him off on another rhapsody. Desire and shame, shame and desire. His own words for his own feelings were that they were mad and dirty.

The madness was there all right, the madness that through the long hours of day and night, when he attained divinity through language, murdered his eyes, his nerves and later his stomach. He went far into far latitudes but he always came back. He came back with such weird reliability. He had to. He had to cope with poverty, piracy, lawsuits. Money was always on their agenda, or rather the absence of it. Borrowing and Lending. Checking the prices of food, of furniture, hotel rooms and much much later, the cost of mental institutions. He had dreams of grandeur. There were some very fine furs he wanted to buy for Nora. There was a necklace that he had made for her in Dublin, while at the same time he was sending his brother a telegram to say that he was arriving on the morrow, penniless. He suggested a linoleum they get for the kitchen, the shade of curtains and the armchair where he could loll. He asked his brother for Jesus' sake not to attack him with bills.

He attended to his own talent, not in the interest of bombast or self-aggrandisement, but rather like a faithful watchman. He had the fixity of the great and therefore no need of vanity. He estimated that three shillings would be a reasonable price for *Ulysses*. A tiresome book, he admitted. At the same time he was dogged by fear that the printing house would be burnt down or that some untoward catastrophe would happen to it. He assisted Miss Beach in wrapping the copies, he autographed the de luxe editions, he wrote to influential people, he hawked packages to the post office. He knew that the illustrious would change their minds many a time before settling down to a final opinion and he knew that many another would know as much about it as the parliamentary side of his arse. If there was a good review he rejoiced, simply because it might lead to another sale. If there was a bad review he asked sagely what method of suicide he ought to embark on. He was a distant man. Ambiguous. He wrote reams and reams of letters and yet there was no knowing for certain what he truly felt about the people he wrote to. A slitherer, Jesuitically trained, and with a scorching wit. Getting shamrock so that it was a cloudscreen, a sham screen and from that to something else, derived from Syrian or Burmese or Heaven or Hell. Metamorphosis it is called. Then back to his bath buns. If he had a sign on his person it would be "Beware of the Miserere." He liked regional dishes. He liked a white wine that was named St. Patrice. He knew that Oxford was where the best shirts were made. He asked an affluent friend for a spare tie and upon getting it was filled with a deferential effusion. Blind as only the visioned can be. His mind a conglomeration of colour, trinities, rainbows, double rainbows, Joyce knows what. Iridescent and onomatopoeic and sensifacient, all together. He must have often longed to have his brain dry-cleaned or exposed to the gales of the Atlantic Ocean. When he learned that the wild flowers of Carthage survived the devastation of centuries he likened that indomitableness to the lilts of children. He had two children, Lucia and Giorgio.

It was where his family pinged and impinged that his profound heart was
bared. He believed that a mysterious malady had caught hold of them when
they were small, in Switzerland. Lucia wanted to be a dancer and then an
artist. Giorgio wanted to be a singer. Neither of them achieved their ambitions. At first he feared that their existence might sever him and Nora. As
they grew older their needs became paramount. When they were absent
from home he wrote daily and maundered into many languages because he
liked to think that they were multilingual. For his son he copied out songs,
sent sheet music, wished maybe that he be another John McCormack whom
he both admired and ridiculed in that sparring way of his. Never the genius
but always the father, livening them up with some story, some little memory
that danced through his mind. Always in the cause of the "mafacule," always.

Fathers and daughters. That terrible clench. He named her Lucia after
the patron saint of eyes. She had to have an operation to have one of hers
straightened. First she wanted to be a dancer, then an artist, a graphic artist.
She was given to premonitions. She had the wisdom of the serpent and the
gentleness of the dove, as he said. Again as he said, she was gay, sweet and
ironic, but given to bursts of anger and eventually she had to be put in a
straitjacket. He strove to right her. He must have minded terribly not being
God, he who had nearly attained a divinity through language. He praised her
rubrics, her lettering, her designs. Long before he had loved the graphic fantasies of the old Irish monks. She was not Cezanne, as he noted, but he
wanted her life to have point. It was more than fatherly concern, he saw into
her. He tried to save her from institutions but she passed the line of demar-
cation, made too far a walk, out into the mental Azores, and had to be committed. One asylum was called St. Nazaire. So like Nazareth. So like Joyce.

Towards the end of his life there came a thaw, a burstingness. He was
famous then. There were picnics arranged in his honour. When he went to
his favourite Paris restaurant the orchestra played "It's a Long Way to
Tipperary." He was bowed to, at the opera. But it was not fame that caused
him to mellow so, surely it was growth. He called on people, sent greetings,
blessings, telegrams, entertained those he met with his clear tenor tones. He
sent Mr. Yeats an autographed copy of "Work in Progress" and said that if
Mrs. Yeats cared to unsew the first pages of *Ulysses* he would happily sign it
for them. He sent *Pomes Penyeach* to the Library at Galway University. They

had a special reading desk made and he was delighted that his book, with
Lucia's letterings, was on display for all the ex-hooligans to see. The spleen
was growing out of his mind. He was the father of his family, a scattered family. He remembered Christmas, birthdays, old friends, he lifted a glass to old
times. He had come to a height. He had achieved monumence both in his
work and in his being. In neutral Switzerland where he and Nora went to be
near Lucia he got pains that could only be relieved by morphine. The doc-
tors and surgeons had a consilium and took him to the Red Cross hospital
where they operated. There was a hole in his stomach resulting from an ulcer
that had been his constant and undiagnosed companion for years. Two days
later he died. It was January. He was bordering on sixty. It is hard not to
believe in immortality, considering the death of dear Mr. Joyce.

Brendan Kennelly

(b. 1936)

"Am"

Brendan Kennelly was born in Ballylongford, County Kerry, in 1936. He was an accomplished Gaelic footballer. He studied at Trinity College and Leeds University. Although always close to his Kerry background, he has lived for many years in Dublin and taught as a professor of English at Trinity College.

He is a prolific poet, prose writer, novelist, and editor. Some of his output includes *Cast a Cold Eye* (1959, with Rudi Holzapfel), *The Rain, the Moon* (1961, with Rudi Holzapfel), *The Dark about Our Loves* (1962, with Rudi Holzapfel), *Let Fall No Burning Leaf* (1963), *The Crooked Cross* (1963), *My Dark Fathers* (1964), *Good Souls to Survive* (1967), *The Florentines* (1967), *The Penguin Book of Irish Verse* (1970, editor), *Bread* (1971), *New and Selected Poems* (1976), *Cromwell* (1983), *A Time for Voices: Selected Poems, 1960–1990* (1990), *Euripides' Medea* (1991), *The Book of Judas* (1991), *Poetry Me Arse* (1995), *The Man Made of Rain* (1998), *The Singing Tree* (1998), *Glimpses* (2001), and *The Little Book of Judas* (2002).

"All songs are living ghosts that long for a living voice," Kennelly has said. He has consistently argued that poetry is a visionary enterprise, and he often cites as model and inspiration the work of Patrick Kavanagh. His poetry, as well as having a considerable command of rhetoric and lyricism, often articulates unexpected ideas. This unconventional poem below is an example. It navigates through the pathology of fanaticism and the self-deceptions of ideology in an unusual sequence of images and propositions. It voices the excuses for hatred; the illusions of resistance. In a country where many of these things have been irritants and sources of violence, this poem is a potent, surprising and suppressed critique.

When I consider what all this has made me
I marvel at the catalogue:
I am that prince of liars, Xavier O'Grady,
I am Tom Gorman, dead in the bog,
I am Luke O'Shea in Limerick prison,
I sell subversive papers at a church gate,
Men astound me, I am outside women,
I have fed myself on the bread of hate,
I am an emigrant in whose brain
Ireland bleeds and cannot cease
To bleed till I come home again
To fields that are a parody of peace.
I sing tragic songs, I am madly funny,
I'd sell my country for a fist of money.

I am a big family,
I am a safe-hearted puritan
Blaming it all on the Jansenists
Who, like myself, were creatures on the run.
I am a home-made bomb, a smuggled gun.
I like to whine about identity,
I know as little of love as it is possible
To know, I bullshit about being free,
I'm a softie crying at the sound of a bell,
I have a tongue to turn snakespittle to honey,
I smile at the themes of the old poets,
Being lost in myself is the only way
I can animate my foolish wits.

Do I believe myself? I spill
My selves. Believe me, if you will.

Seamus Heaney

(b. 1939)

"In Memoriam Francis Ledwidge"

Seamus Heaney was born in 1939 in Derry in Northern Ireland. He studied at St. Columb's school. In 1957 he went to Belfast, to the Queen's University, graduating in 1961. In 1965 he married the writer Marie Devlin. The following year his first volume, *Death of a Naturalist*, came out. Heaney continued to publish over the next three decades—translations, essays, drama, but most notably poetry marked by rare degrees of lyric craft and with a wide and generous sense of the complications of an Irish identity. His volumes of poetry include *Death of a Naturalist* (1966), *Door into the Dark* (1969), *Wintering Out* (1972), *North* (1979), *Selected Poems, 1965–1975* (1980), *Station Island* (1984), *The Haw Lantern* (1987), *New Selected Poems, 1966–1987* (1990), *Seeing Things* (1991), *The Spirit Level* (1996), *Opened Ground: Poems, 1966–1996* (1998), *Electric Light* (2001), and *District and Circle* (2006).

Heaney's critical work includes *Preoccupations: Selected Prose, 1968–1978* (1980) and *The Government of the Tongue* (1988), as well as translations, including a highly successful translation of *Beowulf* in 1999. In 1995 he was awarded the Nobel Prize for poetry for "works of lyrical beauty and ethical depth, which exalt everyday miracles and the living past." In his fine Nobel address he said: "It is difficult at times to repress the thought that history is about as instructive as an abattoir." He was commenting on the ordeal of violence in Northern Ireland. But his words could equally be applied to the wounded identities that have flowed like tributaries into what the nineteenth-century Irish patriot and poet Thomas Davis called "the river of the Irish mind." This is the theme of the poem reprinted below.

In many of his best poems Heaney writes with the force of a private lyric poet conscripted to a public situation. It makes for a reluctant, compelling music. This poem is about Francis Ledwidge, who died in World War I. Heaney describes him as "our dead enigma." His wonderful evocation of Ledwidge's multiple identities—from Catholic boy to British soldier to Irish poet—serves as a critique of tensions that go to the heart of Irish writing.

The bronze soldier hitches a bronze cape
That crumples stiffly in imagined wind
No matter how the real winds buff and sweep
His sudden hunkering run, forever craned.

Over Flanders. Helmet and haversack,
The gun's firm slope from butt to bayonet,
The loyal, fallen names on the embossed plaque —
It all meant little to the worried pet

I was in nineteen forty-six or -seven,
Gripping my Aunt Mary by the hand
Along the Portstewart prom, then round the crescent
To thread the Castle Walk out to the strand.

The pilot from Coleraine sailed to the coal-boat.
Courting couples rose out of the scooped dunes.
A farmer stripped to his studs and shiny waistcoat
Rolled the trousers down on his timid shins.

At night when coloured bulbs strung out the sea-front
Country voices rose from a cliff-top shelter
With news of a great litter —"We'll pet the runt!"—
And barbed wire that had torn a friesian's elder.

Francis Ledwidge, you courted at the seaside
Beyond Drogheda one Sunday afternoon.
Literary, sweet-talking, countrified,
You pedalled out the leafy road from Slane.

Where you belonged, among the dolorous
And lovely: the May altar of wild flowers,
Easter water sprinkled in outhouses,
Mass-rocks and hill-top raths and raftered byres.

I think of you in your Tommy's uniform,
A haunted Catholic face, pallid and brave,
Ghosting the trenches with a bloom of hawthorn
Or silence cored from a Boyne passage-grave.

It's summer, nineteen-fifteen. I see the girl
My aunt was then, herding on the long acre.
Behind a low bush in the Dardanelles
You suck stones to make your dry mouth water.

It's nineteen-seventeen. She still herds cows
But a big strafe puts the candles out in Ypres:
"My soul is by the Boyne, cutting new meadows. . . .
My country wears her confirmation dress."

"To be called a British soldier while my country
Has no place among nations. . . ." You were rent
By shrapnel six weeks later. "I am sorry,
That party politics should divide our tents."

In you, our dead enigma, all the strains
Criss-cross in useless equilibrium
And as the wind tunes through this vigilant bronze
I hear again the sure confusing drum

You followed from Boyne water to the Balkans
But miss the twilit note your flute should sound.
You were not keyed or pitched like these true-blue ones
Though all of you consort now underground.

Eiléan Ní Chuilleanáin

(b. 1942)

"Pygmalion's Image"

Eiléan Ní Chuilleanáin was born in County Cork in 1942. She studied English and history at University College Cork. She did her graduate work at Oxford University. She has taught at Trinity College in Dublin for many years. Her work, over several decades, shows a continuing interest in history, language, and sexuality. She is a powerful lyric poet, both reticent and commanding, canvassing issues of history and sensibility in poems that are often poised between a musical sensibility and a dark modernism.

Her volumes of poetry include *Acts and Monuments* (1972), *Site of Ambush* (1975), *The Second Voyage* (1977, 1986), *The Rose Geranium* (1981), *The Magdalene Sermon* (1989), *The Brazen Serpent* (1994), and *The Girl Who Married the Reindeer* (2002). She and Medbh McGuckian also translated the poems of Nuala Ni Dhomhnaill in *The Water Horse* (2001). She has been an editor of the literary magazine *Cyphers*, published in Dublin. Her work can be experimental and surreal, associating image and argument in new and surprising ways. She often interlaces a complicated, modern Ireland with the older, lost Gaelic Ireland—in the process producing fascinating and individual lyric shadows.

The poem reprinted below continues that project. Several themes and images are laid skillfully over each other: The coming to life of an image. A valley laid waste in some undefined way. And above all, a woman entering her own existence in terms of language. The poem is both mysterious and forceful, suggesting new and old traits of the Irish imagination, including the power of the land and the loss of language.

Not only her stone face, laid back staring in the ferns,
But everything the scoop of the valley contains begins to move
(And beyond the horizon the trucks beat the highway.)

A tree inflates gently on the curve of the hill;
An insect crashes on the carved eyelid;
Grass blows westward from the roots,
As the wind knifes under her skin and ruffles it like a book.

The crisp hair is real, wriggling like snakes;
A rustle of veins, tick of blood in the throat;
The lines of the face tangle and catch, and
A green leaf of language comes twisting out of her mouth.

Seamus Deane

(b. 1940)

"Return"

Seamus Deane was born in County Derry in 1940. He was educated at Queen's University and received his doctorate at Cambridge University in England. He is a poet, critic, and novelist. In his book *Reading in the Dark* (1966) he tracks the experience of boyhood in Northern Ireland and the struggles of coming of age and discovering a self in a violently divided society.

In his writing he has expressed the indivisible nature of political and private vision. Growing up in Derry, he experienced the tensions between the two at first hand. In an interview he remarked: "I don't suppose that there was any point at which I ever felt that there was a visible gap between what people call politics and my private life. The two things were always integrated. I learned that a political system, especially when it's a rancid one, as in Northern Ireland, has an effect on personal relationships—in fact, it spreads right through the whole society. Especially when the political system is based on various forms of coercion and colonization."

Among his nonfiction writings are *Celtic Revivals: Essays in Modern Irish Literature, 1880–1980* (1985), *A Short History of Irish Literature* (1986), *The French Enlightenment and Revolution in England, 1789–1832* (1988), *Strange Country: Modernity and Nationhood in Irish Writing since 1790* (1997), and *Foreign Affections: Essays on Edmund Burke* (2005). His books of poetry are

Gradual Wars (1972), *Rumours* (1977), and *History Lessons* (1983). He is the general editor of *The Field Day Anthology of Irish Writing* (1992).

    In the poem reprinted below, the continuation of the Irish past is shadowed through landscape. It is an exploration of the relation between human nature and nature, which is the opposite of pastoral: the land is afflicted by its history; history cannot be erased by the land. This shifting, disappearing sense of identity, as well as the tenuous connection with a place, is a characteristic of newer Irish writing. Here it has the added poignance of the ghost of political violence standing in the wings, watching every word.

> The train shot through the dark.
> Hedges leapt across the window-pane
> Trees belled in foliage were stranded,
> Inarticulate with rain.
> A blur of lighted farm implied
> The evacuated countryside.
>
> I am appalled by its emptiness
> Every valley glows with pain
> As we run like a current through;
> Then the memories darken again.
> In this Irish past I dwell
> Like sound implicit in a bell.
>
> The train curves round a river,
> And how tenderly its gouts of steam
> Contemplate the nodding moon
> The waters from the clouds redeem
> Two hours from Belfast
> I am snared in my past.

Crusts of light lie pulsing
Diamante with the rain
At the track's end. Amazing!
I am in Derry once again
Once more I turn to greet
Ground that flees from my feet.

Derek Mahon

(b. 1941)

"In Carrowdore Churchyard"

Derek Mahon was born in 1941 in Belfast, where he received his early education. He went on to Trinity College Dublin, then moved to London in 1970.
Mahon's powerful, formally constrained poetry has often reflected the
wistfulness and acute perspective that result from self-imposed exile.
Although born into a generation of writers whose poetry was conscripted
by the Northern conflict, his comments on it—whether poetically or in
criticism—have been oblique rather than direct.

In his preface to *The Sphere Book of Irish Poetry* in 1972, however, Mahon
wrote indirectly about his own identity. In an eloquent and striking passage,
he suggested a new and different poetic constituency, one difficult to define
and complex in origin: "These are the Northern poets . . . Protestant products
of an English education system, with little or no knowledge of the Irish
language and an inherited duality of cultural reference. They are a group
apart, but need not be considered in isolation, for their very difference
assimilates them to the complexity of the continuing Irish past." He went
on to say: "Conor Cruise O'Brien has defined the Irish poet as one who is
'involved in the Irish situation and usually mauled by it' and this is as true of
the Northern poets as it is of Clarke or Kavanagh. Whatever we mean by 'The
Irish situation' the shipyards of Belfast are no less a part of it than a country
town in the Gaelthacht."

Irish themes are an integral part of Mahon's work, which is often inflected by estrangement and experiment. From the start his work has displayed a delicate, open-ended relation with European poetry. He is an authoritative translator of Philippe Jacottet; Samuel Beckett is certainly a model. Mahon's books of poetry include *Night-Crossing* (1968), *Lives* (1972), *The Snow Party* (1975), *Poems, 1962–1978* (1979), *The Hunt by Night* (1982), *Antarctica* (1985), *Selected Poems* (1991), *The Yaddo Letter* (1992), *Collected Poems* (1999), and *Harbour Lights* (2005). "The continuing Irish past," as Mahon calls it, is present in this elegy for Louis MacNeice, which—in contrast to MacNeice's own poem of self-exclusion included earlier in this book— places the Northern poet firmly back on his own ground. "All we may ask of you we have," the poem says, suggesting an exemplary relation between twentieth-century Irish poets.

(At the Grave of Louis MacNeice)

Your ashes will not stir, even on this high ground,
However the wind tugs, the headstones shake.
This plot is consecrated for your sake,
To what lies in the future tense. You lie
Past tension now, and spring is coming round
Igniting flowers on the peninsula.

Your ashes will not fly, however the rough winds burst
Through the wild brambles and the reticent trees.
All we may ask of you we have; the rest
Is not for publication, will not be heard.
Maguire, I believe, suggested a blackbird
And over your grave a phrase from Euripides.

Which suits you down to the ground, like this churchyard
With its play of shadow, its humane perspective.
Locked in the winter's fist, these hills are hard

As nails, yet soft and feminine in their turn
When fingers open and the hedges burn.
This, you implied, is how we ought to live —

The ironical, loving crush of roses against snow,
Each fragile, solving ambiguity. So
From the pneumonia of the ditch, from the ague
Of the blind poet and the bombed-out town you bring
The all-clear to the empty holes of spring,
Rinsing the choked mud, keeping the colours new.

Michael Longley

(b. 1939)

"Wounds"

Michael Longley was born in Belfast in 1939. He read Classics at Trinity College
in Dublin. His poems have canvassed his divided inheritance, and his own intent
to resolve it. His father fought in the British Army at the battle of the Somme.
Some of Longley's collections of poems include *Ten Poems* (1965), *No
Continuing City: Poems, 1963–1968* (1969), *Lares* (1972), *An Exploded View:
Poems, 1968–1972* (1973), *Fishing in the Sky: Love Poems* (1975), *Man Lying on
a Wall: Poems, 1972–1975* (1976), *The Echo Gate: Poems, 1975–1979* (1979),
Selected Poems (1981), *Poems, 1963–1983* (1985), *The Ghost Orchid* (1995),
Ship of the Wind (1997), *Broken Dishes* (1998), *The Weather in Japan Cape*
(2000), *Snow Water* (2004), and *Collected Poems* (2006).

For Irish writing in the 1970s, especially in Northern Ireland, violence was
an ethos that summoned imagination. But it was extraordinarily difficult to
maintain the poise of craft and voice while answering that summons. To
uncover the reality of a daily violence, while keeping the issues of identity and
craft together without compromise, seemed a truly arduous task. Longley's
poem reprinted below, "Wounds," manages it. The poem locates the horror of
violence in the daily actions of ordinary people. But it also peels back that skin
of identity, history, and choice by which too much Irish writing has remained
concealed. The remembered violence gives the poet access to the present
version.

Of "Wounds," Longley has said: "The Edwardian dream ended in 1914; mechanised slaughter became the norm, and the world has never been the same since. At the age of 16 my father had enlisted in 1914, one of thousands queing up outside Buckingham Palace. He joined the London Scottish by mistake, wearing an unwarranted kilt. . . . He recalled the lice, the rats, the mud, the tedium, the terror. Somehow, my father's existence, and his experience, the stories he passed on to me, gave me a kind of taproot into the war."

Here are two pictures from my father's head —
I have kept them like secrets until now:
First, the Ulster Division at the Somme
Going over the top with "Fuck the Pope!"
"No Surrender!": a boy about to die,
Screaming "Give 'em one for the Shankill!"
Wilder than Gurkhas' were my father's words
Of admiration and bewilderment.
Next comes the London-Scottish padre
Resettling kilts with his swagger-stick,
With a stylish backhand and a prayer.
Over a landscape of dead buttocks
My father followed him for fifty years.
At last, a belated casualty,
He said — lead traces flaring till they hurt —
"I am dying for King and Country, slowly."
I touched his hand, his thin head I touched.

Now, with military honours of a kind,
With his badges, his medals like rainbows,
His spinning compass, I bury beside him
Three teenage soldiers, bellies full of
Bullets and Irish beer, their flies undone.
A packet of Woodbines I throw in,
A lucifer, the Sacred Heart of Jesus

Paralysed as heavy guns put out
The night-light in a nursery for ever:
Also a bus-conductor's uniform —
He collapsed beside his carpet-slippers
Without a murmur, shot through the head
By a shivering boy who wandered in
Before they could turn the television down
Or tidy away the supper dishes.
To the children, to a bewildered wife,
I think "Sorry Missus" was what he said.

Michael Hartnett

(1941–1999)

"A Visit to Croom 1745"

Michael Hartnett was born in Croom, County Limerick, in 1941. From child-
hood he was bilingual and his tense, passionate relation to both English and
Irish characterized his achievement as a poet. His first book, *Anatomy of a
Cliché*, was published by Poetry Ireland in 1968. In 1974 he left Dublin and
began to reconsider his relationship with the Irish language. He went to live in
Templeglantin, just five miles from Newcastle West. In 1975 he published
Farewell to English and stated his commitment to writing only in Irish from
then on. English, he said, was the "perfect language to sell pigs in." He
published a number of volumes of poetry in Irish: *Adharca Broic* (1978), *An
Phurgóid* (1983), and *Do Nuala: Foighne Chrainn* (1984).

Hartnett did, however, return to writing in English. He brought out
several later books in that language, including *A Necklace of Wrens* (1987),
Poems to Younger Women (1989), and *The Killing of Dreams* (1992). He
continued to work in Irish, doing translations, including *Selected Poems of
Dáithí Ó Bruadair* (1985) and *The Poems of Aodhaghán Ó Rathaille* (1999). His
Collected Poems appeared in two volumes in 1984 and 1987.

One of the distinctions of Hartnett's work is his acute sense of two languages, their history and the tensions between them. He transited from Irish
to English, and back again with passion and clarity. In the process he changed
and amplified his concept of the poet in either tongue. William Yeats and

Dáithí O'Bruadair, Anglo-Irish and Gaelic icons, were blended into a concept of the poet as both outcast and oracle. It is a rich, idiosyncratic perspective on Irish poetry. This inspired double vision gets into the poem reprinted below. It appears informal and at the edge of irony. With a closer look, however, the poem can be seen as a suppressed critique of Irish writing: this snapshot of the old Bardic order in decline, of poets losing their language in the eighteenth century, confirms the vulnerability and power of the poet's life.

The poem is set in the eighteenth-century court of Maigue poets in Limerick, whose name came from the river that flows past Croom. They are credited with inventing the limerick. To the speaker of the poem, however, the poets of the court are simply unaware, in their insular world, of the dangers surrounding them. This poem calls back to Daniel Corkery's poignant and outraged evocation of the Bardic poets from *The Hidden Ireland*, an excerpt of which is printed earlier in this book.

For Séamus Ó Cinnéide

The thatch dripped soot,
the sun was silver
because the sky
from ruts of mud to high blaze
was water:
white-washed walls were silver,
limeflakes opened like scissored pages
nesting moss and golds of straw
and russet pools of soot:
windows small as ratholes
shone like frost-filled hoofprints,
the door was charted
by the tracery of vermin.
Five Gaelic faces stopped their talk,

turned from the red of fire
into a cloud of rush-light fumes,
scraped their pewter mugs
across the board and talked about the king.
I had walked a long time
in the mud to hear
an avalanche of turf fall down,
fourteen miles in straw-roped overcoat
passing for Irish all along the road
now to hear a Gaelic court
talk broken English of an English king.
It was a long way
to come for nothing.

John Banville

(b. 1945)

"Bloomsday, Bloody Bloomsday"

John Banville was born in Wexford County in 1945, where he was educated at the Christian Brothers' and St. Peter's College. He came to Dublin and began his career as a journalist writing for the *Irish Press*. He worked for many years in journalism—progressing from subeditor on the *Irish Press* to literary editor with the *Irish Times*. His first novel, *Long Lankin*, was published when he was only twenty-five. Since then he has pushed the boundaries of an essentially realistic Irish tradition of fiction, always driving toward experiment and play and invention. In a conversation, years ago, he spoke of his perception of two entities: the novel and the art of the novel. It is to the second that he has adhered.

Banville has published *Nightspawn* (1971), *Birchwood* (1973), *Doctor Copernicus: A Novel* (1976), and *Kepler: A Novel* (1981). Each new publication proved his gifts as a stylist. His models have never been the realistic writers of the Irish 1930s, with their Chekhovian acts of homage. Rather, his heroes were the masters of experiment. Beckett and Nabokov are exemplary presences at the edge of his work. Nevertheless, he resists the idea that his style is in any way exclusive. "There is not a sentence anywhere in my work," he said in a 2005 interview, "which, in terms of syntax, grammar, and vocabulary, would not be understood by an eight-year-old equipped with a dictionary. I would not expect a child to absorb the nuances of meaning and suggestion in those sentences, but I do strive to make them as clear as mirror-glass, with all the ambiguity that implies. The Mandarin's gown would sit very awkwardly on my frame."

With the publication of *The Book of Evidence* (1989), *Athena* (1995), *The Untouchable* (1997), *Shroud* (2002), and *The Sea* (2005), Banville widened both his ambitions and his audience. A dark wit and a deliberate inwardness keep his writing on course in its attempt to explore further ways to expand the entire project of Irish fiction. One of his strengths is the ability to make a sharp, telling critique, even when it requires a certain amount of iconoclasm: for instance, taking an anarchic and yet illuminating look at the way Irish writing is made and received. As a critic, he is never predictable. He is often irreverent, about himself as well as his subject. In this exasperated view of the hundredth anniversary of Bloomsday, he points up, in a witty and revealing way, the need for every Irish writer to be self-made.

Very many years ago, when I was growing up in the town of Wexford, on the southeast coast of Ireland, I dearly wished to get hold of a copy of James Joyce's *Ulysses*. I had read *Dubliners* and *A Portrait of the Artist as a Young Man*, and had even written, on a big black Remington borrowed from my Aunt Sadie, a number of lugubrious short stories in what I thought was the Joycean manner, mainly devoted to the subject of death and all centered on a neurasthenic young hero whom no one truly understood, whose soul was much given to swooning and who went under different names but was always me.

I had no doubts that my nascent literary endeavors showed me already to be one of Joyce's direct heirs — if not, indeed, the heir — but I was in a hurry to put these childish efforts behind me and get on to the real thing. I had met Stephen Dedalus in the *Portrait*, but Leopold Bloom was the man I was after, as (perhaps more important) Molly was the woman.

Technically, it would have been possible for me to buy a copy of *Ulysses*, not perhaps in the pleasant backwater of Wexford but certainly in Dublin, since the book was not and never had been banned in Ireland, another of those curious anomalies that abound in the tangled relations between his native country and the writer whom a teacher at Joyce's old school, the Jesuit-run Clongowes Wood College, is reputed to have referred to as "not one of our successes." It would have required strong nerves, however, for a boy from the boondocks to venture into Fred Hanna's or Hodges Figgis, Dublin's main bookshops, and lisp aloud his shameful desideratum. Also, and not incidentally, he would have been hard put to come up with the cover price of the Bodley Head hardback, the only edition then available.

In Ireland in those days — I am speaking of the late 1950s — Joyce's masterpiece was known, outside academe and a few rare progressive households, only by repute, and mostly ill repute at that. *Ulysses*, it was believed, certainly by the majority of the Irish Catholic petite bourgeoisie, was one of the dirtiest books ever written. In the smut stakes, it had rivals like *Lady Chatterley's Lover* and *Tropic of Cancer*, of which we had heard tell, yet Joyce's novel was viewed with special horror. Not only was it written by an Irishman and a Catholic but it was fairly boiling with blasphemy as well as sex, and in places with the two scandalously combined. When, later on, at the age of 17, I at last bought my first copy of *Ulysses* — in a Liverpool bookstore from an émigré Irish shop assistant — my mother threatened to "put that book on the back of the fire!"

Even before that momentous purchase, I knew more about *Ulysses* than many a person who had actually read it. Wexford's public library was voluminously stocked with critical studies of Joyce, and I devoured them all, understanding little of their import but enthralled by their aura of arcane, priestly exegesis and grateful for the extended extracts quoted from the sacred text. Indeed, when I came to read *Ulysses* itself, I had the same pleasant series of jolts of recognition that the first readers of *The Waste Land* must have experienced when they encountered echo upon familiar echo in Eliot's thickly allusive text.

One mighty tome of Joyce scholarship that I borrowed from the Wexford library, written by an American academic whose name I have long since forgotten, devoted the entirety of an extensive section on *Ulysses* to the parallels between the Stephen Dedalus–Leopold Bloom relationship and that of Sherlock Holmes and Dr. Watson. As a result, for many years I assumed that

Holmesian rather than Homeric parallels formed the true substructure of
the book — so when I came to read Stuart Gilbert's study of *Ulysses*, directly
inspired (directly dictated, some would say) by Joyce himself, I was baffled
by the lack of reference, amid all that complex mesh of designated corre-
spondences, to the sleuth of Baker Street and his trusty Achates. Ever since,
I have wondered about the exact function of academic scholarship when
applied to works of art.

Joyce liked to boast that *Ulysses* was so detailed a portrait of Dublin that
if the city were to be destroyed — an eventuality that in his darker moments
of Hibernophobia he would probably have welcomed — it could be rebuilt
brick by brick, using his book as a model. In his essay "The Precession of
Simulacra," the French savant Jean Baudrillard recalls the story by Jorge Luis
Borges in which the Empire's cartographers spend years drawing up a map so
detailed that when it is done it covers exactly the territory of the Empire,
and imperial decline is plotted by the fraying of the map until only a few
shreds remain. If we were to revive the fable today in our media-dominated
world, Baudrillard suggests, the map would have engendered the Empire,
and "it would be the territory whose shreds are slowly rotting across the
map."

Dublin, even well into the 1960s, when I came to live there, was in many
respects still the city that Joyce had known and that he celebrated with
maniacal exactitude in *Ulysses*. All now is changed. True, most of the streets
and many of the buildings through which Joyce's characters circulate on
their way to eternity are still in existence, but the heart of the place is a
transplant from Silicon Valley by way of the poppy fields of Afghanistan:
Ireland is the world's largest exporter of computer software, and its capital
city is a serious importer of the hardest of hard drugs. Where now is the
"real" Dublin?

One must beware setting up Joyce as a founding father of the Irish tourist
industry. Our minister for the arts, tourism and sport bids us "rejoyce" this
June 16, the 100th anniversary of Bloomsday, but in Dublin, as elsewhere,
Ulysses remains one of the most talked about and least read works of world
literature. There is nothing wrong with a party — a breakfast of bacon,
sausage, black and white pudding and that quintessential Irish dish, hash
browns, will be served to a crowd of 10,000 rejoycers on O'Connell Street —

but Roddy Doyle's public outburst against *Ulysses* earlier this year was probably less a literary judgment than an instance of the exasperation many of us
feel at the pervasiveness and bathos of the Joyce myth.

BLOOMSDAY (a term Joyce himself did not employ) was invented in
1954, the 50th anniversary, when the novelist Flann O'Brien and the writer
and magazine editor John Ryan organized what was to be a daylong pilgrimage along the *Ulysses* route. Accounts of the venture are given by Ryan in his
book of reminiscences, *Remembering How We Stood* — renamed by Dublin
wits *Remembering How We Staggered* — and in *No Laughing Matter*, a biography
of O'Brien by the poet Anthony Cronin, who was one of the pilgrims.
Cronin's downbeat version of the "structured and, in a way, humorless"
event is probably the more accurate one. The tour began at the architect
Michael Scott's house beside the Martello tower in Sandycove, where the
effects of the drink that Scott had laid on caused a scuffle between O'Brien
and the poet Patrick Kavanagh. As might be expected, matters went down-
hill from there, and the pilgrimage was abandoned halfway through, when
the weary Lestrygonians succumbed to inebriation and rancor at the Bailey
pub in the city center.

Cronin was the instigator of another Bloomsday event in 1982, when writers from around the world were invited to Dublin to celebrate Joyce's own
centenary. Among the many notable artists who came was — yes — Borges,
who by then was in his 80s and totally blind. He was collected from the air-
port by a couple of volunteer meeters-and-greeters, who deposited him in
his suite at the Shelbourne Hotel and went off to do more meeting and
greeting. When they returned, late in the day, Borges was still in his room,
and in fact had not left during the intervening hours. What was he to have
done, Borges asked, since he did not know the city or anyone in it? Ever
since, when I hear talk of Bloomsday celebrations, that, I am afraid, is the
image that springs immediately to mind: an old, blind writer, one of the
greatest of his age, sitting alone in a hotel room overlooking an unseen St.
Stephen's Green.

Micheal O'Siadhail

(b. 1947)

"Tight-Wire"

Micheal O'Siadhail was born in 1947. His childhood was spent in Ireland. "I suppose I started writing as a boy," he has said, "because I had such strong feelings that I had to express them in some way. I loved music and color, but I was surrounded by a tradition of words. Poems as a child moved me so deeply that I wanted to hold on to that extraordinary excitement." He went to Clongowes and Trinity College Dublin. He completed his studies at the University of Oslo.

A noted linguist, O'Siadhail has written academic studies of the Irish language, including *Learning Irish* (1988) and *Modern Irish* (1989). His publications include *The Leap Year* (1978), *Rungs of Time* (1980), *Belonging* (1982), *Springnight* (1983), *The Image Wheel* (1985), *The Chosen Garden* (1990), *Hail! Madam Jazz: New and Selected Poems* (1992), *A Fragile City* (1995), *Our Double Time* (1998), *Poems, 1975–1995—Hail! Madam Jazz: New and Selected Poems* (1999), *The Gossamer Wall* (2002), and *Love Life* (2005).

Despite his authoritative and scholarly command of the Irish language, O'Siadhail's poetry is clearly set in a contemporary Ireland. Whereas the literature of the Irish Revival acted as a narrow focus, screening out details of background life and activity that were not thought to be relevant, the poems of a new Ireland, as it appears in his work, increasingly have a wide lens. In this brief, graceful poem about the anomaly of the circus in a provincial town,

O'Siadhail edits in the information of this ordinary Ireland, in all its surprise and awkwardness. What he insists on is the reality of what is actually there: no longer the romantic foreground, but a detailed and daily prospect.

Strolling fields behind the tent I glance
Figures leaving glares of light.
Wild applause inside.
Elephants to dance;
Now the acrobats delight
Children, now the juggling clown,
Someone hand a faded dressing gown.
Steadied, out she'll stride

Over guy-wires, over littered mud and cans
Past an empty pony stall
Slipping in among
Hung-out clothes and vans.
There she'll seem too small and frail.
No one saw who stepped the wire,
Those who clap her clap their own desire.
Someone always young

Slinging ropes between two garden sheds
Full of reckless festive grace
Seems to dare to flout
Endless overheads
Nothing underwrites but space.
Thrills of business just for fun
Touch the dreams of things we might have
Steadied, she'll step out.

Tom Paulin

(b. 1949)

"Desertmartin"

Tom Paulin was born in 1949 in Leeds, England. His mother was from Northern Ireland, his father was English. While still a child, he moved back to Belfast, at a time when sectarian tensions could not help but be part of the most secure and ordinary childhood. Much of Paulin's work has considered the divisions in the society he grew up in. He has not been afraid to see the scars of ideology and soured faith in the small towns, customs, histories, and inheritances of the North. The poem below considers the effect of these divisions.

Paulin is a poet, essayist, and literary critic. He has written a noted commentary on William Hazlitt, the radical British writer of the Romantic movement. Much of his own interests as a writer have been in seeking out the ways political and imaginative radicalism—with one constantly informing and shaping the other—can renew and refresh the forms of writing. His books include *A State of Justice* (1977), *The Strange Museum* (1980), *The Book of Juniper* (1981), *Fivemiletown* (1987), *The Wind Dog* (1999), *The Faber Book of Political Verse* (1986, editor), *Minotaur: Poetry and the Nation State* (1992), *The Day-Star of Liberty: William Hazlitt's Radical Style* (1998), and *The Road to Inver: Translations, Versions, and Imitations, 1975–2003* (2004). The poem "Desertmartin" locates "the parched certainties" of inflexible belief in a town where "the free strenuous spirit" has suffered because of it.

At noon, in the dead centre of a faith,
Between Draperstown and Magherafelt,
This bitter village shows the flag
In a baked absolute September light.
Here the Word has withered to a few
Parched certainties, and the charred stubble
Tightens like a black belt, a crop of Bibles.

Because this is the territory of the Law
I drive across it with a powerless knowledge —
The owl of Minerva in a hired car.
A Jock squaddy glances down the street
And grins, happy and expendable,
Like a brass cartridge. He is a useful thing,
Almost at home, and yet not quite, not quite.

It's a limed nest, this place. I see a plain
Presbyterian grace sour, then harden,
As a free strenous spirit changes
To a servile defiance that whines and shrieks
For the bondage of the letter: it shouts
For the Big Man to lead his wee people
To a clean white prison, their scorched tomorrow.

Masculine Islam, the rule of the Just,
Egyptian sand dunes and geometry,
A theology of rifle-butts and executions:
These are the places where the spirit dies.
And now, in Desertmartin's sandy light,
I see a culture of twigs and bird-shit
Waving a gaudy flag it loves and curses.

Medbh McGuckian

(b. 1950)

"Gateposts"

Medbh McGuckian was born in Belfast in 1950. She was educated at the Dominican convent and the Queen's University of Belfast. She is a poet, editor, and teacher. Her poems are original, volatile, and superbly mysterious. She should be seen as a first-rate experimental writer in a tradition of such writing that over the years has become a defining force in Irish literature.

McGuckian's work has consistently involved Ireland, the Irish situation—violence, division, and the stresses on language—even when she is not writing about it directly. "I would say much of the contempt and resentment and what some would call intolerance of my work locates it in this particularly savage culture," she said in an interview. "I think it has the duality of here, the slipping cloaks of Irish/English, British/Europeans, and an isolated anxiety at being an island within an island beyond an island."

Her volumes of poetry include *The Flower Master* (1982), *Venus and the Rain* (1984), *On Ballycastle Beach* (1988), *Marconi's Cottage* (1991), *Captain Lavender* (1994), *Selected Poems* (1997), *Drawing Ballerinas* (2001), *The Face of the Earth* (2002), *Had I a Thousand Lives* (2003), and *The Book of the Angel* (2004). The frequent layers of meaning in her work are deceptive and shimmer from one side of symbol to the other side of sense, like mirrors. She is an associative imagist, close to certain strategies of modernism. But she is also—although sometimes in disguise—a powerful narrative poet.

In the following poem, for instance, there are hints of Irish history, of the Irish landscape. They are partially mediated through gender—through the hat, the gate, the holy well, the bread farls, the bed-wing warmed by the chimney breast. They are also shadowed by unspoken things. There are suppressed stories here, as there so often are in McGuckian's poems; and, moreover, a suppressed eroticism in a nation that has often resisted that dimension of its own story.

A man will keep a horse for prestige,
But a woman ripens best underground.
He settles where the wind
Brings his whirling hat to rest,
And the wind decides which door is to be used.

Under the hip-roofed thatch,
The bed-wing is warmed by chimney breast;
On either side the keeping-holes
For his belongings, hers.

He says it's unlucky to widen the house,
And leaves the gateposts holding up the fairies.
He lays his lazy-beds and burns the river,
He builds turf-castles,
And sprigs the corn with apple-mint.

She spreads heather on the floor
And sifts the oatmeal ark for thin-bread farls:
All through the blue month
She tosses stones in basins to the sun,
And watches for the trout in the holy well.

Paul Muldoon

(b. 1951)

"Anseo"

Paul Muldoon was born in Armagh, Northern Ireland, in 1951. He was educated at the Queens University in Belfast. He now lives in the United States.
Like his contemporary Medbh McGuckian, Muldoon's poetry is lyric and
experimental; he often rejoices in allusion, closely woven texts, sleights of
language, and a ludic approach to even serious subjects. Yet underlying these
surfaces, the concerns of history, of Ireland, of the illusions of memory and the
deceptions of history, keep returning. He has always given credence to the
sheer force of location in shaping Northern Irish poetry. In an interview in 1995
he commented: "Obviously one of the things that poets from Northern Ireland
and beyond had to do was try to make sense of was what was happening on a
day-to-day political level. It would be odd if they hadn't tried to do so."

The counterpoint between the Northern Irish situation and the play
and shimmer of some of Muldoon's best poetry is important. It suggests a
sensibility ready to alchemize solid surfaces into mercurial ones, and impure
events into pure language. Indeed, language itself becomes history in a
Muldoon poem. This puts Muldoon directly in the line of such writers as Myles
na Gopaleen. It should also be said, however, that he is the most transnational
of Irish poets, with clear affinities to such American poets as Robert Frost. His
delight in language and his virtuoso technical abilities allow him to be, in
Marianne Moore's phrase, "a literalist of the imagination."

Muldoon's work includes the following publications: *New Weather* (1973), *Mules* (1977), *Why Brownlee Left* (1980), *Quoof* (1983), *Paul Muldoon: Selected Poems, 1968–1983* (1986), *Meeting the British* (1987), *The Prince of the Quotidian* (1994), *New Selected Poems: 1968–1994* (1996), *Hay* (1998), *Moy Sand and Gravel* (2002), and *Sixty Instant Messages to Tom Moore* (2005) as well as *Horse Latitudes* (2006). Although it appears clear and direct, the poem below, like so many of Muldoon's poems, is an experimental narrative. It follows an Irish word—*anseo*—from common to menacing usage. It is both a political poem and—as so often in Muldoon's work—a linguistic subversion. The subtle, careful weaving together of language and event, of words in common use shadowed suddenly by the uses of violence, builds into a powerful image. It suggests new challenges of language and history—two subjects of Muldoon's work that have endured.

When the master was calling the roll
At the primary school in Collegelands,
You were meant to call back *Anseo*
And raise your hand
As your name occurred.
Anseo, meaning here, here and now,
All present and correct,
Was the first word of Irish I spoke.
The last name on the ledger
Belonged to Joseph Mary Plunkett Ward
And was followed, as often as not,
By silence, knowing looks,
A nod and a wink, the master's droll
"And where's our little Ward-of-court?"

I remember the first time he came back
The master had sent him out
Along the hedges

To weigh up for himself and cut
A stick with which he would be beaten.
After a while, nothing was spoken;
He would arrive as a matter of course
With an ash-plant, a salley-rod.
Or, finally, the hazel-wand
He had whittled down to a whip-lash,
Its twist of red and yellow lacquers
Sanded and polished,
And altogether so delicately wrought
That he had engraved his initials on it.

I last met Joseph Mary Plunkett Ward
In a pub just over the Irish border.
He was living in the open,
In a secret camp
On the other side of the mountain.
He was fighting for Ireland,
Making things happen.
And he told me, Joe Ward,
Of how he had risen through the ranks
To Quartermaster, Commandant:
How every morning at parade
His volunteers would call back *Anseo*
And raise their hands
As their names occurred.

Gerald Dawe

(b. 1952)

[EXCERPT FROM]

"Anecdotes over a Jar"

Gerald Dawe was born in Belfast in 1952 and educated at the University of
Ulster at Coleraine and University College Galway (now National University of
Ireland, Galway). He is a poet, teacher, and essayist. He has argued forcefully
for the recovery and inclusion of the strengths of the Protestant imagination
within Irish writing, and for the rich inheritance that is there to be recognized.
His volumes of poetry include *Sheltering Places* (1978), *The Lundys Letter*
(1985), *Sunday School* (1991), *Heart of Hearts* (1995), *The Rest Is History: A
Critical Memoir* (1998), *The Morning Train* (1999), *Stray Dogs and Dark Horses*
(2000), and *Lake Geneva* (2003).

In the dark and witty excerpt below, Dawe makes several important
points. He heralds his piece with Sean O'Faolain's warning: "The lesson of our
time is that Irish writers cannot any longer go on writing about Ireland." He
then shows, in this account of visiting an interviewer in Holland with a preset
view of Irish writing, that all national literatures can manufacture their own
exclusions—and that those exclusions quickly translate into the narrow
expectations of readers, scholars, and those who broker a country's literature
into a nation's canon. Of an earlier encounter, where these preconceptions
were also in evidence, he writes: "It was my first experience of the weight of
assumption and expectation which bears upon the two words 'Irish Poet.'"

His own Northern Protestant inheritance, woven in and out of his love for

the west of Ireland—a subtle amalgam of affinities and loyalties—is ignored
in this piece. Instead, the interviewer searches for the ordained themes of Irish
identity. This brief excerpt serves as a cautionary tale about the simplifying of
a literature and the damage done by such simplifications.

> The lesson of our time is that Irish writers cannot any longer go on
> writing about Ireland, or for Ireland within the narrow confines of the
> traditional Irish life-concept; it is too slack, too evasive, too untense.
> SEAN O'FAOLAIN, "FIFTY YEARS OF IRISH WRITING,"
> STUDIES, 1962

I was in Holland in 1981 with Richard Murphy, on a reading tour, and in
Amsterdam we were separately interviewed. The keen radio interviewer
wanted me to talk about "vio-lence" and "pol-it-ic-al repression" and later on,
in a taxi, I heard my own voice, with estranged *gravitas*, struggling to answer
him. It was obvious that the good Dutch radio man had clear ideas about
Ireland and wanted to have them confirmed in double-quick time before
moving on to the next item — William Burroughs, if I am not mistaken, who
was sitting in a marble-like pool of silence, cane-in-hand and Trilby hat, like
a spectral clerk of works.

It was my first experience of the weight of assumption and expectation
which bears upon the two words "Irish Poet." Five years later, in a packed
hotel in Sydney, for the city's Poetry Festival, the sign on the door revealed
"Irish Poet" reading along with Les Murray and Tom Murphy. Through the
steamy night, lots of people milled in and out but, half-way through my stint,
a (drunken) voice came from the back of the hall: "You're not following in
the footsteps of Heaney." This question, complaint or statement (I was
never sure which), was patently true since I stood reading my own poems
and they had little to do with Seamus Heaney's. But I understood and sym-
pathized with what the man meant.

Probably an expatriate, here he was amongst a mixed bunch of "ex-pats"
of all kinds and on stage was this poet, from Ireland mark you, reading
poems *not* about the Ireland he knew, or thought he knew: O'Faolain's "tra-

ditional life-concept." And, if you weren't insulted, the poet was actually talking about Edward Carson, for Christ's sake, and little towns in the north no one ever heard of. What he was hearing simply did not *fit* and he was having none of it.

Another quirky illustration might be sufficient to indicate the weight of expectation that lies upon this notion of the Irish poet, whether at home or abroad. It is a fascinating subject in itself since its powerful influence, particularly *via* the States, has rarely been touched upon by critics of writing from Ireland.

Quite recently, I met an EC literary journalist accompanied by an avid Irish intellectual trend-spotter. In the brief exchange I was asked several questions: about "the loss of Irish," colonial history, identity crises, and the role of women writers in modern Ireland. This menu of issues, of which I had personally little experience, amounted to an agenda and it became crystal-clear that *poetry* had very little to do with it except to serve as a springboard for someone else's flights of fancy. Irish poets were influenced by Irish poets and Irish history, O.K. Game set and match. As for Europe . . . ?

When I muttered something about coming from a Protestant background in Belfast and living in the west of Ireland, a professional smile glazed over what remained of their time. Critical comment on that background, indeed, on any sense of alternative influences, arguments or literary ideals, went out the window, *pronto*. May as well talk about green blackbirds.

Frank McGuinness

(b. 1953)

"Our Lady of Kylemore Abbey"

Frank McGuinness was born in Buncrana in County Donegal, Northern Ireland, in 1953. He was educated at University College Dublin. From the start his plays have been concerned with the power of region, the injuries done by language, the force and upheaval of sexuality, and, especially, the continuing conflicting loyalties of Irishmen, as expressed in his play *Observe the Sons of Ulster Marching Towards the Somme* (1985). In this play the Irish Protestant inheritance is viewed through the lives of eight characters; it has—in the span of two decades—become a classic of the Irish repertory.

McGuinness is a prolific playwright who also written screenplays and poetry. Some of his plays include *The Factory Girls* (1982), *Baglady/Ladybag* (1985), *Innocence* (1986), *Carthaginians* (1988), *Mary and Lizzie* (1989), *The Bread Man* (1990), *Someone Who'll Watch over Me* (1992), and *Dolly West's Kitchen* (1999). He has adapted several plays: *Yerma* (Federico García Lorca, 1987), *Rosmersholm* (Henrik Ibsen, 1987), *Peer Gynt* (Henrik Ibsen, 1988), *Three Sisters* (Chekhov, 1990), and *The Threepenny Opera* (Bertolt Brecht and Kurt Weil, 1991).

He has also written two collections of poetry, *Booterstown* (1994) and *Stone Jug* (2003). The poem below is a fascinating, experimental view of a sacred figure. It echoes Paula Meehan's dark portrait of the Virgin at Granard and John McGahern's representation of what is sacred in the Irish imagination. These iconic symbolisms have never quite left Irish writing, and this poem is an instance of it.

I appeared out of purdah on this mountainside,
A statue overlooking the lake at Kylemore, White
And hard faced. They called me the mother of God, as if
He needed a mother, as if I needed a God.

There are those who wonder about my present position.
A woman suspended on a pedestal. I don't like it
But it's a living, and it beats what I used to do.
This involved melting the salt from the sea,

Writing the Bible in the salt so distilled, dipping
The parchment in fresh water and giving solace
To men who weep, to women giving birth to a mountain.
Mercy made me Our Lady of Kylemore Abbey.

From that day on though, I lost all heart, all interest,
Receiving the worship of lonely girls, rowing in the lake,
Girls like myself once, waiting for husbands to sail
Into fertile places. They never arrived, these husbands —

They had wives at home to conquer. Yet I loved
The smell of their ships. They caught fish, I fire,
And used it to burn their boats. They drowned then in the arms
Of other women. My husbands dead, I went into purdah

And veiled my face, Our Lady of Kylemore Abbey.
I dressed in this white and gave to the poor.
I gave them the mercy that once hardened me
When I was raw and awkward but full of grace.

Theo Dorgan
(b. 1953)
"Twentieth-Century Irish-Language Poetry"

Theo Dorgan was born in County Cork in 1953. He is a poet, editor, translator, and noted activist in Irish poetry. His overview (excerpted below) of poetry in the Irish language is characteristic of his broad, humane, and informative view of the state of Irish poetry. For many years he was the gifted administrator of a leading arts organization, Poetry Ireland, in Dublin.

His books and publications include *The Ordinary House of Love* (1991), *Rosa Mundi* (1995), and *Sappho's Daughter* (1998). He has also published a volume of selected poems in Italian, *La Case ai Margini del Mundo* (1999), and a Spanish translation of *Sappho's Daughter*, *La Hija de Safo* (2001). He has edited *The Great Book of Ireland* (1991, with Gene Lambert), *Revising the Rising* (1991, with Máirín Ní Dhonnachadha), *Irish Poetry since Kavanagh* (1996), *Watching the River Flow* (1999, with Noel Duffy), and *The Great Book of Gaelic* (2002, with Malcolm Maclean). He has been series editor for the European Poetry Translation Network.

This essay is an important addition to the debate on poetry in the Irish language registered by other writers throughout this book. It tracks the history of false starts, hopes, and deferments that for some writers over-shadowed the dream of recovering the Irish language as a mainstream literary instrument. He outlines with subtlety and force the tensions between an old

226

language and a modern Ireland; between the vitality of the moment and what he calls here "a heavy and inescapable ancestral burden."

At the dawn of the twentieth century, borne up on the rising tide of national feeling, nurtured by the Gaelic League's recuperative work on the poetry of the past, an Irish-speaking optimist might have predicted a flood of new poetry in the language as a feature of the coming times. He, or she, would have been both incautious and destined to be disappointed. The first Gaelic poet of serious achievement in the new century, Máirtín Ó Direáin, would not even begin to think of writing poetry in Irish until 1938, and would say at the outset "Níor chabhair mhór d'éinne againn san aois seo an aon uaill ná mac alla ó na filí a chuaigh romhain inár dteanga féin" — No cry or echo from the poets who went before us in our own tongue would be of help to any of us in this time.

Apart from Ó Direáin, no poetry of true value would appear in the Irish language until Seán Ó Ríordáin published *Eireaball Spideoige* in 1952. Consumptive, lonely and unillusioned, Ó Ríordáin was a kind of alienated pietist whose work strikes the first truly modern note in Gaelic poetry. Refusing the succour of sentimental loyalty to the forms and tropes of the high Gaelic tradition, his agonised soul-searching is a local version of the doubt and existential anguish which now seems so characteristic of the European mid-century. But Ó Direáin's reluctant, even angry abandoning of the Arcadian peasant dream does not quite make him modern, in the sense that Eoghan Ó Tuarisc, say, writing self-consciously under the shadow of the Bomb, is modern. Paradoxically, Máire Mhac an tSaoi, immersed as she is in the poet-scholar tradition, becomes modern precisely because of her ability to play off a distinctly independent and contemporary sensibility against the structures and strictures of inherited traditions. Seán Ó Tuama, with his Corkman's ancestral yearning for the Mediterranean, and Pearse Hutchinson, drawn to Galicia and Catalonia, find distinctive contemporary voices in Irish outside the sway of world-girdling English; one might say the same of Tomás Mac Síomóin, heavily and productively indebted to a Continental sensibility which owes more to Pasolini than to Pearse.

Caitlín Maude, who died tragically young, and Michael Hartnett, to whom we will return, both born in 1941, carry the mid-century: the former as a feminist *avant la lettre*, the latter as a gifted poet in both Irish and English, translator of Ó Bruadair, eidetic companion to the present generation even in death. Maude and Hartnett, as with the generation following swiftly on their heels, were more of the present moment than of Ireland, in the important sense that the Gaelic world was for them a repository of enormous resource for the living of a life, far more than it was a heavy and inescapable ancestral burden. They and their successors are of post-Catholic, post-nationalist Ireland, the Ireland that was beginning to struggle to its feet at about the time they began publishing their youthful verses.

If the Gaelic League had, as it were, an afterlife following the establishment of the Irish Free State it was not vivifying, but the reverse. We can see it now as an admirable project of recovery and recuperation which carried within itself the metal fatigue of Victorian sentimentalism. The lost Gaelic order towards which it flung out a bridge was aristocratic, disdainful, Catholic and doomed. Apt in and for its time, the poetry of that order was spectacularly ill-suited to the grubby, dour, post-colonial truth of the infant Republic which would seize on it as the epitome of native high culture and, by force-feeding it in the schools, rob it of its political charge while unconsciously undermining its power as art. The insular, primitive nationalism of the new ruling class seized on the rich poetry of the 17th and 18th centuries as a shining string of baubles, the pathetic jewels of the poor who do not recognise their own poverty nor understand where their true wealth is to be found. By resolutely closing out the modern in favour of an idealised and unreal nexus of virtuous peasant and cultured Lord, the State, through its "education" system, made the disjunction between a glorious poetry of the past and a possible poetry of the present both absolute and prescriptive. Seeking, for perhaps the best motives, to celebrate the high poetry of a comparatively recent past, it silenced the present.

There were, to be sure, disruptions. Frank O'Connor, no cherished treasure of the State, published a muscular translation of *Cúirt an Mheán-Oíche*, *The Midnight Court*, in 1945, followed by *Kings, Lords and Commons* and *A Golden Treasury of Irish Poetry 600–1200* (with David Greene), both in 1959. These books, paradoxically, awakened his English language readers to the intrinsic riches of the Gaelic poetic tradition, and helped make it possible to see in a positive context work which, unfortunately, the State had helped stigmatise as backward and unworthy of serious attention.

There were disruptions, and there was also a nourishing silence. Away from the eyes of the State and the new professional class of Gaeilgeoirí, in "unforgiven places," as Tony Curtis puts it, Irish continued to be spoken as a living, adaptive and ambitious language. On building sites in Coventry as much as in the botháns of Kerry and the fire stations of Boston and Chicago, with neither fuss nor fanfare, the language endured and mutated, as all living languages do, out of sight and out of mind. There is nobody more secretively rebellious than a man or woman who is assured by the well-off that poverty is an admirable thing; nothing is better suited to the life of a language than the secrecy of the poor; and nothing more appeals to a rebel than a language in which to access simultaneously both a hidden past and an unborn future. The rebels, as it happens, were waiting in the wings.

When Nuala Ni Dhomhnaill and Michael Davitt, Gabriel Rosenstock and Liam Ó Muirthile arrived in University College Cork, they were coming to themselves as poets in what Che Guevara, in a different context but at more or less the same time, described as "an objectively revolutionary situation." They would found, and be published in, a radical journal, *INNTI*.

The power of the State to contain reality had withered. The electronic age and the first world generation were upon us, rock and roll had thundered out across the world and the short-lived counter culture, for a dizzy moment, held the commanding heights. The first trans-national generation had arrived to claim its place in the sun, and considerably to the surprise of the tweeds and Fáinne brigade this brash and exuberant generation of poets was as unremarkably at home in the Gaeltachts as in the hip, wide world.

Nuala Ni Dhomhnaill, born in Lancashire, brought up in Nenagh and in the Gaeltacht of Corcha Dhuibhne, was a natural rebel with a profound sense of the riches of the folk tradition, as source both of story and syntax. Michael Davitt, son of a CIE worker, and Liam Ó Muirthile from the heart of Cork City found themselves wildly at home in the Gaeltachts of Corcha Dhuibhne and Cúil Aodha, party and privy to a racy reality the pietists of the language had ignored or tried to forget. There was a true exuberance in the air, perhaps more soberly shared by Gréagóir Ó Dúill and Micheal Ó'Siadhail (his own preferred spelling) in other places, a sense that, as John Montague put it, "old moulds are broken" and that a new world, a new language was both possible and necessary. An Irish language, to put it this way, that could contain LSD and Gabriel Rosenstock's abiding faith in the wisdom-literature of the East.

The wily and sceptical Seán Ó Tuama offered a bracing counterpoint to their wilder enthusiasms, perhaps, as Seán Ó Riada brought a demonic precision to the music he did so much to uncover and make new again, in the same place and at the same time, but for all that, the *INNTI* poets were essentially unruly and individual as much as they were ever a school. Their education helped shape but does not explain them.

They were excoriated as shallow barbarians, dabblers in the shallows of the language, polluters of the unsullied, sex-free, drug-free paradise of the Gael. Contemptuous of the carefully nurtured and comfortable state-within-a-state which the professional Gaeilgeoirí had so profitably and quietly nurtured, they earned, in some quarters, genuine, spitting hatred. It is true that their focus was on the immediate, the lyric instant of the body present to itself, the street as theatre of the present moment, the exalted state of mind as both norm and normative. In that sense they were very much of their time, in fact so much of their time that, disconcertingly, they were of the avant-garde in a way that few of their English-language contemporaries were. Formally and thematically, they were ripping through received forms and received wisdom in unprecedented ways; perhaps only Paul Durcan, at that time, was doing in English what these poets were doing in Irish. This cleavage with the past, especially with the immediate past, was so shocking that, in effect, the shock anæsthetised itself. They were out and through into a new, unexpected re-appropriation of the past almost before they, themselves, realised what was going on.

It should be noted that the rising generation of poets were both heartened and inspired to a more capacious sense of their inheritance by the visits to Ireland of Scottish Gaelic poets, singers and musicians organised by Colonel Eoghan Ó Néill, and by the reciprocal visits to Scotland which would enter into the folklore as well as the poetry. The sense of a cognate tradition and of a comradeship in struggle became and remains an amplification and a quickening of commitment to the language, to a life in the language.

We live in a changed landscape now. Biddy Jenkinson can forge, as she has done, a lapidary and rigorous language of her own, steeped in the cold water of the language, and be and feel free to do so. Áine Ní Ghlinn can dare her poems to the edge of cold prose, write of the most painful things, and occasion no reproach that she lacks the classical frame of reference. Cathal Ó Searcaigh, whose beginning was in Kerouac, whose delight is in an unabashed gay sensibility, can write of Nepal and Gort 'a Choirce and sex satisfactory and unsatisfactory and know he will be read and heard as a poet of the living moment. These things are true, and remarkable. Louis de Paor and Colm Breathnach are the first of the post–*INNTI* generations, each a true and individual poet, both of them born into a new kind of liberty.

The cleavage is absolute between our now and our past, insofar as that past was constructed as an ideal reservation without whose walls there could be no salvation. The cleavage is, also, an illusion: language comes down to us as a living stream, defying all efforts to shape and contain its course. It is literally not possible to engage with the present of a language, to write in a language, without being informed by the past of that language. What is different is that the poet today can pick and choose where to immerse herself in the past, can come to the past as part of the project of making his own, unique existential self as a poet. There is an essential freedom in this relationship to the past, a freedom which is at base a kind of absolute humility and without which there can be no genuine respect for the life and work of those who have gone before us.

When Michael Hartnett, Mícheál Ó hAirtnéide, came "with meagre gifts to court the language of my people," when he turned from English to Irish, to his own immediate present as well as the living present of Ó Bruadair and Ó Rathaille, it was a gesture read in one of two ways: it was quixotic and arbitrary, or it was a choice made in the face of forces, ahistorical powers, he was helpless to resist. With the passage of time, and following his uncriticised and civilly-received return to English, it is possible now to see that Hartnett's choice was made in response to a simple imperative: the words sought him out, and the words were in Irish.

And this, I think, is where we are now. When poets now living make their poems in Irish, they are making poems, not obeisances, not signs made in the name of a tradition but the elements themselves of a free, living tradition. Poems. In Irish. No more, and no less.

Colm Tóibín

(b. 1955)

[EXCERPT FROM]

"Lady Gregory's Toothbrush"

Colm Tóibín was born in County Wexford in 1955. He studied at University
College Dublin and afterward went to Barcelona. His novel *The South* (1990)
and his nonfiction book *Homage to Barcelona* (1994), both about his time in
Spain, marked out what would be continuing themes: a profound sense of the
adventure of other places, both as a critique of and an escape from the Irish
experience. In 1982, Tóibín became the editor of a news magazine, *Magill*. His
journalism tracked a time of social change and upheaval in Ireland. His second
novel, *The Heather Blazing* (1992), revisited the Irish sensibility, making a
profound study of the repression and pain of Irish social life.

In recent years Tóibín has addressed twin themes of alternate sexuality
and how the literary imagination can be eroticized and transformed. This is
true of *The Story of the Night* (1997), set in Argentina during the Falklands
war, and of his novel *The Master* (2004), which explores the isolation and
achievement of Henry James. This last is a landmark novel in contemporary
Irish literature, boldly seeking out the inner weather of a stylistic master from
a different tradition.

Despite being a prolific fiction writer and journalist, Tóibín has never let
lapse his exasperated and affectionate commentary on the Irish tradition. He
is one of the contemporary Irish writers who best proves the consistency and
richness of the conversation between past and present. By the exuberance and
productivity of his critical writing, he has added to it greatly.

This excerpt is part of the addition. It comes from a biographical essay he
wrote on Augusta Gregory. In it he examines aspects of her life: her patrician
status, her idealization of Irish rural life, her devotion to a literary Renaissance
that all but eclipsed her. It is not a reverent piece, but by its wit and clarity
it signals the energy with which Irish writers continue to live the past of Irish
writing. It warms and animates vexed questions of Lady Gregory's authorship
of some of Yeats's work—particularly, as here, *The Countess Cathleen*. Above
all, it lifts her out of the passive role she has been assigned in many accounts
of the Irish Revival and, by so doing, restores her to the contradictions of
her life.

3

Cathleen ni Houlihan was Yeats's third play. At Coole in the summer of 1901,
Yeats told Lady Gregory of a dream "almost as distinct as a vision, of a cottage where there was well-being and firelight and talk of a marriage, and into
the midst of that cottage there came an old woman in a long cloak" who was
"Ireland herself, that Cathleen ni Houlihan for whom so many songs have
been sung, and about whom so many stories have been told and for whose
sake so many have gone to their death." This woman would lead the young
man of the house away from domestic happiness to join the French who had
landed to fight the British at Killala in County Mayo in 1798.

It is now absolutely clear that this play *Cathleen ni Houlihan* was actually
written by Lady Gregory rather than Yeats. The idea belonged to Yeats and
Yeats wrote the chant of the old woman at the end. But he could not write
naturalistic peasant dialogue, and the play depends on the naturalistic setting,
the talk of money and marriage, the sense of ease in family life in a small holding. In the manuscript held in the Berg Collection in the New York Public
Library, Lady Gregory has written in pencil on the first section of ten pages
"All this mine alone" and "This with WBY" at the beginning of the second
section. James Pethica has described how Lady Gregory managed in the play
to temper Yeats's tendency "to symbolize rather than to represent life" and
grounded the development of the play within a realistic framework.

In her journal for 1922, Lady Gregory said that she wrote "all but all" of *Cathleen ni Houlihan*. Lennox Robinson stated that "the verses in it are the poet's, but all the homely dialogue is Lady Gregory's. Indeed Yeats has told me more than once that the authorship of the play should be ascribed to her." Willie Fay also reported that Lady Gregory had written all of the play "except the part of Cathleen."

It is clear that Lady Gregory contributed "directly and abundantly," in James Pethica's phrase, to Yeats's work for the theater, especially to *On Baile's Strand*, *The Pot of Broth*, *The King's Threshold*, and *Deirdre*. In his dedication of *Where There Is Nothing* to Lady Gregory in 1902, Yeats wrote:

> I never did anything that went so easily and quickly; for when I hesitated, you had the right thought ready, and it was always you who gave the right turn to the phrase and gave it the ring of daily life. We finished several plays, of which this is the longest, in so few weeks, that if I were to say how few, I do not think anybody would believe me.

In public Yeats gave Lady Gregory some credit for this collaboration, but he never acknowledged the extent of her work on *Cathleen ni Houlihan*. In a diary entry in 1925 Lady Gregory complained that not giving her name with the play was "rather hard on me." Elizabeth Coxhead, in her literary portrait of Lady Gregory, wrote that "when her family . . . urged her to stake her claim, she always refused with a smile, saying that she could not take from [Yeats] any part of what had proved, after all, his one real popular success."

The play was performed with George Russell's play *Deirdre* in Dublin in April 1902 with Maud Gonne playing Cathleen. Lady Gregory, according to Roy Foster, attended one rehearsal and "slipped away to Venice well before the first night." Yeats, in an interview with the *United Irishman*, said that his subject was "Ireland and its struggle for independence." "Apparently," Roy Foster wrote, "neither of them anticipated the response to their joint production." The hall was packed every night, and the effect of the play was powerful. It was short and stark, with no subplots or stylized dialogue until Cathleen herself appeared, and its message was clear: that young men would have to give up everything for Ireland. The audience and the ordinary people on the stage were as one, and both were visited by this haunting force, a woman both old and young, Platonic Ireland, who would pull them toward heroism and away from everyday materialism. The critic Stephen Gwynn attended the performance and wrote:

I went home asking myself if such plays should be produced unless one was prepared for people to go out to shoot and be shot. . . . Yeats was not alone responsible; no doubt but Lady Gregory helped him to get the peasant speech so perfect; but above all Miss Gonne's impersonation had stirred the audience as I have never seen another audience stirred . . .

George Bernard Shaw later said that it was a play "which might lead a man to do something foolish." By 1904, Yeats was ready to deny that "it was a political play of a propaganda kind," but he was not convincing. Many years later, he would wonder, "Did that play of mine send out / Certain men the English shot."

Two other one-act plays to which Lady Gregory gave her name as sole author, *Gaol Gate* and *The Rising of the Moon*, both produced and published over the next few years, made no bones about her support for rebellion. Lennox Robinson wrote that *Cathleen ni Houlihan* and *The Rising of the Moon* "made more rebels in Ireland than a thousand political speeches or a hundred reasoned books."

How she managed her two separate worlds in these years is a mystery, but she managed superbly. In these same years, she could write Yeats a description of a dance at Coole:

> Our dance last night went off splendidly, lasted till three o'clock this morning, I wished you could have been there it was such a pretty bright sight, the drawing room cleared and lighted by close of fifty wax candles, the supper served on the twenty silver dishes, all the table silver and flowers and tempting dishes. . . . We were about thirty, chiefly cousins of Robert's and also two or three officers and a sister of Lord Westmeath's, Lady Emily Nugent. It was the merriest dance I ever saw (my experience has not been great, Buckingham Palace and Indian Viceregal and Embassy Balls chiefly).

In *Cathleen ni Houlihan, The Rising of the Moon,* and *Gaol Gate*, indeed in the story of Cuchulain himself, the lone male hero was ready to sacrifice himself. He was an idealistic, inspirational figure, free from the mire of the struggle for land which preoccupied most Irish peasants in these years. In *Cathleen ni Houlihan*, the family's desire for more land is something the son will have no truck with now that the old woman has come to the house and the French have landed at Killala. There was no grubby land-hunger in the rhetoric of these heroes.

Thus it was easier for Lady Gregory to apply the same zeal to collecting her folklore as to collecting her rents. She was, however, on at least one occasion, frightened enough by what she herself had created to write to Frank Fay in 1907: "I particularly didn't wish to have *Gaol Gate* [produced in Galway] in the present state of agrarian excitement, it [might] be looked on as a direct incitement to crime."

Her plays could incite crime; and when crime came close to her, it kept her awake. In May 1912 she wrote to Yeats about her tenants:

> Dear Willie, I am in great trouble this week — my brother wrote last week that he had had a meeting with the tenants but that they could not come to terms at present. Then Monday was rent day and he wired "Tenants demand 6/ — in the pound reduction — no rents paid." This was a shock and gave me a sleepless night and in the morning I had a letter from him saying the tenants are trying to blackmail us — and that he is making preparations to seize their cattle end of this week or beginning of next, which will he thinks bring them to reason, especially as the bulk of them are really anxious to pay.

She wrote to her son that their agent "was sure that the seizures would bring them to their senses. . . . He had arranged to start from Gort at 7 o'clock Friday morning, with eight Gort men, four Coole men and twenty police; to begin with the stock of the small tenants, and to sweep that of the larger ones as well."

The cattle raid in Coole did not take place, however, since a settlement was negotiated. Robert, who was away, owned the estate and the rents were his income. "I hope you think I have done right," she wrote to him, "I have done what I think best for your happiness." This is the key to understanding Lady Gregory's role as landlord at Coole. The cold, ruthless tone in her letters to Yeats and Robert about the tenants was not because she was a landlord's daughter who could not shake off this tone. She held Coole for Robert. It was his heritage and his inheritance. However much she may have changed in other matters, she remained steadfast in this.

4

Lady Gregory's mixture of high ideals and natural haughtiness gave her an inflexibility and sturdy determination which were invaluable when dealing with those who opposed her. Her gifts for governing men, her passion and precision, as Yeats put it, came into their own in the early years of the twentieth century when she became involved with the Abbey Theatre.

Her first battle was with Miss Horniman, the tea heiress from Manchester who bankrolled the theater in its early days and made great demands on the management and fellow directors while also making a pitch for the affections of W. B. Yeats. In many letters to Yeats, Lady Gregory deplored Miss Horniman's "vulgar arrogance and bullying" and suggested that she "should be locked up." She also called her "cracked," "a blood sucker," "a crocodille," "the Saxon shilling," "wicked," "a mad woman," "insane," and "a raving lunatic." If this was not enough to dislodge her, Lady Gregory pulled rank. "I have never treated her as an equal," she wrote to Yeats, "without regretting it." And later: "I think it is a mistake treating tradespeople as if they had one's own table of values."

This hauteur and invective were accompanied, however, over several years by Lady Gregory's slow and deliberate and tireless preparations to have Miss Horniman removed. While Miss Horniman ranted and raved, Lady Gregory never lost her nerve. By early 1911, she had succeeded.

This readiness to do battle, this tough attitude toward opposition, made all the difference when the artistic integrity of the Abbey Theatre was under attack. The importance of Yeats's and Lady Gregory's collaboration at the Abbey was not so much that words of theirs sent out certain men the English shot, as that during the time when they ran the theater a number of enduring masterpieces were produced, notably the plays of Synge and O'Casey, and also George Bernard Shaw's *The Shewing-up of Blanco Posnet.* Both Yeats and Lady Gregory maintained their relationship to a peasant culture they had dreamed into being, and at the same time made no effort to repudiate their own Anglo-Irish heritage. This gave them an enormous advantage in both Ireland and London: they were members of a ruling class who lost none of their edge or high manners or old friends while espousing a new politics and a new art in Ireland. They were independent and they did what they liked, subject to no peer group or class pressure. It was the mixture of ambiguity and arrogance in their position which made them ready for the exemplary battles they were now to fight for artistic freedom in Ireland, the right to stage the plays of Synge, Shaw, and O'Casey. They, and no one else, had the strength of will and the class confidence and the belief in their

cause to do battle with the rabble, the Catholic Church, the Lord Lieu-
tenant, and, when the time came, the new Irish state.

The young Catholic revolutionaries who had been so inspired by the simple message of *Cathleen ni Houlihan* were not ready for the mocking ironies
and wild paganism of John Millington Synge's *The Playboy of the Western
World*, which the Abbey Theatre first produced in 1907. Yeats and Lady
Gregory were ready to stand up to them, insisting on their own nationalist
credentials, but reverting also to Ascendancy hauteur. After a week of riots
in the theater against the presentation of Irish peasants as less than holy,
there was, on Yeats's suggestion, a public debate held in the Abbey on
February 4. Yeats took the stage, announcing that he spoke as the author of
Cathleen ni Houlihan. Referring to a priest in Liverpool who had withdrawn
a play because of the public's objection, he said of the Abbey directors, who
were all Protestants: "We have not such pliant bones and did not learn in the
houses that bred us a suppliant knee." The audience would have understood
this very clearly as a statement of arrogant Ascendancy values over suppliant
Roman ones. When Yeats's father in the same debate referred to Ireland as
an island of saints and scholars and then, sneeringly, referred to "plaster
saints" ("his beautiful mischievous head thrown back," as Yeats described
him many years later in "Beautiful Lofty Things"), the audience would also
have understood his remark as an insult to Catholicism.

Lady Gregory's nephew led a group of Trinity students to the theater to
defend the play and offer what was perhaps most missing in the debate — a
rendering of "God Save the King." And as the disturbances continued in the
theater, the Abbey directors, as property owners, knew what to do: they
called the police, who arrested rioters. The calling of the police did not win
them many friends in nationalist Ireland. In 1909, two years after *The
Playboy*, Lady Gregory placed the conflict between the Abbey directors and
the Catholic nationalist mob in terms both stark and superior: "It is the old
battle," she wrote to Yeats, "between those who use a toothbrush and those
who don't."

Greg Delanty

(b. 1958)

"Leavetaking"

Greg Delanty was born in Cork City in 1958. While at University College Cork, he edited the college literary magazine, *Quarryman*. His first poems were published around this time. He traveled to the United States in 1986 and became a citizen in 1994. He is the Artist in Residence at Saint Michael's College in Vermont.

In a recent interview he spoke eloquently about the reach and reward of living between two traditions, two places, and seeking to integrate them. "I've lived here for most of my writing life," he says of the United States, "and have been an American citizen for more than twenty years. I even ran for the Green Party in the elections. I see myself as both part of the Irish poetic tradition and part of the American tradition. I'm recasting myself from the hellbox of America, and picking from the spirit fonts of the Irish and U.S. traditions where I feel and think they suit, sometimes mixing the fonts, and sometimes dipping into the font trays of other traditions."

Delanty's volumes of poetry are *Cast in the Fire* (1986), *Southward* (1992), *American Wake* (1995), *The Hellbox* (1998), *The Blind Stitch* (2001), *The Ship of Birth* (2003), and *Collected Poems 1986–2006* (2006). With Nuala Ni Dhomhnaill, he edited *Jumping Off Shadows: Selected Contemporary Irish Poetry* (1995). The poem below, from *Cast in the Fire*, recalls one of the oldest themes—and one of the most frequently recurring—in Irish writing: the sundering from land

and home, the persistence of farewells, the abandonments brought about by

distance.

After you board the train, you sit & wait,
    to begin your first real journey alone.
You read to avoid the window's awkwardness,
    knowing he's anxious to catch your eye,
        loitering out in never-ending rain,
to wave, a bit shy, another final goodbye;
you are afraid of having to wave too soon.

And for a moment you think it's the train
    next to you has begun, but it is yours,
and your face, pressed to the window pane,
    is distorted & numbed by the icy glass,
        pinning your eyes upon your father,
as he cranes to defy your disappearing train.
Both of you waving, eternally, to each other.

Paul Durcan

(b. 1944)

"Making Love Outside Áras an Uachtaráin"

Paul Durcan was born in Dublin in 1944. His family came from County Mayo, and his work reflects a strong feeling for the west of Ireland. His anarchic, powerful poems often work best when they are dealing with place and displacement. He went to University College Cork and studied archaeology and medieval literature. The sensibility in his work—irreverent and deeply involved with linguistic play and logical reversal—occasionally brings in the subjects of his undergraduate education.

His books of poetry include *Endsville* (1967, with Brian Lynch), *O Westport in the Light of Asia Minor* (1975), *Sam's Cross* (1978), *Jesus, Break His Fall* (1980), *Ark of the North* (1982), *The Selected Paul Durcan* (1982), *Jumping the Train Tracks with Angela* (1983), *The Berlin Wall Café* (1985), *Teresa's Bar* (1986), *Going Home to Russia* (1987), *Daddy, Daddy* (1990), *Crazy about Women* (1991), *A Snail in My Prime: New and Selected Poems* (1993), *Give Me Your Hand* (1994), *Christmas Day* (1997), *Greetings to Our Friends in Brazil* (1999), *Cries of an Irish Caveman* (2001), and *The Art of Life* (2004).

Because Durcan's work is often comic and has both a populist and popular dimension, it is easy to miss his real identity as a poet: he is, first and foremost, a serious, original, and surprising political poet. The poem reprinted below is an example of this. His poems about Ireland often seek out the small, shimmering incidents and fragments of experience that are, in fact, the first signs of repression. Durcan's work—as is the case with this poem—often displays a brilliant antiauthoritarianism.

When I was a boy, myself and my girl
Used bicycle up to the Phoenix Park;
Outside the gates we used lie in the grass
Making love outside Áras an Uachtaráin.

Often I wondered what de Valera would have thought
Inside in his ivory tower
If he knew we were in his green, green grass
Making love outside Áras an Uachtaráin.

Because the odd thing was — oh how odd it was —
We both revered Irish patriots
And we dreamed our dreams of a green, green flag
Making love outside Áras an Uachtaráin.

But even had our names been Diarmaid and Gráinne
We doubted de Valera's approval
For a poet's son and a judge's daughter
Making love outside Áras an Uachtaráin.

I see him now in the heat-haze of the day
Blindly stalking us down;
And, levelling an ancient rifle, he says "Stop
Making love outside Áras an Uachtaráin."

Ciaran Carson

(b. 1948)

"Belfast Confetti"

Ciaran Carson was born in Belfast in 1948 into an Irish-speaking family. In his poetry and prose he considers questions of language, meaning, and traditional speech and its violation by both historical and present-day colonialism. "I write in English," he has said, "but the ghost of Irish hovers behind it; and English itself is full of ghostly presences."

Among his publications are *The New Estate* (1976), *The Irish for No* (1987), *Belfast Confetti* (1990), and *First Language: Poems* (1993). He has written prose, including *The Star Factory* (1997) and *Fishing for Amber* (1999). His most recent novel is *Shamrock Tea* (2001). His translation of *Dante's Inferno* was published in 2002. His most recent collection is *Breaking News* (2003). Carson is also an accomplished musician and a scholarly commentator on Irish traditional music, as can be seen from his 1996 book, *Last Night's Fun: About Time, Food, and Music*.

Carson's work has skillfully and eloquently drawn together elements of language, nationhood, and contemporary disjunction. Often local, it is never provincial. He writes of places and events in a fresh, truculent way. His technical reach in a poem is idiosyncratic and persuasive, with signature long lines and powerful images. The poem below is a case in point. It manages a poignant and powerful collision between two central concerns of Carson's poetry: history and language. By giving the poem the ironic title of "Belfast

Confetti," Carson signals just how dark a marriage this has been. And how the
bitter wedding of meaning and violence touches every life in its vicinity.

Suddenly as the riot squad moved in, it was raining exclamation
      marks,
Nuts, bolts, nails, car-keys. A fount of broken type. And the
      explosion
Itself — an asterisk on the map. This hyphenated line, a burst of
      rapid fire . . .
I was trying to complete a sentence in my head, but it kept
      stuttering,
All the alleyways and side-streets blocked with stops and colons.

I know this labyrinth so well — Balaclava, Raglan, Inkerman,
      Odessa Street —
Why can't I escape? Every move is punctuated. Crimea Street.
      Dead end again.
A Saracen, Kremlin-2 mesh. Makrolon face-shields. Walkie-
      talkies. What is
My name? Where am I coming from? Where am I going? A
      fusillade of question-marks.

Nuala Ni Dhomhnaill

(b. 1952)

[EXCERPT FROM]

"Why I Choose to Write in Irish, the Corpse That Sits Up and Talks Back"

Nuala Ni Dhomhnaill was born in Lancashire in northwestern England in 1952. When she was five years old, her parents returned to the Dingle peninsula in County Kerry, where she grew up. The rest of her childhood was spent in the Gaelthacht, and her mother was a native speaker. She was an undergraduate at University College Cork, where she studied English and Irish. After this, with her husband and children, she traveled in Europe for some years and later returned to live in Dublin.

For all the freedom that the Irish language conferred, the Ireland of the 1960s, especially outside Dublin, was sexually and socially repressive. Enough so for Nuala Ni Dhomhnaill to comment wryly: "Living in a puritanical Irish social setting has made it difficult even for heterosexuals to come out of the closet." Much of her poetry—all of which is written in Irish and translated by other Irish poets—addresses a charged interplay of instinct, anger, and language. Many of her themes visit and revisit the moment and the meeting between the body and systems of repression—whether linguistic or historical.

Her first collection of poems, *Dealg Droighin*, was published in 1981, and she has since published *Féar Suaithinseach* (1984), *Rogha Dánta* (1988), *The Astrakhan Coat* (1992), and *Pharaoh's Daughter* (1991). *The Water Horse* was published in 1999. Her *Selected Essays* was published in 2005. From the beginning, Nuala Ni Dhomhnaill has been an advocate for the Irish language.

She has argued with subtlety and force for its necessary continuance in a national psyche and its place in a national literature. As a central Irish poet, she has identified the consequences attendant on losing the language. In another part of the essay excerpted below she states: "I would think that the preservation of minority languages such as Irish, with their unique and unrepeatable way of looking at the world, would be as important for human beings as the preservation of the remaining tropical rainforests are for biological diversity."

The excerpt comes from her important essay on the Irish language, which was first printed in the *New York Times* in January 1995. With its eloquence and its unswerving honesty, it continues the conversation taken up by other writers included elsewhere in this book on the centrality of the Irish language to Irish literature. It also explores what the loss of the language could mean for a single imagination.

How does all this affect me, as a poet writing in Irish? Well, inasmuch as I am human and frail and prone to vanity and clamoring for attention, of course it disturbs me to be misunderstood, misrepresented and finally all but invisible in my own country. I get depressed, I grumble and complain, I stand around in rooms muttering darkly. Still and all, at some fundamental level it matters not one whit. All I ever wanted was to be left alone so that I could go on writing poetry in Irish. I still remember a time when I had an audience I could count on the fingers of one hand. I was perfectly prepared for that. I still am.

But it has been gratifying to reach a broader audience through the medium of translations, especially among the one million who profess some knowledge of Irish. Many of them probably had good Irish when they left school but have had no chance of using it since, for want of any functional context where it would make sense to use the language. I particularly like it when my poetry in English translation sends them back to the originals in Irish, and when they then go on to pick up the long-lost threads of the language which is so rightly theirs. I also find it pleasant and vivifying to make an occasional trip abroad and to reach a wider audience by means of dual-language readings and publications.

But my primary audience is those who read my work in Irish only. A print run for a book of poems in Irish is between one thousand and fifteen hundred copies. That doesn't sound like much until you realise that that number is considered a decent run by many poets in English in Ireland, or for that matter even in England or America, where there's a much larger population.

The very ancientness of the Irish literary tradition is also a great source of strength to me as a writer. This works at two levels, one that is mainly linguistic and prosodic and another that is mainly thematic and inspirational. At the linguistic level, Old Irish, though undoubtably very difficult, is much closer to modern Irish than, say, Anglo-Saxon is to modern English. Anyone like me with a basic primary degree in the language and a bit of practice can make a fair hand of reading most of the medieval texts in the original. Thus a *few* lines into a text on, for example, Mor of Munster taken from the twelfth-century Book of Leinster but dealing with seventh-century material and written in, at the latest, tenth-century Irish, I am hauled up short at a rather difficult word, "*aimilliui*." I understand the grammar of the sentence, and how the word functions in it, but what can it possibly mean? Then as I ponder the word, repeating it aloud and making allowances for more than one thousand years of linguistic development, suddenly I've got it: it is the word "*aimliu*." This is not only still occasionally heard in West Kerry speech, but I can even remember the last time I heard it uttered, on the tongue of Mike Long, a farmer of Cahiratrant, as we sat chatting on his ditch while he took a break from bagging potatoes. Talking about a well-known local rascal who had quite coolly helped himself to a large quantity of his neighbour's hay, he declared, "Fágfadsa aimliú air!" — he would leave a "deformity" upon him if he caught him. This depth of resonance is of untold linguistic and psychological strength.

Thematically, too, the older literature is a godsend, though I am only now slowly but surely beginning to assess its unique possibilities to a modern writer. There are known to be well over four thousand manuscripts in Ireland and elsewhere of material from Old to modern Irish. Apart from the great medieval codices, only about fifty other manuscripts date from before

1650. Nevertheless, the vast majority of the material painstakingly copied down after this time is exemplary of much earlier manuscripts that have since been lost. A lot of this is still catalogued in ways which are unsatisfactory for our time.

Many items of enormous psychological and sexual interest, for example, are described with the bias of the nineteenth century as "indecent and obscene tales, unsuitable for publication." On many such manuscripts human eye has not set sight since they were so described. Most scholarly attention has been paid to pre-Norman Conquest material as the repository of the unsullied well-springs of the native soul (those cultural nationalists again!), with the result that the vast area of post-Conquest material has been unfairly neglected. The main advantage of all this material to me is that it is proof of the survival until even a very late historical date of a distinct *Weltanschauung* radically different from the Anglo mentality that has since eclipsed it.

Because of a particular set of circumstances, Irish fell out of history just when the modern mentality was about to take off. So major intellectual changes like the Reformation, the Renaissance, the Enlightenment, Romanticism and Victorian prudery have never occurred in it as they did in the major European languages. One consequence is that the attitude to the body enshrined in Irish remains extremely open and uncoy. It is almost impossible to be "rude" or "vulgar" in Irish. The body, with its orifices and excretions, is not treated in a prudish manner but is accepted as "*an ndduir,*" or "nature," and becomes a source of repartee and laughter rather than anything to be ashamed of. Thus little old ladies of quite impeccable and unimpeachable moral character can tell risqué stories with gusto and panache and enter into an animated banter where every word is not only a double but often a triple or even quadruple entendre. The language is particularly rich in what the French call *polysemie*, words with many different meanings, which get stretched like elastic. And because it is a highly inflected language, word order is much less rigid than it is in English, say; the copula, for example, can be used instead of a substantive at the beginning of a sentence to allow for expectations to be set up and then demolished. Thus the skillful use of syntax alone can be the cause of wholesale hilarity, and has resulted in some of the best laughs of my life. It is with great personal difficulty that I buckle down to the relatively staid and straight-faced literalness that passes for civilised conversation anywhere in Ireland east of the Shannon. In Irish you can get away with murder. "Is there a word for sex in Irish" indeed! Is there an Eskimo word for snow?

By now I must have spent whole years of my life burrowing in the Department of Folklore at University College Dublin, and yet there are still days when my hands shake with emotion holding manuscripts. Again, this material works on me at two levels. First is when I revel in the well-turned phrase or nuance or retrieve a word that may have fallen into disuse. To turn the pages of these manuscripts is to hear the voices of my neighbours and my relatives — all the fathers and uncles and grandfathers come to life again. The second interest is more thematic. This material is genuinely ineffable, like nothing else on earth.

Sebastian Barry

(b. 1955)

[EXCERPT FROM]

"Driving Mrs. Synge"

Sebastian Barry was born in Dublin in 1955. He is a poet, playwright, and novelist. In all these forms he has explored the wrenching choices made by those who are outsiders in a nation. His play, *The Steward of Christendom* (1995), is about divided loyalties and the bewilderment of the effect of new histories on old attachments. It was built around the character of his own maternal great-grandfather, who was the chief superintendent of the Dublin Metropolitan Police (DMP) from 1913 to 1922. Similarly, his novel *A Long, Long Way* (2005) followed the fortunes of Willie Dunne, a recruit to the Royal Dublin Fusiliers in World War I. Uncovering these hidden histories, Barry is tracking the dilemma of earlier Irish writers such as Francis Ledwidge— included earlier in this book—who lived between two worlds.

In an interview about the novel, Barry said: "It is part of the grace of the Irish people that if a wrong or an absence is pointed out, they usually will listen with a certain pointed humanity. It has been wonderful to me the attitude of audiences around the country in their willingness to hear about Willie and his friends. To understand them, to identify with them, and silently and with enormous friendship to salute them." His publications include *The Water-Colourist* (1983), a volume of poems. His novels are *The Whereabouts of Eneas McNulty* (1998), and *Annie Dunne* (2002), set in Wicklow in the 1950s. His plays include *Boss Grady's Boys* (1990), *Our Lady of Sligo* (1998), and *Whistling Psyche* (2004).

In this excerpt from Barry's article on J. M. Synge he visits some of the landscapes that influenced Synge and considers his continuing importance to Irish writers. The Margaret Synge mentioned married a nephew of the playwright.

When Synge is mentioned, I always hear Tom Murphy, one of the greatest living Irish playwrights, saying that Synge was the master, Synge "the finest of us all." And yet it is easy to forget how long long ago Synge flourished, how long long ago he died. Margaret talks about Pestalozzi John as if he had died maybe in the forties, the nineteen forties; so maybe it is a Synge characteristic that they, each of them, seem present and correct in all ages.

Well, they all live there in the heaven of Margaret Synge's memory. I have to confess here I think Margaret Synge a heavenly person. Her decorum is musical. Her composure is inspiring. Her friendship is to be hoarded. Maybe old/young/eternal John Millington Synge was like that. I suspect so. His brother Sam loved him, always a good sign. Although he preferred to ignore the fact that his brother had connections with the dubious world of the theatre.

It may be strange now to think Synge was fallen upon by the commentators of his day for the use of the word "shift" in a play. What he actually wrote was (Christy speaking):

> It's Pegeen I'm seeking only, and what'd I care if you brought me a drift of chosen females, standing in their shifts itself, maybe, from this place to the eastern world.

The "maybe" is good.

Of course, the whole play is perfect and brilliant. It is language (the language he didn't speak, the language he heard with his eyes) gone to heaven, and emerged as the Elizabethan tongue of elaborate angels. There is no limit to the elaboration of the speeches, the nuts in them, or the joy, the thing he emphasized that plays must have (I feel bad about my own plays when I read that. I suppose he is right). The exuberance of Christy's words is of a brain that has ten thousand dancers in his head, and all of them in their shifts, and no "maybe" about it.

Well, at last Margaret brings me — directs me — to Lough Nahanagan. (Before I forget, Rathvanna, mentioned in *The Tinker's Wedding* and elsewhere, is an invented name, she says, quite a rare thing, if not singular, for Synge.) Lough Nahanagan is one of the places, Synge says (in his book), where a language is spoken "more Elizabethan than the English of Connaught." The other places he mentions in this respect are Aughavanna (just up the hill, as I said, I must go there some day and stop and see if they still do speak that English. I doubt it), Glenmalure, where my own people, Dunnes and Cullens, were peasants over seven generations at least, and whose language I certainly learned as a child, and sits deep in my tongue to this day (I hope and pray).

But Lough Nahanagan is not so far from The Seven Churches as it happens. It is a region of mortarless walls, deserted lead mines and the like, and a river, and a fine, well a wonderful, waterfall, down which Margaret Synge tells me a lady fell to her death. I ask her if she committed suicide, but Margaret says she didn't think so, though she might have pulled her chair too close to the falls with something vague in mind. Otherwise, apart from thoughts of that lady, there is no one about except a few very cold tourists, who might even be Irish, but everyone is a tourist up here, except Margaret. (Her old map across her lap has pencil markings on it that turn out to have been written there by her father years ago. It is a wonderful rare map, with all sorts of secret information on it that the world will never know. Such maps are extinct.) Even Lough Nahanagan is not quite "at home," at least it is invisible from the road. It is said there are good trout up there, if crazy in the head, and I can believe it. But they must be lonely. It is fearsomely lonely. There are no people going about speaking a language "more Elizabethan than the English of Connaught." There is no one at all to call Synge, or Mrs. Synge, or even myself, a foreigner.

Synges themselves are few on the ground, although we do stand later on sacred ground, "the Synge paddock" as Margaret calls it, a little Victorian enclosure where Synges lie in the Synge churchyard, including her marvellous John. "I'll be lying in there," she says, pointing to some unpromising dockleaves, and I ask her of her kindness to stay alive at least another twenty years, if only for my sake (I am selfish in my friendships and care nothing for anyone else). She says she will, and she will likely keep her word.

It is the word of a Synge. Fifteen thousand words of a Synge made the greatest play in the Irish canon, *The Playboy of the Western World*. It is a very nice thing that the Western world he refers to is actually Mayo, where once I lived myself. I always think of Mayo as a little Northern (not Connemara, not Galway, the traditional West). It could have been *The Playboy of the North Western World*. His other plays, apart from *Riders to the Sea*, are set in Wicklow, in the "eastern world" of Christy's speech. And I think it is true that they all speak the same, the characters, so it is a very democratic language, and he has bestowed his discoveries in language on the entire nation, as if that English he heard through the floor in Wicklow were really an Irish — a National tongue. Even the ancient grandees in *Deirdre of the Sorrows* speak the same language. It is a measure of Synge's elegant love, that he could fish such a language up from a Wicklow kitchen and spread it all over the country.

We go into the church and Mrs. Synge shows me the stone that remembers the death of young Captain Synge. The Fall of the House of Synge, she calls it, but it is one of her singing pleasantries. The house of Synge is quite eternally alive. The people are gone from Lough Nahanagan, and the tinkers from Ballinaclash, and even Rathvanna, that never existed; The Beauty of Ballinacree is gone, Sarah Casey herself, they are gone from the lonely glens and the back roads of Rathdangan, where Synge saw the Tinkers gathered every year to choose a yearly wife. The descendants of those Travellers used to come up our own farmyard and rattle the latch on Sarah Cullen and Annie Dunne, and frighten the life out of us children. That's how it was in those times, and I have written about it without ever thinking till this moment that I lived as a little boy of four in the land and the language of Synge. I write this little rambling essay here under those very mountains, of Kiltegan, Ninevah and Kelsha. All those people are gone, my own included, but the house of Synge will never be gone. For it is a house made of such words that no wind can touch it, government disdain it, or mortal life leave it empty.

Mary O'Malley

(b. 1954)

[EXCERPT FROM]

"Locus Pocus"

Mary O'Malley was born in Connemara, County Galway, in 1954, the eldest
of ten children. Her father was a fisherman. She graduated from University
College Galway and now lives in Moycullen. Her collections of poems are *A
Consideration of Silk* (1990), *Where the Rocks Float* (1993), *The Knife in the
Wave* (1997), *Asylum Road* (2001), *The Boning Hall* (2002), and *A Perfect V*
(2005).

O'Malley writes a sharp lyric line, salted with tones of irony and
energized by rhetoric. Many of her poems consider the difficulties of being a
female poet in the iconic traditions of the Irish language and the rural inheritance, and the tensions produced by them. Living in the west part of Ireland,
she knows these tensions between languages and traditions firsthand. In a
poem called "Received English," she eloquently suggests the struggle to
remake the old formulae in a new generation:

> It was hard and slippery as pebbles
> full of cornered consonants
> and pinched vowels, all said
> from the front of the mouth
> no softness, no sorrow, no sweet lullabies
> until we took it by the neck and shook it.

We sheared it, carded it, fleeced it
and finally wove it
into something of our own,
fit for curses and blessings.

More important, O'Malley, with her lyric abilities and astringent intelli-
gence, belongs to and strengthens a generation that has questioned, and in
some cases deflated, the claims of the Irish Revival. Decades later, the tendency of writers like J. M. Synge to idealize the lives that O'Malley's people
knew as a real enterprise, comes under scrutiny.

In an excerpt from this powerful and testing reconsideration of Synge,
she writes about what Irish writing is, and how it needs to change when its
early, iconic politicizations are found to have simplified and excluded the lives
that are its subject. This is not a new tension in Irish writing. But its restatement here is powerful, painful, and rewarding.

As a young child I picked carrageen and picked spuds and salted fish. All
these activities were carried out in the cold lash of April, or the bitter wind
of November, so the body's memory insists. I know the salting was actually
done in summer, the minute the fish were gutted and washed. This task I
also carried out, when I was old enough to be trusted with a knife. My
fingers were thin and they reddened and froze more quickly than anybody
else's, I was nervous and lacked dexterity so I did all of these things badly,
but as the eldest I had to show some sort of example.

While we were not as dependent on the sea as an island would be, we
depended on it for sustenance, for beauty and for escape to America. The sea
was capricious. The ability to predict weather had to be matched by the ability to know where and when the fish were to be found, as well as how to
catch them. The sea could be miserly, ensuring a winter of want and poverty,
or it could, without warning, be lavish.

As in fishing villages the world over, the men were either "out on sea" or
the currachs were in. When I was nine or ten the family moved to a house

with a view of the quay and my father got a bigger boat, a twenty eight footer, the *Grainne Mhaol*. The dominance of the sea was then complete; I depended on it for dreams.

The season was short, the winters long and life often brutal. In summer, the boats went out and money came in. If weather threatened or the boat was late, one of us children would be sent down to the pier head to look over the stormwall and scan the grey for a sight of the boat. If there was further cause for concern, a fast child was sent to see if anything could be spotted from further along the shore and finally — and I only remember this happening half a dozen times — someone was dispatched to see if the men had landed in the next village, and if not, whether anyone else was in. The fears were never voiced, but even the youngest child felt the tension — we learned it with our prayers.

Aillbebrack in the nineteen-fifties and early sixties was far closer to the world of Synge's *Aran Islands* than it was to Dublin or to the Galway of today. This small village at the edge of the Atlantic in the area was known to outsiders as Connemara, but to people from other parts of the region, and to us, it was known as Errismor.

Such knowledge, or lack of it, was one of the many small signifiers that told us whether someone was a stranger or not. Another was how they spoke. Not alone the accent, but more importantly the use of the telltale phrase. Even the children in every locality in Ireland could, before television, tell who came from within its borders and who from without after a few minutes of conversation.

The history of a people works on their language; the language limits what they can express of their world. When a language is lost in the place to which it is native, the effects are by definition more extreme than when this happens because of migration or immigration. This part of Connemara spoke an English not alone wedded to its deeper Irish grammatical structure, but moulded into a shape that could to some extent express the place and history of those who lived, and lost, in it. "The limits of our language are the limits of our world," Wittgenstein says. For ourselves, or for others? This is, in some ways central to how I read Synge, and to the critical essays and commentaries that I have read about him.

My grandmother and parents, my uncles and the neighbours spoke an English that was far from standard. "We're going out after the pots" or "He's over after the cattle" or "Think will herself be looking for more flour?" "I hear there was great gaisce altogether at Taimin over in Keogh's." "By the cross of Christ, I'll lay that fella out with a kick" would not be out of the question. Such language is easy to exaggerate and it is no surprise that Synge lost the run of himself in *The Playboy*.

There is a very clear line between parody and poetry, but the ear has to be finely tuned to the idiom and every nuance to achieve one and avoid the other. Daniel Corkery has described this linguistic minefield more than adequately in his *Synge and Anglo Irish Literature*, and I think that in essence he is right. He also says, to paraphrase wildly, that as a Protestant in love with the notion of the wild natural man, Synge didn't understand the nature and place of Catholicism, and this lack of understanding led him astray in *The Playboy*. Corkery is referring to the use of profanity, certain aspects of the overtly sexual talk and behaviour in the play that cause it to be read as parody, if not insult.

In other words, when Synge wanted pagan, he saw only pagan. He intended not to insult but to express what he saw as the great sport and heroics of the unfettered peasant. But the peasant world was guided by one god with two sets of saints and two kinds of knowledge, the old and the Roman. There was little direct conflict between the two.

As a child, I never gave any thought to the fact that our three main saints, Brigid, Cailin and Mac Dara were never on the calendar. I knew St. Patrick wasn't either and if I thought about it at all, I put it down to them being somehow native because St. Patrick, wherever he was from, is legitimized by the same type of half heroic story as the other three, and all gave their names to known places.

Synge wrote *The Playboy* in a ferment of sexual frustration, and it shows. When he arrived in mis Meain at the age of twenty-seven with a sack of books and a broken heart, he had an eye for the beauty of the girls, and they must have had great sport with him on an island well out in the Atlantic at the end of the nineteenth century.

When I read *The Playboy* sometime in my teens I thought it was ridiculous. I was mildly offended, not at anything in the play, but that educated people thought it had something to say about the kind of life lived by my ancestors and their like. . . .

Thomas McCarthy

(b. 1954)

"Black Flags at a Party Meeting"

Thomas McCarthy was born in County Waterford in 1954. He was educated at University College Cork. On being a poet, he once wrote: "I am not sure why I first began to write poems. It had something to do with the rich boredom and loneliness of my childhood. Yes, that boredom was rich. With boredom in my pockets, I travelled to many places, made many friends in my imagination. Poets are born, not made. But I think that there are many more poets born than ever live to see their talent exposed and matured by practice. Most people will have the poetry knocked out of them, mainly by being kept physically busy. For poetry is born in that oasis of lethargy and dreaming."

McCarthy is one of the first Irish poets to be born into the new Republic of Ireland, constituted in 1948. He inherited the calm and complacency, as well as the considerable inner contradictions, of what Sean O'Faolain called "the grocer's republic." Some of his strongest poems are about the political parties of the 1950s—the organizing, the self-deception, the rhetoric of a new state. His published volumes of poetry include *The First Convention* (1978), *The Sorrow-Garden* (1981), *The Non-Aligned Storyteller* (1989), *The Lost Province* (1996), *Mr Dineen's Careful Parade: New & Selected Poems* (1999), and *Merchant Prince* (2005). His fiction includes *Without Power* (1991) and *Asya and Christine* (1992). He has also published a memoir, *The Garden of Remembrance* (1998).

In the poem "Black Flags at a Party Meeting" he gives voice to Ireland's flirtation with fascism in the 1930s, and by so doing, he shows the intent of new Irish writing to recover an awkward historical past.

The black flag is a Fascist tag. My father,
we've been there too long before
in the land of anger, land of fear.

The anger that has overtaken you
has touched me too. I want to hunt
the anonymous historian. I want to chase
him into a corner and say *I'll never forget!*

I know how they left you with scars —
but there's no historian of the *might have been*
to count those who died at the precipice.
Fold that flag and let your face be seen.

An elbow on the nose, a baton in the mouth,
a blueshirt or a green pushing through a crowd:
come home to memory where these are understood.

Rita Ann Higgins

(b. 1955)

"I Asked Him about the Horses"

Rita Ann Higgins was born in 1955 in Galway, where she has remained her entire life. She writes about the place and the people. In the process she has brought a vigorous voice to lyric poetry in Ireland, tapping into her own experience, registering new tones and powerful dissent, and frequently contesting the conservatism of both the social and literary conventions around her. Her publications include *Goddess on the Mervue Bus* (1986), *Witch in the Bushes* (1988), *Goddess and Witch* (1989), *Philomena's Revenge* (1992), *Higher Purchase* (1996), *An Awful Racket* (2001), and *Throw in the Vowels* (2005). Her plays include *God-of-the-Hatch-Man* (1990) and *Face Licker Come Home* (1991). These were produced by the Punchbag Theatre Company. Also, her collection *Down All the Roundabouts (or No One Is Entitled to a View)* was published in 1999.

In an interview Higgins once said: "All I care about is the fact that I was able to say what I wanted without an oppressive regime or anything else preventing me from doing so. I have always had a voice, I just didn't have a channel for it." Her work has uncovered new registers of protest and narrative for Irish poetry. It is often experimental, sliding in and out of fragmentation, half speech, and yet all the time keeping a music of sense close to the Irish vernacular. In the following poem, "I Asked Him about the Horses," she recreates a half conversation. As is characteristic in a Higgins poem, the voice drives the poem forward, splintering the narrative with shadows of misunderstanding, swerves of half words, and almost-sentences.

"Don't talk to me about horses
they're running backwards
one let me down badly
in a Yankee yesterday,
the gennet"

More lotto talk,
"England have the lotto now,
what they can't steal from us
they copy"

More mano over there talk
more when I get out things will be different talk
back then to safer ground
a hurricane called Gordon is devouring Florida
a place for Irish weather
a place for every horse since Arkle
a race for mints

"Go on, go on I tell you,
take one, one for the bus."

Roddy Doyle

(b. 1958)

"Wild and Perfect: Teaching The Playboy of the Western World"

Roddy Doyle was born in Dublin in 1958. He grew up in Kilbarrack and graduated from University College Dublin. He worked as a teacher until 1993,
teaching English and geography in a school where the students called him
Punk Doyle because of his earring. In 1993 he became a full-time writer. In
an interview Doyle spoke of his wariness of the change: "I was determined
not to cut myself off from all of that. I had to make sure I kept an eye on the
real world. It came up to my desk when I was a teacher."

His novels have had success from the beginning. *The Commitments*
(1987), *The Snapper* (1990), and *The Van* (1991) have all been made into films.
Known as the Barrytown trilogy, they introduced into Irish writing a new
reality—the bittersweet acoustic of voices under pressure—and a new
perspective on the hard-pressed world of working-class Dublin. It has been a
transforming energy for contemporary Irish writing. In these books, he said in
an interview, he was content "just to let the characters do their own roaring,
and I kept the descriptions as bare as possible." Later novels, however, such as
Paddy Clarke Ha Ha Ha (1993) and *A Star Called Henry* (1999), show a turn
inward: the reappearance of the narrator and lyric elegy added to realism.

Even in a country as abrasive as Ireland, there are tendencies to be reverent with the literary past. Doyle is free of these. To prove its worth, that past,
like any other, has to survive its present. It has to come into the daily furnace of

the contemporary world—and there is no hotter variant of that than a North Dublin school. Doyle's wonderful account here of teaching J. M. Synge's *The Playboy of the Western World* to irreverent teenagers is comic and compassionate, as well as being a vivid and challenging critique on what makes a work of literature survive its moment. The pupils are a hard sell. And yet there is something moving and instructive here in this account of how the reticent, wounded, Anglo-Irish sensibility of Synge and the skeptical students of a hard-pressed modern Ireland find one another. With Roddy Doyle as their Virgilian guide.

The best thing about *The Playboy of the Western World* is the voices. The thing is full of culchies. It's a teacher's dream. Try finding enough students willing to read the parts in Hamlet.

"Hands up who wants to be Laertes."

Hands stay down; eyes hit the desk. You're standing in front of a roomful of very shy, aspiring vets and accountants. Not an actor or a chancer among them.

But come back in six months with *The Playboy*.

"Hands up who wants to be Shawn Keogh."

"Sir!"

"Sir!"

"Me sir!"

"Sir!"

"Me, me, me, me, me!"

"What about the Widow Quin?"

"Oh God, pick me!"

I was an English teacher for fourteen years. I spent hours, days, months trying to convince young people that the irony in *Persuasion* was worth their attention. "There's a good laugh on the next page; I swear."

I spent hours and days trying to convince them that Wordsworth wasn't an eejit. "They're only flowers, Sir. Calm down."

That Yeats wasn't an eejit—"Sir? Why didn't he just ask her to go with him?"; that every sentence and line they read wasn't, automatically, the work of an eejit.

It was a constant fight. I stood at the front of the room and said, "Open up _____ " (Choose any one of the following: *Persuasion, The Charwoman's Daughter, Heartbreak House*, most of the pages in *Soundings, Portrait of a Lady, The Greatest of These* — and the list goes on. The horror!)

The command to open the text was always followed by a groan. A real groan. The dreadful, wet sound of young minds being squeezed. I was killing these children. But there were plenty of good days. The students were easily convinced that Shakespeare was the business. They loved Edmund. They loved Lady Macbeth. They loved Iago. They loved *Wuthering Heights*. They loved Heathcliff and Cathy. They loved hating the other characters. They loved the passion and the cruelty. They loved *Lord of the Flies*. They loved Piggy, and the "stuff" coming out of his head. They loved the posh English boys shoving, hitting — killing each other. "Sucks to your asthmarr!"

They loved the fact that these kids could have been themselves; they loved the honesty of the book, the language, and the simplicity of the story — the theme: children, given the chance and the island, will eat one another. And they loved — God, they loved — *The Playboy of the Western World.*

"Sir!"

"Sir!"

"Me!"

It was, at first, the opportunity to do the voices. The room was suddenly full of Christys and Pegeen Mikes. Even the girl I chose to read the stage instructions became a culchie, an R.T.E. continuity announcer circa 1981. "Impty barrels stind near di counter."

It was mad, wild stuff. A laugh. These Dublin kids got it out of their systems. Every Garda who'd ever told them to move their arses, every teacher who'd ever looked sideways at them, every priest who'd ever let his Mass go over the thirty-five minutes — they all got a slagging in the first few pages of *The Playboy*.

"Where's himself?"

Shawn Keogh, "a fet ind fair young min," is the first male character to walk onstage. In the first few days of reading, Shawn came from Kerry, Donegal, Galway, Offaly, Limerick, Wexford and, bizarrely, Scotland. One boy in the class could do a good Sean Connery and decided not to waste it.

"Where'sh himshelf?"

James Bond had just walked into the shebeen, but Pegeen Mike didn't even look up. If I remember correctly — and I probably don't — the first Pegeen Mike, having beaten off the opposition, decided to stick with her own accent. So, for the first five or six pages, Pegeen Mike Flaherty, "a wild-looking but fine girl," came from Briarfield Grove, Kilbarrack, two minutes walk from the Dart station.

"Isn't ih long the nights are now, Shawn Keogh, to be leavin' a poor girl wi'h her own self countin' the hours to the dawn o' day?"

James Bond's response was lost in the roars and wolf-whistles.

It was fun, but not much else, at first. The first few pages were very slow. Pegeen's shopping list on the first page seemed unnecessarily verbose, and we were expected to watch her write it. And what did those words mean? "A hat is suited for a wedding day." Did she want a hat? And what was a hat doing on a shopping list? Where were the eggs and the bread? And why all the names on the first two pages? Philly Cullen and Red Linahan, the mad Mulrannies and Father Reilly, Marcus Quin, "got six months for maiming ewes." It was one line, stop, next line, stop, just like reading Shakespeare for the first time, until they got the hang of it, until they could see it, and hear it, and it began to make great sense.

It did make great sense. And, along the way, it was often hilarious. One of the great successes of my career in teaching came to me unexpectedly, when Shawn Keogh delivered the line, "I'm after feeling a kind of fellow above in the furzy ditch." The Shawn that morning was from somewhere near Kerry, but his accent fell away when he got to "fellow" and he realized what he'd just read, and the other twenty-nine boys and girls in the room realized what he'd just read, and the silence — it lasted less than a second — became a cheer that became a bigger cheer, and bigger, and Shawn Keogh looked at his desk, and under his desk, for the hole he hoped would swallow him whole, and burp. And, after the laughter died and Shawn Keogh redis-covered his spine, I never before saw such keen scholarship; every student was flying through the pages, looking for more lines like that one. I hoped the principal or vice-principal would walk in now; I hoped anyone would walk in. I was listening to the sound of utter concentration. I had control and engagement. And I had silence. No threat or bribe would ever again be as effective. And I had it, the sound of well-used silence — it's very, very rare — for two long minutes, until someone found Shawn Keogh's line about "the naked parish."

"What page, what page?" — and that started another scramble.

Then someone else found the Widow Quin talking about "the gallant hairy fellows are drifting beyond," and that got me up to the bell and the coffee break. I bought myself a Twix. At first, the language of *The Playboy* was as far away from these Dublin kids as the language of Chaucer and Shakespeare. Even the simple question from the Widow Quin, "What kind was he?" needed a good looking at before it became, "What was he like?" or something nearer their words. "There's harvest hundreds do be passing these days for the Sligo boat." Again, it needed staring at. What was a "curiosity man"? And what did "Tuesday was a week" mean? But, as with Shakespeare, the staring was well worth the time. "Harvest hundreds" brought a story about one girl's grandfather who went from Donegal to Scotland every year to pick potatoes. And, more than twenty years later, I still meet ex-students who smile and say, "Tuesday was a week."

The Playboy was a hit. It wasn't just because they could become culchies for the day. They copped on to the story and, unlike the language, the story was immediately theirs. I taught *The Playboy* in the early '80s, when many of these kids were going to join the "harvest hundreds." The play was about people on the edge of the rules, and the kids I taught knew that place. Today, that part of north Dublin is often featured in the Property sections — the schools, the sea, all the recently discovered amenities. Back then, it looked much as it does now but, more than once, I saw the word "ghetto" used to describe it. It was no more a ghetto than Ranelagh, but these kids knew the hurt of being written off. They knew the power and fun of language; language was one of the things they owned. Slagging was a sport and an art. The best slag I heard was this: "Your granny'd climb out of her grave for a half-bottle of gin." Change it a bit and it could be a line from *The Playboy*; it might even have been in the first draft. It's a *Playboy* line because *The Playboy* is a slagging play. The slags fly across and back across the stage. Pegeen Mike and the Widow Quin, the big women of the play, are particularly good at it — "there's poetry talk for a girl you'd see itching and scratching." Slagging is a huge part of the play's energy. Shakespeare knew a well-aimed slag. So did Synge. And so did my students.

And they knew a great story. "Tell us a film," I'd ask one particular student when I was feeling lazy, and he'd stand up and deliver the plot of whatever video he'd watched the night before. I'd seen some of the films; he was much, much better. Is wasn't just entertainment. I could see that on his face, and I could see it in the faces of the others watching and listening. It was vital; it was power. He had them. These minutes might have been the high-point of his life. It's not just the plot of *The Playboy*. It's the man in the middle, Christy, telling the story, making himself up, assembling himself with words. I don't know what age he's supposed to be, what age Synge had in mind when he made him cough offstage, before he walks on, "a slight young man . . . very tired and frightened and dirty." He's a teenager. (So is Pegeen Mike.) He's lost and he's shy. But he talks; he makes up his story. He's listened to, and he has power.

Then there's Christy's story. ". . . wasn't I a foolish fellow not to kill my father in the years gone by." Sophocles only had it half-right. No true Irish boy wants to sleep with his mother. But killing the Da is a different proposition. "I just riz the loy," says Christy, "and let fall the edge of it on the ridge of his skull." Once they knew that a "loy" was kind of a shovel and that "riz" meant lifting it over his Da's head, all faces in the room lit up. These were teenagers, and all fathers are eejits, and worse than eejits. What else would you do with a shovel? Christy was their man. Better yet, the dead man walks onstage. The play has become a horror film, one of those really funny ones. Then Christy gets to fight his Da again, and he wins again. Old Mahon takes his beating and likes it. Christy pushes him offstage, and follows him. "I'm master of all fights from now." For the boys in the room, the play ends there. The girls read on, to Pegeen's lament — "I've lost him surely" — but the boys are offstage with Christy.

The fears of the boys and girls, their dreams, their current selves — they're in *The Playboy*. And — a must for all good school texts — as we read or watch, we see the central characters grow out of their pain, and learn. The first time we see Christy, he's gnawing a turnip. By the end of the play, he's biting Shawn Keogh's leg.

I loved teaching *The Playboy*, it more than made up for *Persuasion*. It's a great school play because it's wild and perfect, much like the average teenager.

Anne Enright

(b. 1962)

Introduction
to As Music and Splendour,
by Kate O'Brien

Anne Enright was born in Dublin in 1962. She is a novelist and short story writer. She studied in Dublin, where she received her degree from Trinity College. She then went to the University of East Anglia, where she did a master's in creative writing. One of her teachers and influences was the late British novelist Angela Carter. In 1986, Enright began work in Irish television. She produced a late-night program called "Nighthawks." Her first book, a volume of short stories called *The Portable Virgin* was written at this time and published in 1991. "I'd come home on Friday, go to the pictures, then write all weekend," she said in an interview.

Enright's first novel, *The Wig My Father Wore*, was published in 1995. Her second novel, *What Are You Like?*, was published in 2000. *The Pleasure of Eliza Lynch* was published in 2004, and a new novel, *The Gathering*, is due in 2007. In 2004 Enright wrote a reflective book on becoming a mother, called *Making Babies: Stumbling into Motherhood*. "I only write what I can," she has said, implying the limits and strengths of the storyteller's vision. In the same interview she remarked: "I like to fetishise objects. I find if you stare at them long enough they become funny. You stop being able to 'read' them." These comments suggest the sometimes comic, often surreal, and edgy worlds of her fiction. Enright belongs to a new generation of Irish fiction writers—a generation less reverent, more diverse in style than the Irish realists of the early part of the twentieth century. The challenges are different; the approach is often more international.

In this introduction to *As Music and Splendour* by Kate O'Brien, Enright looks back, with compassion and insight, to a more enclosed sexual and social world. "These images of authenticity," she writes of O'Brien's treatment of women, "were the stock of Catholic nationalism, whose ideal of the lovely Irish girl did not include her falling in love with other women, in a carnal sort of way." Enright's eloquent, candid treatment of O'Brien's world reveals a distance between the past and the present of Irish writing, especially in the way in which women writers address the silences of a society.

The twenty-first century presents a new problem to the writer discussing human intimacy. Anything buried or half hidden or forbidden can be found, explicit and open and wrapped in carry-out latex, on the Internet. This blight of the obvious infects, not just the secrets in a novel, but the way in which those secrets are revealed. It is useful — when our methods are so undermined — to look at writers on the other side of this river of flesh; ones for whom the obvious was not allowed.

Two of Kate O'Brien's earlier novels, *Mary Lavelle* (1936) and *The Land of Spices* (1941), were banned in Ireland — the latter because of a passing reference to homosexuality. This hurt her deeply, but O'Brien was a flower of the Irish convent school system, and not easily thwarted. She was also very proud. Clare, one of the two protagonists in *As Music and Splendour*, may be a lesbian, but this is not the point of her character, quite. The novel — O'Brien's last — was published in 1958. Irish censorship had grown less severe, but to speak of sex between women would still have been inflammatory. O'Brien solved the problem, quite deftly, by speaking about love instead.

Lesbianism is not Clare's problem; her problem is the same as that of her great friend, Rose: she must find her voice. The girls meet at a school in Paris where they have been sent, fresh from provincial Ireland, to train for the great opera houses of Europe. They are young, they can sing — they could break your heart. The novel follows them to a *maestro*'s house in Rome, where they fall in and out of love with their fellow students, and then through their first seasons as fledgling *divas*, aiming for La Scala, and beyond.

O'Brien loves greatness — she loves to talk of it and imagine it, and the final humility it might require. "Don't you know that nothing can be settled about us while we live?" says a character in *The Land of Spices*, echoing, perhaps, the weary megalomania of writers everywhere. Greatness is the fantasy of the novel and its romance. Opera provides O'Brien with a world of high endeavour, in which a woman can become an *assoluta*: something absolute, something beyond. For this she will need talent, discipline, emotional complexity and purity of intent. This is an ideal that is also available to readers, whether they can sing or not, because the only way to attain it is to become more completely yourself. *As Music and Splendour* produced in me a huge and sighing nostalgia for a time when "self-expression" meant the expression of something fine. O'Brien is a convent existentialist. She believes in girls. She believes in what they can become. Her belief is made more fierce — more pure, even — by the fact that she wrote at a time when girls rarely became anything much, as the world saw these things.

Still, this relentless interest in the educated heart. O'Brien believes in teachers in a way that is rare among writers; the *Bildungsroman* usually prefers the more accidental lessons that life sends our way. Duarte, Clare's natural maestro, teaches her "with speed, impatience and merciless accuracy: indeed with a compressed passion in every instruction that compelled her wits to race with him, and that brought — she could hear and feel herself — great elasticity and extension to her voice." Teaching is a labour of love, to the extent that it is often confused with desire — and when desire is thwarted, then teaching will do. Clare's friend Thomas is gallant enough when disappointed in love, but he flings himself weeping in her lap when she tells him she will study the role of Alceste with someone else.

The self in Kate O'Brien's work is the intractable human substance of Catholicism, it is something that must be moulded and pummelled and broken and reshaped. There is no quarter, and so this most romantic of writers is also the most unsentimental. Perhaps Clare's lesbianism has a function here: it requires a way of writing about girls that is not solved by marriage; it frees up the ending, and allows their lives to be treated with as much uncertainty and rigour as the lives of boys.

Away from Ireland, Clare and Rose leave Catholicism quite simply behind. "We are sinners," says Clare, as they take to love, instead. They do this as part of their musical education — who could sing Verdi, if she never had a broken heart? — and they are helped by the simplicity of Catholicism itself: "Rose and I know perfectly well what we're doing. We are so well instructed that we can decide for ourselves. There's no vagueness in Catholic instruction." All of this is as pragmatic and uneasy as their feelings about the country they have left behind. Catholicism, like Ireland, is "over there" — it seems that O'Brien is tired of clawing at both of them from the inside. In this late novel, she retains the questions of Catholicism, while ditching the answers it is so keen to supply.

Clare's problem is, first and foremost, a spiritual one. At the age of sixteen, "she had to balance herself, unaware of her ordeal, on the sharp and dipping ring — made of light — where the spirit has to decide with the flesh between union and divorce." This is the challenge set to her voice, which is a cool, androgynous, intellectual instrument, as set against the joyful virtuosity of Rose. The question is not what kind of flesh Clare should indulge in, but whether she should indulge at all. This is not a problem of sexuality, but of art, and it can be resolved only by artistic means. In order to become a true artist, however, Clare must experience sexual love.

Many arias run through *As Music and Splendour*, but one that lingers is "*Che faro . . .*" from Glück's *Orfeo ed Euridice*. If you look behind to see if she is following, Euridice will be lost to you. This is the discovery Clare makes — that all love is impossible, that it fades as you try to grasp it. In the face of this realization, gender is a detail; gender is just a question, sometimes, of logistics.

And still, the music yearns and insists that love is possible so long as we are true. Gender may be a detail, but it is an essential one. Clare has no other option. There is no one else for her to be. When Thomas does finally rage at her, she thinks, "I can't be stormed at. There is nothing here for him to storm."

There is something about Clare's heart that cannot be altered, and this romantic essentialism is echoed in the way she harkens to the Irish landscape, to ideas of purity and home. She dreams of being back "under a rain she knew, among stones and empty lanes, and looking at grey sea and a wet pier, and hearing her grandmother's sweet, good voice calling her in out of the wet to her tea." These images of authenticity were the stock of Catholic nationalism, whose ideal of the lovely Irish girl did not include her falling in love with other women, in a carnal sort of way. With these images of Ireland, O'Brien, at her most haughty and subversive, claims the higher ground.

O'Brien loves her characters' Irishness. Rose is hailed as La Rosa d'Irlanda by the Italian audience. She possesses, in her easy emotional grace, a large helping of what O'Brien calls the "over-saluted and over-mocked Irish charm." For all her wanderings, there is a core that does not change in Rose, either. Perhaps O'Brien is as partisan as any narrow Catholic nationalist when she says that you can take a nice Irish girl anywhere — anywhere at all: "she did not change in anything, save to grow more like herself, the honest and merry and tender-hearted one, the level-headed and benevolent one, that she could have been foreseen to become in any walk of life, from Lackanashee to Milan and back again."

Then again, perhaps it is true.

But this sense of an essential, unchanging self has its downside too. Clare, new to love, observes herself and her own emotions. "Another Clare, the familiar one of always, was about her usual business, and was able to watch this newcomer coolly enough from the wings. And the newcomer knew this, and knew it with a sense of relief that puzzled and sometimes saddened her. One does not change, she thought, one does not escape."

Clare never does have a great moment of revelation about her sexuality. In a world where the obvious is never stated — can never be stated — things merely are. She comes back from a day spent with her lover, and Thomas sees her on the stairs, and knows more about her than she, perhaps, knows about herself.

Much later, he will call her a "stinking lily," a phrase that is quite marvellously unpleasant, combining the image of chastity with that of rot. But by now Clare is sure of her heart. Thomas insists on the illusion of love, its essential selfishness and impossibility. "When it's of love we think, Clare, we're alone with it." Clare replies that it is "just possible" we are not alone, that love is reasonable, that it can be given and returned. This hint of possibility gives people the ability to "bear love, and look at it quietly even in themselves." It also "makes them write poems, I suppose, and operas —"

"Makes them sing?"

"Yes, I think so."

And so the only explicit conversation in the book about Clare's intractable heart turns out not to be about lesbianism, but about the absolute and the possible, and the space between the two where the artist and the lover both make their home. O'Brien is too proud to discuss something so delicate and important as sexuality on other people's terms.

Perhaps it is my convent education that makes me think there is something thrilling in writing about women's problems in this way. The ardency of her beliefs and the ferocity of her disdain make me think of Kate O'Brien as a figure of almost medieval romanticism: a religious knight. She has, in her time, been accused of arrogance, but she is not so much arrogant as *interested* in arrogance, its pitfalls and delights. She is an extraordinarily resilient writer. She resists the dross — of whatever decade — and so endures.

Dermot Bolger

(b. 1959)

"Poem for a Newspaper"

Dermot Bolger was born in 1959, in Finglas, a suburb of Dublin. He is a noted poet, playwright, and fiction writer, although he has said that the novel interests him most. He is also an activist publisher, with a strong sponsorship of innovative Irish writing through his founding of New Island Books. Of his method of writing, he has said: "I'm inclined to climb the highest tree and jump off and see what happens next. I know writers that do plot their books intricately—and they're very fine books—but to me, if I know too far ahead what is going to happen, the book ceases to be a journey for me."

His novels are *Night Shift* (1982), *The Woman's Daughter* (1987, revised and enlarged 1991), *The Journey Home* (1990), *Emily's Shoes* (1992), *A Second Life* (1994), *Father's Music* (1997), *Temptation* (2000), *The Valparaiso Voyage* (2001), and *The Family on Paradise Pier* (2005). His plays are *The Lament for Arthur Cleary* (1989), *Blinded by the Light* (1990), *In High Germany* (1990), *The Holy Ground* (1990), *One Last White Horse* (1991), *Greatest Hits, One Act Plays* (1997), *April Bright/Blinded by the Light* (1997), and *The Passion of Jerome* (1999). His poetry collections include *The Habit of Flesh* (1980), *Finglas Lilies* (1981), *No Waiting America* (1982), *Internal Exiles* (1986), *Leinster Street Ghosts* (1989), *Taking My Letters Back: New and Selected Poems* (1998), and *The Chosen Moment* (2004).

Bolger has continually questioned the set texts of Irish identity, and he has repeatedly argued for a more open, more plural society. He is one of the newer Irish writers who proves that a tradition that began with grand promises and a deep belief in Irishness has in some ways had to lease its authority to younger writers with subtle questions and necessary iconoclasms. The piece below, "Poem for a Newspaper," with its deft, bleak sense of what does not survive—of the ironies and emptiness of trying to arrange the future—is an eloquent if oblique commentary on that.

Imagine this poem boxed
Among columns of newsprint
In a paper you have half-read.

This is the night you move
into your first house.
How eerie the rooms seem:

Bare light bulbs,
Strips of unfaded carpet
Like sunken graves that mark

Where furniture once stood.
Paint tins have been stacked
Beside the spare mattress.

Tomorrow new carpets will arrive.
You finger the tacks and knife,
Already hearing in your mind

The trundle of a tricycle,
Bare feet, muffled by underlay,
Racing to greet you coming home.

It is midnight when you start.
This poem is your only witness
As you rip the old carpets up

To make the floorboards your own.
The house is naked for you to possess her,
Yet all you can do is lay newspaper down.

II

Decades pass and you will be dead
When somebody lifts those carpets.

The house stripped bare as they glance
Through these lines you half-began,

Trying to fathom your unknown life,
Your thoughts as you worked, through them.

Paula Meehan

(b. 1955)

"The Statue of the Virgin at Granard Speaks"

Paula Meehan was born in Dublin in 1955. She was raised in the inner city and educated at Trinity College and Eastern Washington University. She has written poems, prose, and plays. Her voice is one of the most distinctive in contemporary Irish writing. Meehan has given workshops in prisons and inner-city communities. Her drama and her poetry draw on sources that are notably engaged with the contemporary world, involved with both its challenge and its suffering. Her work is politically committed: rigorous, eloquent, and often radiant with anger and argument. The language of lived experience, of daily encounters, of the ordinary world has proved to be a source rather than a stumbling block for her vision. Her books of poems include *Return and No Blame* (1984), *Reading the Sky* (1985), *The Man Who Was Marked by Winter* (1991), *Pillow Talk* (1994), and *Dharmakaya* (2000). A play, *Cell*, was produced and published as a book in 2000.

The poem below, "The Statue of the Virgin at Granard Speaks," comes directly from the rare mix of imagination and commitment that Meehan can manage. In 1984 a teenager was found dead in a field in Granard, a small town in Ireland. With this young woman was her dead baby. She had died giving birth to the baby, near a grotto with a statue of the Virgin Mary. In this poem, like John McGahern elsewhere in this book, Meehan questions the power and darkness of Catholic faith and its continuing presence in the Irish imagination. The narrative—as such writing often is in Ireland—is deeply antiauthoritarian. It inhabits the voice of an iconic religious symbol while laying bare, through craft and language, the self-deceptions of faith and the toxic language of evasion and hypocrisy.

The power of this poem evokes an article on craft that Meehan wrote: "A deeply felt poem can achieve extraordinary formal power under the very pressure of utterance, the way when you have to get to the other side of the river, when your very life depends on it, a raft slung together of driftwood and tyres will be as beautiful and fit for the journey as a vessel carefully crafted by a master boat builder."

It can be bitter here at times like this,
November wind sweeping across the border.
Its seeds of ice would cut you to the quick.
The whole town tucked up safe and dreaming,
even wild things gone to earth, and I
stuck up here in this grotto, without as much as
star or planet to ease my vigil.

The howling won't let up. Trees
cavort in agony as if they would be free
and take off — ghost voyagers
on the wind that carries intimations
of garrison towns, walled cities, ghetto lanes
where men hunt each other and invoke
the various names of God as blessing
on their death tactics, their night manœuvres.
Closer to home the wind sails
over dying lakes. I hear fish drowning.
I taste the stagnant water mingled
with turf smoke from outlying farms.

They call me Mary — Blessed, Holy, Virgin.
They fit me to a myth of a man crucified:
the scourging and the falling, and the falling again,
the thorny crown, the hammer blow of iron
into wrist and ankle, the sacred bleeding heart.

They name me Mother of all this grief
Though mated to no mortal man.
They kneel before me and their prayers
fly up like sparks from a bonfire
that blaze a moment, then wink out.

It can be lovely here at times. Springtime,
early summer. Girls in Communion frocks
pale rivals to the riot in the hedgerows
of cow parsley and haw blossom, the perfume
from every rushy acre that's left for hay
when the light swings longer with the sun's push north.

Or the grace of a midsummer wedding
when the earth herself calls out for coupling
and I would break loose of my stony robes,
pure blue, pure white, as if they had robbed
a child's sky for their colour. My being
cries out to be incarnate, incarnate,
maculate and tousled in a honeyed bed.

Even an autumn burial can work its own pageantry.
The hedges heavy with the burden of fruiting
crab, sloe, berry, hip; clouds scud east,
pear scented, windfalls secret in long
orchard grasses, and some old soul is lowered
to his kin. Death is just another harvest
scripted to the season's play.

But on this All Soul's Night there is
no respite from the keening of the wind.

I would not be amazed if every corpse came risen
From the graveyard to join in exaltation with the gale,
A cacophony of bone imploring sky for judgement
And release from being the conscience of the town.

On a night like this I remember the child
who came with fifteen summers to her name,
and she lay down alone at my feet
without midwife or doctor or friend to hold her hand
and she pushed her secret out into the night,
far from the town tucked up in little scandals,
bargains struck, words broken, prayers, promises,
and though she cried out to me in extremis
I did not move,
I didn't lift a finger to help her,
I didn't intercede with heaven,
nor whisper the charmed word in God's ear.

On a night like this, I number the days to the solstice
and the turn back to the
light.
                    O sun,
center of our foolish dance,
burning heart of stone,
molten mother of us all,
hear me and have pity.

Joseph O'Connor

(b. 1963)

[EXCERPT FROM]

"Reading John McGahern"

Joseph O'Connor was born in Dublin in 1963. He has written fiction, screenplays, and plays. He has also written a critical study of the Irish poet Charles
Donnelly, who died in the Spanish Civil War. O'Connor belongs to a new
generation of Irish writers who look outward rather than inward. He is interested in other places, other perspectives. It is both poignant and revealing
then that his article below about John McGahern, and his acknowledgment of
McGahern's influence, amounts to a tribute to one of the most rooted of all
Irish writers.

 Among O'Connor's published works are *Cowboys and Indians* (1991), *True
Believers* (1991), and four novels: *Desperadoes* (1993), *The Salesman* (1998),
Inishowen (2000), and *Star of the Sea* (2003). His nonfiction includes *Even the
Olives Are Bleeding: The Life and Times of Charles Donnelly* (1993), *The Irish
Male at Home and Abroad* (1996), and *Sweet Liberty: Travels in Irish America*
(1996). His stage plays are *Red Roses and Petrol* (1995), *The Weeping of Angels*
(1997), and *True Believers* (1991). His screenplays include *A Stone of the Heart*
and *The Long Way Home*.

 O'Connor is one of the Irish writers who has transited between historically based fiction and novels set in the immediate, contemporary world. In
his novel *Star of the Sea*, for example, he has constructed a powerful fiction
about the Irish famine. He is currently working on another historical novel,

based on the experiences of Irish immigrants in the American Civil War. In the excerpt below from "Reading John McGahern," he writes about his struggle to find a voice as a writer. In the process, O'Connor discovers, alters, and absorbs McGahern's work. It is an eloquent winding together of memory and admiration. It also analyzes the informal, even hand-to-mouth process by which Irish writing finds its way, from generation to generation, into the minds and onto the pages of other Irish writers.

The first short story I wrote was a work of genius. It was austere and lovely, full of elegant sentences and sharp insights. Any reviewer would have called it a *tour de force*. Because the first short story I wrote was by John McGahern.

It's called *Sierra Leone* and it appears in the 1979 collection *Getting Through*, a copy of which had been purchased by my father and was lying around the house. In the story, a couple meets in a Dublin bar to analyse their complicated affair. I was 16 that year. Complicated affairs interested me. My English teacher, John Burns, a wonderful man, said writing could be a beneficial hobby for teenagers. It was the one thing he ever told us that was completely wrong.

Writing was like attempting to juggle with mud. I would sit in my bedroom, gawping at a blank jotter, wishing I had the foggiest inkling as to what might be written. McGahern often wrote about rural Leitrim, but we had no hedgerows or loys in the 1970s Dublin estate I called home. We had no thwarted farmers, no maiden aunts on bicycles, no small-town solicitors, no cattle-dealing IRA veterans. Simply put, there was nothing in Glenageary to write *about*. You could call it the original failure of the creative imagination without which no writer ever got going.

Whenever I tried to write, there was only frustration. I felt as pent up as McGahern's lovers. That's how I recollect these youthful efforts at fiction: a haze of self-conscious fumblings and awkward gropings, second-hand sentences, sentenced to fail. One evening, in dismal hopelessness, I found myself copying out *Sierra Leone* word for word. I ached to write a story. So I wrote one of his.

I must have felt that the act of writing would make the words somehow mine. But, if so, it was an act of literary adultery. I smouldered to know what that feeling was like: to write out a beautiful text from start to finish. I suppose this was comparable to wannabe pop-stars throwing shapes and pulling pouts in the bathroom mirror. But something richer and more interesting was going on, too. McGahern was teaching me to read, not to write: to see the presences hidden in the crannies of a text, the realities the words are gesturing towards. Perhaps this is what pulses at the core of the desire to read: the yearning for intense relationship with words we love. Not just with what they are saying, but with the words themselves. Perhaps every reader is rewriting the story.

The next evening, I transcribed the McGahern piece again. This time I dared to alter a couple of names. The male lead became Sean (my father's name). I christened his girlfriend Deborah (after the punk singer Debbie Harry). Our next-door neighbour, Jack Mulcahy, had his name nicked for the barman. This felt taboo. It was like editing the Bible. I was raised in a home where books were revered. My parents considered it disreputable even to dog-ear a volume's pages. To interfere with a story would have been regarded as a form of sacrilege. Under the spell of McGahern, I became a teenage blasphemer.

Every few nights I'd guiltily rewrite the latest adaptation, changing the grammar here, a phrasing there. I'd move around events, break up the paragraphs, or tell the same story but from a different point of view. I must have written a hundred versions. The heroine's beautiful hair became auburn or black, and finally — exultantly! — strawberry blonde. I learned the importance of punctuation in a story. A question mark could change things. A well-placed full stop had the force of a slap. Before long, I was murdering McGahern's characters, replacing them with my own pitifully scanty puppets. The pub became a discothèque, the couple acquired flares; I engaged them, married them, bought them a house in the suburbs, then a collection of Planxty records and a second-hand lawnmower. The lovers in the story were starting to seem familiar. They would not have appeared out of place in Arnold Grove, Glenageary.

I rechristened them Adam and Eve, after a church on the Dublin quays. I altered their appearances, their way of speaking. I was afraid to admit it, but

I knew who they were becoming. They roamed this fictive otherworld, this Eden designed in Leitrim, talking to each other about all sorts of things: how much they loved novels, how books shouldn't be dog-eared. I could almost feel the firelight of that pub on my face as I watched my parents materialize through the prose.

I'd look at *Sierra Leone*. It became a kind of friend to me. I wanted to know it better, to learn how it ticked. At one point in those years, I feel almost certain, I could have made a fair stab at reciting the entire text by heart. It was breathtakingly simple, as though it had taken no effort to compose. In that, and in other ways, it was like an old Connemara ballad, of the kind I had often heard with my father on our holidays in Galway: so direct, so alluring, so subtly economical. It reminded me of *The Rocks of Bawn*: you wanted to know how it would turn out. It read, in fact, as though nobody had written it — as if it had somehow grown on the page. I recall one of the sentences: "Her hair shone dark blue in the light." That strange ache in the heart caused by precise words.

Each man kills the thing he loves. And so the vandalism continued, night after night, with me editing and rewriting this once perfect story, until gradually, over the span of my teenage years, every trace of McGahern was squeezed out of the text. Sierra Leone had become Glenageary. The story had been desecrated, but at least the resulting ruin was mine.

Perhaps all writers have the story they will tell forever, the idea they will go on exploring, consciously or not, until they run out of masks or find their own way of seeing the world. McGahern's *Sierra Leone* helped me find mine. Every fiction I've begun, every story I've struggled and failed with, has been an attempted reaching-back to that heart-stopping moment of first encountering the power of his art. It's a desire as doomed as any in the history of love stories. But you could spend your time chasing worse.

The Joan Miró Foundation in Barcelona, a city about which McGahern has written with great grace, is somewhat unfashionably arranged by chronology. You start with the child-artist's naive little doodles: his cartoon faces and multicoloured animals. Then you walk through the rooms organised year by year, through a life of struggle to say anything worth saying. You think of Patrick Kavanagh as you move through the still rooms: a man who dabbled in verse, only to have it become a life. Here are the pictures from the young Miró's figurative phase, the bowls of fat oranges, the wine bottles on windowsills. Then the warped guitars, the twisted limbs and mouths. You see him wrestle with the central question of Kavanagh's career: how to balance the satirical impulse with fidelity to the sacred.

And then the stuff gets stranger, wilder, more revolutionary. The faces are leering, the bodies apparently yearning to flee their frames; the world turns upside down before your eyes. And now paint itself begins to be abandoned: there are crazy collages, sculptures, ceramics, electric with the colours of the Catalonia Miró loved. It is a stunning experience to enter the last room and see the three vast canvases that dominate its walls. They hit you the way the opening notes of Beethoven's Fifth do, or those last short plays of Samuel Beckett, in a way you know you will never quite forget. Each painting is an unadorned field of vivid blue, with a yellow snaking line bisecting the plane. The simplicity moves you with incredible force, the idea that at the end of such a long search there is only the very simple, the plain line across colour, the desire to leave a stain on the silence. To stand before these images always brings McGahern to my mind: the man who knew, again like Kavanagh, that in art there will always be two kinds of simplicity. The simplicity of going away and the simplicity of coming back.

Much more could be said about McGahern and Kavanagh, two rural-born Irish writers who chronicled versions of Dublin more memorably than did many a native. Again and again, the city appears in McGahern's work, sometimes at a distance but often centrally. The exquisite short stories are peopled by migrant characters who see the metropolis as a labyrinth of possibilities. Here is a Dublin of tatty dancehalls and uneasy courtships, of kisses in damp doorways and unfulfilled hungerings. His citizens are stalwarts of the city's rural-born workforce, who take the first available bus home to the countryside on a Friday evening and the last one back to bed-sit-land on a Sunday night. They are, in short, like most Dubliners were at the time, and as many are now, despite the new prosperity. Their flings and farewells make for writing of extraordinary beauty with the city as a forlorn backdrop to the search for love. Anyone who has ever lived away from home will find bittersweet beauty in these pages.

McGahern's work acknowledges that Dublin (like capitals everywhere) is largely a community of migrants with conflicted loyalties. And I think of his explorations as opening a way for a number of subsequent writers. In that context it is striking that much of the most compelling fiction about the city has been produced by authors who grew up somewhere else. Ulsterman Patrick McCabe's *The Dead School* and London-born Philip Casey's *The Fabulists* offer powerful reflections on a place that changed radically in the 1970s, as political failure and corruption began to wreak havoc. In *The Book of Evidence*, Wexford-born John Banville produced a gripping novel set in the Dublin of that furtive era, a night-town of whispered secrets and compromised positions. I find it hard to imagine how these novels could have been written without the presence of McGahern on the Irish scene. For me, he looms behind everyone: an Easter Island figure. Every subsequent Irish novelist owes him a debt.

Marina Carr

(b. 1964)

Introduction
to Marina Carr: Plays One

Marina Carr was born in 1964 and grew up in Gortnamona, County Offaly. She was the child of literary parents—her father a playwright and novelist, and her mother (who died when Marina was seventeen) a poet in the Irish language. In an interview some years ago, she said of her childhood background, "My first seven or eight summers were spent running around the fields, eating grass, chasing tractors, picking mushrooms, blackberries, all that stuff. It was quite idyllic for a child. It's a beautiful part of the country and still not very well known."

Carr went to University College Dublin and graduated with a degree in English and philosophy. In her mid-twenties she began writing plays and having them produced in Ireland. "The culture believes in ghosts," she once said, and Carr's drama often seeks out the connections between unseen energies, sometimes dark ones. Her plays have also provided an acoustic chamber for myths of all kinds, often playing on the darknesses of determinism and family relations in Greek tragedy while still exploring a contemporary Ireland.

Carr's main theatrical works include *Low in the Dark* (1989), *The Deer's Surrender* (1990), *This Love Thing* (1991), *Ullaloo* (1991), *The Mai* (1994), *Portia Coughlan* (1996), *On Raftery's Hill* (1996), and *Ariel* (2002). In keeping with her lyrical memories of childhood, she wrote an introduction to her plays in 1999 that evokes them again. Below she locates in her childhood some of the energies and orders that reemerged, years later, in her plays.

When I was a scut we built a theatre in our shed; we lay boards across the stacked turf, hung an old blue sheet for a curtain and tied a bicycle lamp to a rafter at the side of the shed so its light would fall at an angle on the stage. For costumes we wore brown nylons over our faces. There were always robbers in our plays. Even when you weren't playing a robber, you dressed like one, for any second you could be caught or hung or shot. Even the Good Guy dressed like a robber, so if the worst came to the worst he could arrest himself. Everyone was interchangeable. One minute you were the heroine on the swing and the next you were in the stocks pleading guilty to every crime invented. Our dramas were bloody and brutal. Everyone suffered: the least you could hope to get away with was a torturing. And still we all lived happily ever after. Good and bad got down from their ropes or off the rack or out of the barrel of boiling oil, apologized to the Goodie — who was usually more perverse than all the Baddies put together — and made long soliloquies about "never doing it again." Everyone was capable of redemption except Witches. We had no mercy for Witches, but since the Witch had all the power and all the magic, we could never finally throttle her with all the righteous savagery of our scuttish hearts. Just when we had her choked down to her last cheekful of air or had her chest bared for the stake, she'd cast one of her spells and escape on the handle of an old spade.

Scuts know instinctively that morality is a human invention, fallible and variable as the wind, and so our dramas were strange and free and cruel. But scuts also have a sense of justice — bar the Witch, I don't know what she was about — and hence our desire for the thing to end well. We loved the havoc, the badness, the blood spillage, but loved equally restoring some sort of botched order and harmony. Ignorantly we had hit upon the first and last principles of dramatic art. And the Witch? Maybe she was Time. Time we didn't understand or fully inhabit, and yet we respected and feared her. And fell away humbly under her spells and charms and curses. If I'm after anything when I'm writing plays, it's the scuts' view of things as they are or were or should be, and perhaps once in a blue moon be given a sideways glance of it all as the first dramatist might see it and how it should be done.

Colum McCann

(b. 1965)

[EXCERPT FROM]

"Some Strange Vessel"

Colum McCann was born in Dublin in 1965. He belongs to a new generation
of Irish fiction writers who are unsettled with the old landscape of figure and
fiction. More international, less regional, these writers are beginning to
question what themes are left for them to explore, and which ones are
exhausted. By this light there is no special commitment to the old well-
defined Irish themes put forward by earlier generations. Not surprisingly,
perhaps, McCann's most notable novel, *Dancer* (2003), is about the Russian
dancer, Nureyev. The selection of the subject shows a new sense of freedom—
also displayed by writers like Colm Tóibín since the late 1990s—to find a
depth of field and a new resonance, and yet to not be confined to an Irish
geographical reference.

McCann has published short stories, including *Fishing the Sloe Black River*
(1994). His novels are *Song Dogs* (1995), *This Side of Brightness* (1998),
Everything in This Country Must (2000), and *Dancer* (2003). In the excerpt
below from an interview in *The Atlantic Monthly*, McCann makes some telling
remarks about the changes in the psyche of Irish life, and in the likely shifts
which follow in the new cultural and artistic spaces that are opening. He
states the changes that have come for young Irish fiction writers now that
certain fixities of the Irish experience have gone: exile is no longer the same;
there is no need to consider emigration in the light it was once seen in. In

other words there can be no turning back from this shift in motive, expression, and intent. McCann's words track an enormous change. The old landscape of the Irish Revival is now barely visible. The intensity of a stay-at-home literature has disappeared. A new internationalism, a sense that the themes open to the Irish writer are global as well as local—this marks one of the signal shifts in Irish writing in this generation.

KATIE BOLICK: You have said that you are "writing about characters in exile . . . exile from communities, exile from themselves." Like Beckett and Joyce, you have exiled yourself from Ireland. Could you talk about the difference between emigration and exile, particularly for a writer?

COLUM MCCANN: For a long time emigration was one of the most important defining characteristics of Irish society and the Irish imagination, but emigration no longer exists for Ireland in the same way. Fifty years ago, if you left Ireland you were leaving Ireland for good. They would have an American Wake and you would essentially be present at your own funeral. It's a different sort of leaving now. Friends of mine who have moved to London can fly back to Mayo in an hour, whereas it takes four hours to drive to Mayo from Dublin. These changing boundaries form a new cartography, and, in relation, emigration is completely different. It's probably much more poignant for a sixty-year-old Irish woman or man than it is for a twenty-year-old.

Exile also used to be very important for Irish writers, but as Ireland shifts and changes politically, socially, and sexually, so these notions of exile and emigration have to change. Beckett, Joyce, and Wilde were bucking the system, the Catholic Church, small mindedness — basically, they were escaping a very contained culture that they needed to get away from to write about. But Ireland is much more broad-minded now and the Catholic Church has lost its hold. Ireland has become a more open society — and it's difficult to exile yourself from a benevolent place. I've never really felt myself so much in exile, although I have written about characters who are in some sort of exile in *This Side of Brightness* and *Song Dogs*. And less and less do I feel like I've emigrated, although paradoxically I'm longer away from Ireland each day.

[BOLICK]: You have said, "I do think of myself as an Irish writer, but I belong perhaps a little bit more to this breed of international mongrels who have no native land and are comfortable anywhere." Do you see the ranks of this breed swelling as we move into the future? And, if so, just as nations devise their own folklore, will some sort of global folklore evolve?

[MCCANN]: That's a lovely, great question, and something I've just begun to think about. I definitely see the ranks of this breed swelling, sure, and some sort of global folklore has to evolve. I think we're possibly searching for the writer who will make that international folklore available to us in the same way that Don DeLillo made American folklore available to us in *Underworld*. The closest I could think to it right now is Michael Ondaatje — born in Sri Lanka, educated in England, lives in Canada but writes his first novel about a black jazz musician in New Orleans in 1905 — I mean, what a cornucopia, what a geography. I think we're going to see more and more of this sort of internationalism.

Walt Whitman said, "Do I contradict myself? . . . I am large, I contain multitudes" — and that's what writing is all about, too. No answer is ever set in any kind of stone. So when somebody goes out and shoots their mouth off like I'm doing about internationalism and globalization you forget that within that word *internationalism* is the very important word *nationalism*; how is that going to be reconciled? We'll never lose sight of nationalism — in fact, within this notion of internationalism, more and more nationalistic feelings will possibly crop up. But it's hard to talk about these things because it's hard to make a very clear, potent statement about what is right and what is wrong. That's what fiction is about — the big "colorful gray" area in the middle. That's what makes it such a joy to write.

[BOLICK]: You've remarked that had you not gone to America, where "there's a huge bursting out of land and space," but to England instead, your sentences might be "much more clipped and controlled." What would your sentences be like if you had remained in Ireland? How has living in New York City informed your writing style?

[MCCANN]: Language is completely affected by the landscape it inhabits. While I was writing *This Side of Brightness* I found that the sections set in contemporary New York were much more clipped and bare than the sections set in the past. This influence of the landscape on language is the success of certain writers, such as Cormac McCarthy. His recent trilogy could not have been set anywhere other than Mexico and the southwestern United States. The same sort of language mightn't have been so evocative if it was transplanted to another part of the world.

[BOLICK]: You write in *Song Dogs*, "The world rotates on an axis of what-ifs? What if we were somewhere else? What if we sauntered off and just didn't come back?" A few of your characters actually do up-and-vanish from their homes. Why the propensity for disappearing?

[MCCANN]: I've never disappeared as such, although sometimes I want to. I think a lot of us believe our lives are sewn up. John Berger says it best when he says that if he'd known as a child what the life of an adult would have been, he never could have believed it would be so unfinished. Things are in a constant flux. It's not very fashionable, but I love life, and I believe that things disappear and reappear and nothing ever solidifies, no matter how middle-class, housebroken, staid, and solitary someone's life seems to be. That, I think, is what I'm writing about.

[BOLICK]: *This Side of Brightness* chronicles the lives of several poor black urban Americans, some of them homeless. All have had experiences very unlike your own. In anticipation of being accused of cultural exploitation as a writer, you have said, "I think if you try to do something as honestly as you possibly can, then you can do whatever you want." Could you expand on this?

[MCCANN]: For a white, Irish, middle-class writer from Dublin to come in and write a novel about homeless people in New York City, mostly of African-American background — well, I thought there was going to be a little bit more of a hullabaloo. I actually wished there had been, because it's a really important issue for me, and I thought about it long and hard in all sorts of different ways when I was writing the book. All kinds of questions flew around in my brain — Can you morally step into somebody else's world and attempt to recreate it? Is that arrogant? Exploitative? Is talking about race and class a preoccupation of people who are not in that race, or of that class?

If an American writer goes to Ireland and writes a book about the Irish working class, I'm going to read that book with a cynical eye, and if he gets one word wrong I'm going to jump on it. I'll allow an Irish writer writing about the Irish working class, however, to make certain mistakes. So I was very scared when I was working on this book. I went over sections of dialogue with actors from Harlem and southern Georgia, trying to get it right. If you start using devices and playing games with the reader, then you've lost the right to say, "Well, I did something and I did it to the best of my ability." I wanted to be as honest as I possibly could. Ultimately I said, "Fuck it, I stand where I stand, I write what I write."

Emma Donoghue

(b. 1969)

"Future Perfect: Talking with Irish Lesbian Author Emma Donoghue," by Owen Keehnen

Emma Donoghue was born in Dublin in 1969, the youngest of eight children. Her father is the distinguished critic Denis Donoghue. She graduated from University College Dublin in 1990 and in 1997 gained her Ph.D. from Cambridge University. She has been writing full time since then. She now lives in Canada.

Donoghue's first novel, *Stirfry*, was published in 1994, and her second, *Hood*, in 1995. Since then she has published a series of reimagined fairytales called *Kissing the Witch* (1997) as well as a historical novel, *Slammerkin* (2000), inspired by an eighteenth-century murder. Her newer work is *The Woman Who Gave Birth to Rabbits* (2002) and *Life Mask* (2004). In all of these, to a greater or lesser extent, Donoghue has eloquently, and with grace, confronted issues of sexuality and society—issues that have previously been difficult to include in the template of Irish writing. Outside of her fiction Donoghue has crafted an engaged critique in such books as *Passions Between Women: British Lesbian Culture, 1668–1801* (1993) as well as through her editorship of two anthologies, *What Sappho Would Have Said* (1997) and *The Mammoth Book of Lesbian Short Stories* (1999).

Ireland has been, until recently, inhospitable to gay writing and to growing the sort of critique that has been commonplace and essential for decades in other countries. Gay subjects and the identities that enrich them—

cultural, political, erotic—have been slow to come to Ireland. The writer Anne Enright, who is quoted earlier in this book, refers to "Catholic nationalism, whose ideal of the lovely Irish girl did not include her falling in love with other women, in a carnal sort of way." Voices like Donoghue's are particularly important in the discovery and clearing of the valuable spaces around new themes and new energies. The emphasis on how important it is for new gay writers to be able to build communities and restate Irish writing is clear in the interview below. Donoghue's fresh, dissident voice in this 1994 interview— with its candour about creativity and repression—portrays an Irish imagination at a moment of change.

OWEN KEEHNEN: How does Ireland perceive lesbians? Are there role models?

EMMA DONOGHUE: Growing up in Ireland is a little behind, but it's modernizing very quickly. When I was growing up there was no one but Martina Navratilova and she was far away in so many ways. She was much dykier than me, a sports star who lived too far away to be of much use to me, but at least I'd heard of her. I didn't really discover other role models till I was in college, so I grew up in a complete vacuum of images, but actually it allowed me to make up my mind for myself. I wasn't familiar with negative images either; lesbianism was just an unspoken thing in Ireland.

KEEHNEN: Have reviewers in the United States, England, and Ireland treated the lesbianism of the book differently?

DONOGHUE: They have all focused on lesbianism, and in Ireland that's especially fun because I'm not the first publicly out lesbian there, but I'm one of them. In Ireland, the journalists have been very astonished. There was one interview I did with a housewife magazine that said on the cover " 'I always knew I was different,' says Emma," and then you had to turn to page 35 to see what the dreaded stigma was. In Britain and the U.S., it's been a more sophisticated reaction.

KEEHNEN: Are you planning a sequel?

DONOGHUE: No, but I've almost finished my second novel, *Hood*. It's much more ambitious; it's my death novel, a bereavement story. It's about a lesbian couple that's been together since convent school and one of them dies in a crash. The title refers partly to "Little Red Riding Hood" and partly to the hood of the clitoris. I got one review of *Stir Fry* in Ireland that said, "Don't worry, the sex scenes wouldn't offend a bishop." And I thought, "Oh my God, if I'm not offending bishops, I'm not doing the right thing here." So in the second one I'm trying to offend bishops much more. It's really fun mixing in the sex and Catholicism and blasphemy.

KEEHNEN: You've traveled here [in the United States] a great deal; in fact, you were at the Womyn's Music Fest in 1993. What did you think?

DONOGHUE: I adored the Michigan's Womyn's Festival. It restored my idealism in women's communities. Blissful!

KEEHNEN: Are you going back this year?

DONOGHUE: No! I have to go home and finish the novel, and I'm also working on a second play.

KEEHNEN: Before we get to that, in your travels what difference have you noticed between Irish and U.S. lesbians?

DONOGHUE: I think a lot of lesbianism is international, or, rather, I fear it's U.S. culture. We come here and go home with our freedom rings and flags. A lot of lesbians in Ireland seem to have spent some time here. A lot of Irish lesbians emigrate here for fear things will never change at home. But things are. We went this year from complete criminalization of homosexuality to an equal age of consent in one move. I'm hopeful because I'm so fond of Ireland.

KEEHNEN: What's your second play about?

DONOGHUE: It's called *Ladies and Gentlemen* and it's set in late nineteenth-century New York among male and female impersonators in the music halls. They're all true characters.

KEEHNEN: Your first play *I Know My Own Heart: A Lesbian Regency Romance* was performed at Cambridge and in Dublin. What was the greatest challenge you found about creating a drama?

DONOGHUE: Well, with that play the challenge was to take a very unwieldy source, these diaries, and give it a dramatic structure. Diaries are so miscellaneous and in such little bits and pieces that I had to chop them up and put together a story. I had to simplify a great deal because this specific woman seduced so many women that I had to make composite characters; otherwise it would have been a bedroom farce. She seduced all her friends' sisters. So I had to reduce that to one situation. There were lots of questions on how to show sex on the stage. So I had them go up and under the skirts. It worked quite well. I was working with straight actresses and I kept having to say, "Your head is too far away, you would not be achieving anything. Get the head in! Get the head in!" There is an interest in doing productions in New York and San Francisco.

KEEHNEN: Tell me about your nonfiction work, *Passions Between Women: British Lesbian Culture, 1688–1801.*

DONOGHUE: I wrote that on the side. I had funding from the British government to do a Ph.D. on a feminist topic, but I was finding so many fascinating texts that needed looking at in the light of lesbian history, so I sort of went between the pages of my paper and worked on it. Then it was sold to a small feminist press, and I hope to have an American edition soon. It was a big challenge to write a book that would be readable and scholarly. I think that's a challenge that should be met by all academics, especially in areas like queer theory, which should be so rooted in real life but often floats off somewhere. It's completely cut off from the community inspiring the work.

KEEHNEN: Amidst all this productivity you've also managed to get a degree at the University of Dublin and you're currently doing your Ph.D. at Cambridge. What's your thesis?

DONOGHUE: Not a lesbian topic! It's on eighteenth-century writers and their professional friendships — how men and women helped each other and how it inspired platonic friendships, where men and women could be seen as just friends.

KEEHNEN: Do you have any long-term goals?

DONOGHUE: Just to get better and better at writing, particularly fiction.

Conor McPherson

(b. 1971)

"Chronicles of the Human Heart"

Conor McPherson was born in Dublin in 1971. He went to University College Dublin and was a member of the drama society there. His play *The Weir* was performed when he was twenty-six, in 1997. All McPherson's plays have shown a vivid narrative tension. "I think it's just that I really love stories," he said in an interview. Often the action is sustained and realized through wounded characters. His dramatic turns and twists can also bring in a shimmer of the ghostly, the otherworldly, as in *Shining City*, his 2004 play.

McPherson's strategies of dramatic speech include a signature use of monologue. This was obvious in his first play, *This Lime Tree Bower* (1996). The way his characters talk shows some of what he absorbed from David Mamet's work: fragments, hesitations, broken pauses, and words shadowed by other words. Describing his first encounter with Mamet's writing, McPherson said that the language used there was "so much more interesting than rational, considered language; it just seemed like music, somehow."

His plays include *Dublin Carol* (2000), *Port Authority* (2001), *Come on Over* (2001), and *Shining City* (2004). He has also made three films: *I Went Down* (1997) and *The Actors* (2003), which he wrote, and *Endgame* (2001), which he directed. His piece below, written for the *Guardian* newspaper in 2006, considers the achievement of Samuel Beckett and the often mysterious plays and fragments he wrote. McPherson says here of Beckett that "while he is often carelessly described as a twentieth-century European existentialist who created hymns to 'nothingness,' he was in fact an Irish pagan who sought to celebrate the infinite mystery and endurance of the human heart through public rituals."

At one stage in his memoir, *Almost a Gentleman*, the great British playwright John Osborne lets slip his true feelings about his 1950s Royal Court contemporary, Samuel Beckett. He writes with languid derision about the "apostolic awe" Beckett inspired in the Royal Court's founding director, George Devine. "Uncle Sam had the monstrous good fortune of actually looking like one of his own plays, a graven icon of his own texts. The bristled cadaver and mountain-peak stare were the ultimate purifier that deified all endeavour, pity or hope." He goes on to say that, were Beckett's face fatter and less heroic-looking, "the response to that toneless voice might not have been so immediate." He finishes by declaring with barely hidden distaste — and not a little glee — that George Devine was unable to secure an actor to star as Hamm in the English-language premiere of *Endgame* and he "was reduced to having to attempt it himself . . . It was brave but unmoving. It seemed a pretty long chew on a very dry prune [but] I would never have dreamed of saying so."

Obviously, Osborne's view of Beckett is coloured by a natural and (from a fellow playwright's point of view) understandable professional wariness of another big noise on the theatre block at that time. Indeed, the apostolic awe Beckett still provokes in certain theatre practitioners and academics has perhaps not done him any great service in the eyes of his critics. Fandom of Beckett can easily tip into a kind of fetishism typified by theatres who never produce one Beckett play when they can mount whole festivals of his work (as is happening at the Barbican this month), or actors who perform so many of his plays that they become known, almost exclusively, as Beckett actors. But there is no denying his influence. No other modern playwright has inspired so many disparate types of artists and thinkers. He has influenced painters, sculptors, designers, film-makers, philosophers, choreographers, directors, actors, musicians and, of course, writers, in a way that could only have bewildered John Osborne.

In my opinion, Beckett's plays are probably best seen in (ahem) isolation, as each one is a beautifully honed, determined, focused world unto itself. While seeing lots together will raise awareness of the similarity between the plays, it may not help us to see how distinct his best work is, even within his own canon. I believe that his plays will continue to echo through time because he managed to articulate a feeling as opposed to an idea. And that feeling is the unique human predicament of being alive and conscious. Of course, it's a very complicated feeling (and it's a complicated idea), but he makes it look simple because his great genius, along with his incomparable literary power, was the precision and clarity he brought to bear in depicting the human condition itself. That he did it with great warmth, humour and moments of deep sadness, which are some of the most moving one could experience in the theatre, also speaks of his craft as a monumental playwright.

Any perusal of his plays must begin with *Waiting for Godot* (1952). This play has taken on, and will continue to have, a resonance similar to some of Shakespeare's greatest plays. Even people who have never seen it will have some idea of what it is like. In a bare, bleak landscape, two seemingly homeless old men, Vladimir and Estragon, attempt to pass the time while they wait for someone called Godot. The play spans two days (or two evenings really) and during both they experience oppressive boredom, random violence, unfruitful spiritual contemplation, real friendship, uneasy co-dependence, profound longing and, ultimately, a deep, crushing uncertainty. They have problems remembering the day before. They don't know whether to leave or keep waiting. There is no resolution in the traditional sense. But it's really a revolutionary play because it takes the human mind itself as its subject matter and brilliantly dramatises it by splitting it in two.

Vladimir and Estragon speak to each other in the anxious, cajoling way human beings speak to themselves in their private moments. Fears are expressed and dismissed only to be unhelpfully reiterated in slightly different ways. Their feelings of love and hatred for each other jostle and even combine in the same impossible, tiny moment.

Psychologists suggest that the difference between productive thinking and worrying is that productive thinking flows; it moves forward to some kind of conclusion or sense of resolve. Worrying is just the same few unsettling thoughts going round and round like an annoying tune. This is how Vladimir and Estragon communicate, and how they dramatise the subjective experience itself. Their quarrels and musings often conjoin to form a kind of inclusive flow, as though they share one mind, but it always ends in dissatisfaction. For example, near the beginning of act two, when they nervously talk about "all the dead voices":

Vladimir: What do they say?
Estragon: They talk about their lives.
Vladimir: To have lived is not enough for them.
Estragon: They have to talk about it.
Vladimir: To be dead is not enough for them.
Estragon: It is not sufficient.

(Silence)

Vladimir: They make a noise like feathers.
Estragon: Like leaves.
Vladimir: Like ashes.
Estragon: Like leaves.

(Long silence)

Vladimir: Say something!
Estragon: I'm trying.

Without a third party to become a benchmark for their wandering speculations, they are doomed to encircle the same futile topics for ever — and they don't like it. They are waiting for Godot but they are also contemplating suicide. Like Hamlet, they are even powerless to end their lives as they suspect it may only deliver them into another, perhaps even more painful existence. *Waiting for Godot*, like *Hamlet*, is a benchmark in world literature because, in an entirely new way, it presents the anxious, modern, divided self as it witnesses the wanton cruelty of existence, unable to understand it, yet condemned to live it. It is the logical and emotional conclusion to the Cartesian foundation of our contemporary western world: "I think therefore I am." With the existence of thought itself as our only constant, no higher being or deity can adjudicate for the modern rational mind.

Considering that Beckett began writing plays in the aftermath of the hor-
rific genocide of the Second World War, a war in which he fought alongside
the French resistance, it is a testament to his character that the plays, while
skating on the thin ice of our mortality, can be so funny. Godot is full of verbal jokes and visual slapstick routines based upon — what else? — confusion
and misunderstanding. While he opens the wound of the post-religious
mind, at the same time he pours a salve of blessed warmth made possible
only through the communal act of public presentation and laughter. The
very experience of enjoying and understanding the play becomes its optimistic message, as opposed to anything glibly uttered by a character on the
stage.

With his next play, *Endgame* (1957), Beckett shifts his focus from his rumi-
nations on human thinking and turns to an examination of human morals. It
is a masterful play, full of jokes and real profundity, constructed like a vice that
holds its ideas and pursuits centre stage in a riveting and disquieting way.
Where *Godot* is set in an unforgiving, almost featureless exterior, *Endgame* is
set in a kind of claustrophobic bunker. Hamm is blind and unable to walk.
He is attended upon by Clov, who can just about get around, coming and
going from the room to fulfill Hamm's childlike whims. He does so not only
because Hamm holds the combination to the larder that feeds them, but
also because there seems to be nowhere else to go. They can see out of two
grimy little windows, which Clov hoists a ladder to reach, but there is nothing (or "zero") out there. The two other occupants of the room are Nagg and
Nell, Hamm's parents, whom he has consigned to live in dustbins. It is a truly
apocalyptic vision, almost a bulletin from the height of the cold war, with its
constant threat of nuclear annihilation.

But again, I like to see this play as a moving picture of the human mind —
only this time it's what happens in the mind when we think about other
human beings. The characters are racked with notions of responsibility and
our desire to be free of it. Hamm works his way through the play trying to
tell a story, or "chronicle" as he calls it, about how he was asked to take in a
child to save him from starvation. This story causes Hamm great discomfort
as he painstakingly pieces it back together, using many diversionary foot-
notes to prolong its conclusion. We come to understand that he is reluctant
to reveal the ending as it places him in a moral catch-22 situation. If he

refuses to save the child, does he have personal responsibility for his death, even though he did not personally cause it? And if he does save the child, has he accepted a logical responsibility to save anyone who is in a similar situation? He cannot possibly save everybody in the world and he fears that his inability to do so will only cause him further psychic pain.

In response to this puzzling problem, he seems to have chosen to shut down his whole life. He implores Clov (who may be the child he once saved) to "screw down the lids" of the bins where his parents dwell. Cruelty seems easier than mercy to Hamm — it causes him less personal anguish. But Beckett strews the play with great humour and intriguing clues to Hamm's inner distress, suggesting that the sharp sting of moral choice is the price of being alive.

An echo of the reluctant storyteller resurfaces in *Krapp's Last Tape* (1958). Once again we are presented with a divided self, but this time brilliantly and realistically achieved with the presence of a tape recorder. Tucked away in his little "den," Krapp listens back to old diary entries and comments on them with curses and angry fast-forwarding, as he prepares to add a new one. The tension in the play is generated by his search for and, we come to realise, fear of a meaningful moment. He seems to dismiss the recordings of his past selves with disgust, implying that his present self and tonight's recording of it will also be dismissed in the future. His life appears to be an exercise in literally marking time, recording his diminishing sexual adventures and his laughable inability to kick his dependence on alcohol — and bananas.

But Beckett surprises the audience by allowing Krapp to stumble upon his 30-year-old account of a moment of perfect, almost trance-like bliss, in a punt on a stream with a past lover: "We lay there without moving. But under us all moved, and moved us, gently, up and down, and from side to side. [Pause] Past midnight. Never knew such silence. The earth might be uninhabited."

Krapp then attempts to dismiss this account with a new recording but finds himself listening to it again, motionless and spellbound as the play ends. It is a spine tingling few minutes in the theatre, as Beckett illustrates that even our own attempts to duck life's experiences and cast our memories aside is impossible, for to experience even a moment of happiness blesses us with a kind of cosmic faith that is beyond language, and thus beyond denial.

Perhaps the supreme irony at the heart of Beckett's plays, and precisely the point that John Osborne missed, is that while he is often carelessly described as a twentieth-century European existentialist who created hymns to "nothingness," he was in fact an Irish pagan who sought to celebrate the infinite mystery and endurance of the human heart through public rituals. His plays are not easy to perform and none can have been easy to write. But I believe that each one is enormously personal (perhaps this is why he never gave interviews), and while he always mercilessly stripped the work to its barest bones, at the same time he allowed his real feelings to shine through. This is what imbues his plays with their great power. They are also lovingly and respectfully shaped for an audience: this is what has made them enduring. And as long as they are performed with one eye on our spiritual longing, and another on the banana skin, they will continue to endure for generations yet to be born.

Permissions

RICHARD MURPHY, "Wellington Testimonial" from *In the Heart of the Country: Collected Poems.* © 2000 by Richard Murphy. Reprinted with the permission of Wake Forest University Press.

TOM MURPHY, excerpt from an interview with Maria Kurdi from *Irish Studies Review* 12, no. 2 (2004). © 2004. Reprinted with the permission of Taylor & Francis Ltd., www.tandf.co.uk/journals.

MYLES NA GOPALEEN, "Waama, etc." from *The Best of Myles*, edited by Kevin O'Nolan (London: McGibbon & Kee, 1968). Reprinted Flamingo, 1993.

EILÉAN NÍ CHUILLEANÁIN, "Pygmalion's Image" from *The Magdalene Sermon and Earlier Poems.* © 1991 by Eiléan Ní Chuilleanáin. Reprinted with the permission of Wake Forest University Press.

NUALA NI DHOMHNAILL, "Why I Choose to Write in Irish" from *Selected Essays.* © 2005 by Nuala Ni Dhomhnaill. Reprinted with the permission of New Island Books.

CONOR CRUISE O'BRIEN, "Pride in the Language" from *Conor: A biography of Conor Cruise O'Brien: Anthology* (Ithaca: Cornell University Press, 1994). Reprinted by permission of the author, c/o Mulcahy & Viney, Ltd.

EDNA O'BRIEN, "Dear Mr. Joyce" © 1971 by Edna O'Brien. Reprinted with the permission of the Wylie Agency.

KATE O'BRIEN, excerpt from *My Ireland.* © 1962 by Kate O'Brien. Reprinted with the permission of B. T. Batsford, Ltd.

SEAN O'CASEY, excerpt from *Autobiographies.* © 1963 by Sean O'Casey. Reprinted with the permission of The Estate of Sean O'Casey.

FRANK O'CONNOR, excerpt from *An Only Child.* © 1961 by Frank O'Connor. Reprinted with the permission of Random House, Inc.

JOSEPH O'CONNOR, excerpt from *The UCD Aesthetic: Celebrating 100 Years of Irish Writers*, edited by Tony Roche. Reprinted with the permission of New Island Books.

SEAN O'FAOLAIN, excerpt from *The Bell* (December 1944). © 1944 by Sean O'Faolain. Reprinted with the permission of Rogers, Coleridge & White, Ltd.

LIAM O'FLAHERTY, "I Return Home" from *Two Years.* Reprinted with the permission of Random House (UK) Ltd.

MARY O'MALLEY, excerpt from "Locus Pocus" from *Synge: A Celebration*, edited by Colm Tóibín (Dublin: Carysfort Press, 2005). Reprinted with the permission of the author.

MARY O'MALLEY, excerpt from "Received English" from *Where Rocks Float.* Reprinted with the permission of Salmon Publishing, Co. Clare.

MICHEAL O'SIADHAIL, "Tight-Wire" from *Hail! Madam Jazz: New and Selected Poems.* © 1999 by Micheal O'Siadhail. Reprinted with the permission of Bloodaxe Books Ltd.

TOM PAULIN, "Desertmartin" from *Liberty Tree.* © 1983 by Tom Paulin. Reprinted with the permission of Faber & Faber Ltd.

Writers/Works Index

EAVAN BOLAND has published ten volumes of poetry, most recently *Domestic Violence* (2007). She is also coeditor, with Edward Hirsch, of *The Making of a Sonnet: A Norton Anthology* (2007). She is the Bella Mabury and Eloise Mabury Knapp Professor in the Humanities as well as the Melvin and Bill Lane Professor and the director of the Creative Writing Program at Stanford University. Boland is the winner of the Lannan Award for Poetry and lives in Stanford, California, and Dublin.